THE SHOOTING
WEEK-END BOOK

ERIC PARKER

WITH ILLUSTRATIONS BY
BERYL IRVING

LONDON
SEELEY SERVICE
& Co. Ltd.

PRINTED IN GREAT BRITAIN

FOREWORD

I HAVE to acknowledge with thanks the kindness of authors and publishers who have allowed the use of copyright matter:—Messrs. A. & C. Black, for an extract from *Partridges & Partridge Manors*, by Captain Aymer Maxwell; Mrs. H. W. Carlton and the proprietors of the *Field*, for an extract from *Spaniels: their Breaking for Sport & Field Trials*, by H. W. Carlton, and from *New Ways with Partridges*, by Richard Page; Messrs. Gilbertson & Page, for passages from the *Gamekeeper*; Messrs. Longmans, Green & Co., for an extract from the Badminton Library volume *Shooting: Field & Covert*; the proprietors of the Lonsdale Library, for extracts from *Hounds & Dogs* and the *Lonsdale Keeper's Book*; the British Field Sports Association and Imperial Chemical Industries, for extracts of table matter from their Year Books; Mr. Patrick Chalmers; and the executors of the late George A. B. Dewar and Hesketh Prichard.

ERIC PARKER.

CONTENTS

7

CONTENTS

INDEX OF AUTHORS & SOURCES

11

NATURAL HISTORY OF GAME BIRDS

CAPERCAILLIE (*Tetrao urogallus*)

THIS IS the largest of the grouse tribe. Capercaillie is Cabhar Coille, Gaelic for Cock of the Wood—a name not only befitting his size but his character, for there is no other game bird to stand up to him. He is as big as a turkey, with long beard feathers above a purple neck and a green and black breast mottled with white. He has a powerful hooked beak and a crimson bare line over the eye, and his plumage, which is a mixture of browns, greys and greens, is so dark as to appear almost black. The hen's plumage is a rich mixture of reddish and orange browns, with semi-circular markings of darker brown and of white.

Gamekeepers, if they breed pheasants, dislike the "caper," for he will take the pheasants' food: foresters dislike him even more, since his staple diet is the young shoots and leaders of fir and pine. Breeding begins in April; the nest is a hollow scraped among heather at the edge of a wood, or among rough grass in a wood at the foot of a pine or under the shelter of a fallen tree. Here the hen lays from six to twelve eggs, about the size of a heron's, pale orange-brown, spotted and blotched with warm brown of deeper shades.

The capercaillie became extinct in Scotland at the end of the eighteenth century, but it was re-introduced in 1837-8, mainly through the efforts of Sir Thomas Fowell Buxton and Lord Breadalbane. It is now widely established in the Highlands. It was because of its temporary extinction that it has no close time as have other game birds, for in 1831, when the Game Act which is the substance of our Game

Laws was passed, there were no capercaillie in the kingdom for Parliament to think about. So that its close season depends on County Council Orders under the Wild Birds Protection Acts. In its characteristics it is essentially a game bird, for though a cock caper in August, when perhaps he is feeding on berries on the open moor, offers, when he gets up, a mark that could hardly be missed; in winter, beaten out from the branches of pines on a hill, he may darken the sky like the crow in *Alice Through the Looking-Glass*, but I have seen him float out over a valley untouched by cartridges which found no difficulty with high pheasants.

BLACKCOCK: GREYHEN (*Tetrao tetrix*)

This is the second largest of the four members of the family of *Tetraonidae* native to these islands. Like the capercaillies, the cocks and hens differ considerably in plumage. The blackcock is mainly bluish-black, partly tinged with brown; he has a white patch on the wing and another under the tail, which, when he has obtained his full autumn plumage, is strongly forked, much in the same way as the tail of the Australian lyre-bird. The greyhen is mainly light reddish-brown, with crescent-shaped markings of blackish-brown. Blackgame, like their larger relations, do not pair; on early mornings in the spring the cocks gather, seemingly for the purpose of fighting, strutting and posturing and challenging in competition for the hens, from whom the stronger birds take off several wives apiece. These scrape hollows in the heather among the scrubby, half-wooded ground that skirts the moors, and lay six or seven up to as many as ten eggs, of a rich yellow or yellowish-white, spotted with chestnut brown.

It is this habit of polygamy which has led to the convention of not shooting greyhens. If, it is argued, you shoot a greyhen, you kill off a potential mother of a family, whereas it does not matter shooting a blackcock, since those that survive are sure to provide themselves with wives in the following spring. But this convention, I think, is gradually dying out. It is realised that by not shooting greyhens at all, you leave the older hens to become barren and also quarrelsome in their old age, and an old hen who establishes a solitary reign over a chosen part of the moor, and drives off other younger hens who want to nest there, is not an economical proposition. So that in time, I should predict, the ban on greyhen shooting will be lightened, and the birds left to take care of themselves—a development which will bring relief to the youthful or inexperienced who find it difficult at the moment when a greyhen takes wing to distinguish her slower, clumsier flight from the sudden uprising of a grouse.

Another development in customs of blackcock shooting, it is to be hoped, may in time become universal. That is the deferring of the date of shooting young blackgame. Legally, blackcock shooting opens on 20th August. But on that date the birds of the year are no more than callow chicks, who only with reluctance leave their shelter of grass and rushes and fly miserably when they must—a wretched mark for a gun. Whereas a blackcock in October, in his full glory of plumage on the wing, is a bird that flies faster than a driven grouse. A later date for the opening of the season is a change in the Game Laws long overdue—all the more so as it would make no difference to the shooting of old blackcocks in August, who are shot whenever opportunity offers. For as the gamekeeper puts it, knowing the wandering habits and the length of flight of an old blackcock, to-day he is here and to-morrow where is he?

RED GROUSE (*Lagopus scoticus*)

Remarkable as the only British bird which is found nowhere else but in these islands. Red grouse are found in Scotland, the northern and north-western counties of England, Wales, and Ireland; and a few on Dartmoor and

Exmoor, introduced as bought birds from Scotland through a dealer in Yorkshire.

No general description of the plumage of red grouse is possible, for no other British bird varies more in its colouring and marking throughout the year. There is one period—roughly speaking, summer—when all grouse are pretty much alike; their plumage then is mainly black barred with buff. There is a second period—roughly speaking, late autumn—when both sexes have completed their moult, and when they separate themselves—again, roughly speaking—into five types, mainly differing according to locality. These types are:—

(1) *The red form.*—Cocks and hens, but commoner among cocks than hens. Generally speaking, this is a western type, from the Hebrides downwards.

(2) *The black form.*—Cocks and hens, but rare among hens. This is a type widely distributed, from Caithness to Yorkshire, but, generally speaking, not western.

(3) *The white-spotted form.*—Cocks and hens, and the white spotting is found on both red and black forms. This is a Highland type.

(4) *The buff-spotted form.*—Only hens—the commonest form. It is sometimes also spotted with white.

(5) *The buff-barred form.*—Only hens—the Irish type.

Food.—The staple food of the red grouse is heather—the green shoots of *Calluna vulgaris*, the common ling. But of ling they eat also, besides the shoots, the flowers and seed-heads. Of the two other heathers—Bell Heather (*Erica cinerea*) and Cross-leaved Heath (*Erica tetralix*) grouse eat the flowers only of Bell Heather, since the leaves are bitter, and only the flowers of *tetralix*. To these three heather foods they add various berries, buds, flowers, and seeds, of which these are the chief:—

(1) Blaeberry (*Vaccinium myrtillus*).—Whortleberry, bilberry—"whorts" or "hurts." Grouse eat buds, flower-stems, flowers, and berries.

(2) In England, another plant called cranberry (*Vaccinium oxycoccos*), but this is not common in Scotland.

(3) Bear Berry (*Arctostaphylos uva-ursi*).—This belongs to high stony ground; grouse eat the red berries and also the pink clusters of flowers, which appear in June, but which you will find growing with the berries in August.

(4) Crowberry or Crakeberry (*Empetrum nigrum*).—Like a heath with black, shining berries. Grouse eat the shoots, leaf-buds, and berries.

(5) Cloudberry (*Rubus chamaemorus*).—A trailing plant, with fruit like a yellow bramble. Grouse eat the berries and young leaves.

(6) Bog Myrtle (*Myrica gale*).—Grouse sometimes eat the buds in winter.

(7) Creeping Willow (*Salix repens*).—A low-growing plant with silky white leaves, of which grouse are very fond.

(8) Cotton Grass (*Eriophorum polystachion*).—Grouse eat the flowers in spring.

(9) Sorrel (*Rumex acetosella*).—Common on the edge of the moor. Grouse love the seeds.

(10) Field Wood Rush (*Luzula campestris*).—Grouse eat the flowers and seed heads.

(11) Heath Rush (*Juncus squarrosus*).—Grouse eat the flowers and seed heads.

To grind up this food in the gizzard and make it digestible, grouse need grit—white quartz or felspar. Young grouse begin to pick up tiny fragments of quartz when only a few days old, and the fragments of quartz in an old grouse's gizzard may number from 350 to 550 in number, and may measure in bulk as much as an ounce of shot.

Birds pair in an open season as early as January, but pairing may be delayed by snow or hard weather. Nesting begins in April, but eggs are sometimes found in March. The nest is little more than a hollow scraped in shortish heather and lined with a few bents of grass. It is often close to the burn. Six to eight is the usual number of eggs, but clutches are found of ten and twelve. They are brownish-cream in ground colour, thickly blotched with dark chestnut. Incubation lasts twenty-four days. Snow is the great danger during the nesting time—snow in Scotland and rain in

England. The young birds begin with insect food, but soon take to the green shoots of the growing heather.

Heather being the staple food of grouse old and young, it must be the aim of the moor owner wishing to maintain a good stock of grouse to provide as much heather as possible of an edible quality. Old heather will not do; what is wanted is the young green shoots. To obtain a sufficient quantity of these, a sufficient area of old heather must be burned every year, thus ensuring a succession of young crops. The best heather for food is from six to fifteen years old, so that the ideal conditions would be that there should be no heather on the moor older than fifteen years. That means that one-fifteenth of the whole area of the moor should be burned every year. But this is a condition almost impossible to fulfil. On a fair-sized moor—say one with an area under heather of 6,000 acres, of which one-fifteenth would be 400 acres—it is practically impossible to cover the ground. The legal period for burning is 1st November to 10th April, with a possible extension in a wet year to 25th April. But on how many days, owing to the weather, is it possible to burn? The Grouse Disease Inquiry Commission found that on an average, taking dry moors with wet and high ground with low, ten days' burning was about as much as a keeper could hope for, and that if he is able to get all the help he needs—not an easy job—and burns in patches, so that he is able to control the fire and avoid setting a whole hillside ablaze, old and new heather alike—he can burn about 20 acres in a day, or 200 acres in all; just half the amount needed for a 6,000 acre moor. The plain fact is obvious; moor owner and keeper alike must be content with what they can. And even without ideal conditions of burning we do get occasionally very good seasons.

Grouse can be hand-reared, but it is a ticklish business, needing more than an average amount of luck, the chief difficulty being with the care of the mothers. The late Dr. Hammond Smith, writing about grouse that were hand-reared on an "observation area" in Surrey under the auspices of the Grouse Disease Committee, describes experiments made in the years 1906–11. It was definitely proved that success could not be obtained by giving eggs laid by grouse in captivity to foster mothers. Perhaps the wrong kind of fowl was chosen, and matters might have gone better if it had been decided to use bantams instead of ordinary hens; at all events, in the years 1908 and 1909 not a single chick was reared. Three lots of eggs, two of twenty and one of seventeen, were given to Buff Orpingtons in 1908; one hen hatched seventeen and killed them all, another hen hatched eleven and killed them all, and the third hen ate the seventeen eggs given her. The year 1909 was equally unsuccessful, but in 1910 five hen grouse left to sit on their own eggs hatched seven, nine, seven, six, and eleven chicks, and of these forty chicks twenty-three reached maturity.

Very young grouse can be fed with hard-boiled eggs and young heather, but the best food for them is the pupae of ants, taken alive from the ants' nest and scalded—in fact, the so-called "ants' eggs" supplied by the trade, but fresh instead of stale and dry.

PTARMIGAN (*Lagopus mutus*)

Why *mutus*? Because the ptarmigan, although strictly speaking not dumb, has no call like that of the grouse—one of the most welcome sounds of the north—but merely a harsh, guttural croak. It is a sound which many grouse shooters never hear, for the ptarmigan is a bird of the high ground, and is more likely to be seen by the deer-stalker than the tenants of a line of grouse butts. Ptarmigan are the only birds in these islands that change their plumage, as the stoat and weasel and the hare in Scotland change their coats, to white in winter. In the summer the cock is a bird of grey-brown plumage, barred and speckled with black, with white primary wing feathers and white under feathers, while the upper parts of the hen are buff-brown, barred with white and black. In the autumn both change the upper parts and flanks to an exquisitely mottled ash-grey, exactly matching the granites and lichens among which the bird crouches, and this it gradually exchanges for pure white, and then, except for the brilliant scarlet supraorbital comb of the cock, it is invisible against the snow.

Ptarmigan feed on the tips and the fruit of blaeberry and crowberry, and like their cousins the rype of Norway, on the buds of dwarf sallow and birch, for which they will burrow in times of snow. Keepers will tell you that the nests are hard to find; the eggs, except that they are paler in ground colour and less thickly blotched, are like those of grouse.

COMMON PARTRIDGE (*Perdix cinerea*)

One of the most attractive features in the character of partridges is that they choose mates for themselves. You cannot assume that any cock will mate with any hen; the birds make their own choice, and when the cock has chosen his hen—or she has let him know that he may choose her if he pleases—they become a devoted pair, and admirable parents. The time of pairing depends largely on the weather. In a mild season the coveys may break up in January, frost and snow may keep them together into March, and if the birds have paired in a warm January, a cold February may bring the coveys together again.

Partridges nest in May. The hen may lay any number of eggs from twelve to twenty-four, olive-brown in colour, and incubation lasts for twenty-one days. Most of the young partridges in England—they are later as you go farther north —are hatched round about the third week in June, and the little birds are at once taken by their parents into the surrounding crops, where the father tends and teaches them as assiduously as the mother. Here comes the determining factor in the life of the young partridge—the weather. If it remains fine and dry till mid-July the young broods will develop into coveys strong on the wing; if it is cold and wet some are sure to die of pneumonia, and even if hatching takes place in warm and dry weather, a sudden thunderstorm— witness the records of many Ascot weeks—may so drench the crops in which the young birds are sheltering that they have no chance of drying themselves and die of cold. So dependent are old and young partridges on the weather, and so variable is the English climate, that it may be safely said that only about once in ten years are the conditions of spring and summer ideal for the nesting birds. Not until mid-August, when all the corn is cut and carried, can the keeper be absolutely certain of the numbers of birds he has on his ground, though a careful and watchful man will make a pretty good guess.

Cock and hen partridges differ in plumage. A bird with a well-marked dark chestnut horse-shoe on the grey breast feathers is almost certainly a cock, but many hens have more or less distinct horse-shoes, and the test is not absolute. The sexes can be determined with certainty, however, by the wing feathers. In the cock partridge the median wing coverts are marked with a longitudinal pale buff stripe running down the shaft, and on each side of the shaft the feather is mottled with grey or brown. In the hen these feathers have the same pale buff stripe, but instead of being mottled they are barred with buff and dark brown.

To tell an old from a young bird early in the season is simple enough. A "cheeper" or "squeaker," of course—a bird too young to shoot—is obvious. But young birds may very well be full grown in September, and the test then is the feet and legs, which in young birds are yellow and in old birds grey. The yellow gradually gives way to grey, and by December it may have vanished altogether, but for some time after the legs have turned grey the undersides of the toes are still yellow.

There is a chestnut variety of the common partridge, sometimes known as the mountain partridge, in which the plumage throughout is tinged with reddish-brown. Another variety has the rufous colouring very pale, and the rest of the plumage clear grey vermiculated with black, and bearing in the female the characteristic cross-bars in deep brown. Pale varieties and albinistic specimens are not uncommon, and occasionally partridges have, instead of the usual chestnut brown, a black horse-shoe on the breast.

RED-LEGGED OR FRENCH PARTRIDGE (*Caccabis rufa*)

French partridges were introduced into England in 1673. In that year Favennes de Mouchant, gamekeeper to Charles II, wrote a letter asking permission to take *perdrix rouges* in the park or neighbourhood of Chambord, and permission was granted by Charles Colbert, Marquis de Croisy, Ambassador from Louis XIV to Charles II. Copies of these letters, which were found in the Bibliothèque Nationale in Paris, were sent to Lord Leicester at Holkham, who communicated the discovery to the *Field*, in March 1921. The letters are dated in the autumn of 1673.

The plumage of the French bird is handsomer than that of the English. The beak is red, the gorget pale grey fringed with black, the side feathers of the breast and belly are barred with black, grey, and buff, and the legs are red. The cock is distinguished from the hen by a knob like a rudimentary spur on his leg. To tell a young bird from an old, look at the first flight feather; in the young bird the tip, in the first autumn plumage, is yellow. Hybrids between grey and red-leg are reported every September, but they are merely young French partridges which have partially assumed the adult plumage.

French partridge eggs are somewhat larger than English, and are buff speckled with light brown. French partridges are hardier than English, and seem to be immune from certain diseases, generally traceable to cold wet weather, which attack the native bird. Their habit when disturbed is to run rather than fly; when at last they are flushed, they fly straighter than the English bird, and a little slower.

QUAIL (*Coturnix communis*)

This is a summer visitor in varying numbers, which, unfortunately, seem to be less in recent years than formerly. The very hot, dry summer of 1893 was a good year for quail, and another season when there was a considerable influx was 1899. But quail have never been really numerous in any English season. Colonel Peter Hawker in all his long shooting career, 1802–53, only once killed eight and only once seven in a season; he only killed fifty-eight in all, and in many seasons shot none.

Quail, even to a greater degree than partridges, benefit by a dry, fine breeding season. They arrive in May and breed about the end of the month, or in June; the nest is a small, thinly-lined hollow among standing crops, or in rough grass and herbage, and seven to ten or a dozen eggs are laid, rather larger than a missel-thrush's, creamy in ground colour, rather sharply pointed at the small end, and lightly or heavily blotched with rich reddish-brown. The note of the cock consists of three harsh, curious notes which have been imitated by the words "wet my lips." In general appearance the bird is like a plump, small partridge with a short turned down tail. Its food consists of seeds, insects, and small snails.

The proper term for a brood of quail is not "covey" but "bevy."

Landrail (*Crex pratensis*)

Corncrake, dakerhen. This bird, like the quail, unfortunately, appears to be becoming rarer. It is more often seen than heard, but its monotonous "crake-crake—crake-crake," which can be imitated so as to draw a bird across a field by running a stick along the teeth of a comb, is an unfamiliar sound in many places where it used to be a regular accompaniment to the song of the nightingale. It is a very shy, skulking bird, and a head raised above the grass of a May meadow is about as much as is usually seen of it except when it is flushed in the fields during September partridge shooting. It then flies so slowly and heavily, with awkwardly hanging legs, that it is difficult to believe that it can make long journeys across the sea at the seasons of migration—especially as once having been flushed it is impossible to make it rise again.

In size the landrail is rather smaller than a moorhen; in colour it is a mottled reddish-brown above, and pale greyish-white beneath. For nesting it prefers hayfields and young corn; the nest is of dry grass and herbage, and is placed on

23

the ground where the cover is thickest. The eggs are seven to nine or ten in number, creamy buff in ground colour, spotted with reddish-pink and brown, and lighter tones of grey. They are not unlike the moorhen's, but smaller. Its food consists of various seeds, and especially of insects, snails, and slugs.

PHEASANT

COMMON OR BLACK-NECKED (*Phasianus colchicus*)—CHINESE OR RING-NECKED (*P. torquatus*)—MONGOLIAN (*P. mongolicus*)

These three varieties of pheasant, and their crosses, form the main stock of British coverts. *Phasianus colchicus* is sometimes referred to as the "Old English" pheasant, and is doubtless descended from the birds which were in English woods in the time of the Romans. Whether or not they were actually introduced by the Romans will possibly remain a disputed point, since remains of pheasant-like birds have been found in pre-historic caves in France and other places in Northern Europe. But that they were kept in the precincts of Roman villas and that pheasants were reared by Romans from eggs set under domestic fowls is certain. Palladius, the Roman author of *De Re Rustica*, writing at some date between A.D. 300 and 400, gives definite instructions for breeding and feeding, and in the Musée de Bardo near Tunis you may see tessellated floors showing a rich Roman's house and farm, horses, poultry, pheasants and all.

For that reason, that pheasants for hundreds of years have been reared in the same way as poultry, there is not much that is distinct and individual in the bird's natural history. Game farmers pen a cock with five hens as a rule, or in large open pens let the birds run together without exact regard to the proportion of cocks to hens, leaving the stronger cocks to manage as many hens as they please. In a wild state it may happen that a cock and a hen mate as a pair, or the cock may take two wives, which bring up separate families. There is an old belief, or superstition, that the hen pheasant is a bad mother—an idea doubtless due to the fact that a wild hen always loses a few of her brood before they are full grown. But can a bird be called a bad mother who will sit and be drowned in a storm of rain rather than leave her eggs? Or who will attack and drive off any intruder, from a weasel or a dog to a haymaker or even (as I have known it happen) a postman on a bicycle, who should happen to come too near, as she thinks, to her chicks? There is another reason why she loses some of her brood; not that she is a careless mother, but that they are heedless and wandering children. They do not keep close to their parent, as do young partridges; they find themselves on the wrong side of a fence, or wire-netting, and become lost.

For a nest, the hen pheasant scrapes a hollow in the ground, usually among brambles or rank herbage, and lines it with dry leaves or such vegetation as she may find lying about. Ten or twelve is the usual number of the eggs, which are laid in April and May, and are light olive brown, varying a good deal in shade. Occasionally a pheasant will nest in a tree, such as a pollard willow, which provides a convenient platform. Their food is a varied mixture of acorns, grain, berries, and so on, while they eat a great quantity of snails, wire-worms, the grubs of the Bibionidae and other injurious insects, the "spangles" which fall from oak leaves, and roots such as those of silverweed and pig nut. Pheasants have even been found to have swallowed such creatures as small mice and young adders.

Pheasants as a rule roost in trees, the cocks crowing as they go up in the dusk. But they will also roost on the ground, sleeping the night through, for instance, in long heather.

All pheasants inter-breed, so that besides crosses of the black-necked, ring-necked, and Mongolian, varieties of plumage may be traced to the Japanese pheasant, *P. versicolor*, the Prince of Wales's, *P. principalis*, and others. One variety known as Reeves's pheasant has an immensely long tail, and like it, others, such as the golden, silver, and Amherst pheasant, are bred for the beauty of their plumage.

About the year 1926 there occurred a curious outbreak in British pheasant coverts of numbers of dark-plumaged birds which were at first supposed to be of *versicolor* ancestry, but were soon recognised to be a variant first noticed by Lord Rothschild at Elveden in 1888, and known as the melanistic mutant. Why these melanistic mutants should have suddenly appeared at the same time in different parts of the country it was difficult to explain, but the cause of the outbreak was eventually traced to a war-time accident, which resulted in the release from confinement of a batch of descendants of a single melanistic mutant crossed with a common pheasant. Numbers of these birds found their way into the hands of game farmers, and eggs obtained from them, or from hens mated with them, came on the market in the ordinary way, and were bought by owners of coverts in many parts of the country. For a time there seemed to be a possibility that these melanistic birds would prove a dominant type, but either from a change in public taste or from natural causes their numbers season by season became fewer and fewer, until once more the mutant took its place in the bag as merely an uncommon variant.

WOODCOCK (*Scolopax rusticola*)

Mainly a winter visitor, but becoming a resident nester in yearly increasing numbers. The great annual inrush takes place in late October and early November, the largest number arriving at the period of the first November full moon, but probably the determining factor of their movement is an east wind. These winter immigrants are chiefly birds that have bred in Norway, Sweden, Finland, and possibly

Northern Russia; but evidence is still wanting to show how far the birds which breed in the British Isles share in a similar south-westward movement. Of a large number (121) of young birds marked during 1904–10 in Limerick and near Clonmel, eighteen were killed locally though none of them after 10th September. Two Clonmel birds were shot on the same day near Gibraltar in November and one in Holland in October. It looks as if there was a migration from these islands in August or September, but against that as a theory applying to all home-bred birds is the fact that a number of birds marked in Northumberland in 1892 to 1914 were killed near their nesting place from September to March.

Woodcock generally nest in a quiet, shady glade. The nest is a hollow lined with a few dead leaves or bracken. A sitting woodcock is generally found facing the sun, and probably she moves round with it. An old bird will carry her young, if disturbed, between her thighs to a place of safety. Four eggs are laid, pale yellow-brown, blotched and spotted with red-brown and ash-grey. A curious feature in the bird's anatomy is that the ear-opening is situated in front of or under the corner of the eye, instead of, as in other birds, behind the eye.

The sexes cannot be told apart by their plumage, but the pelvic bones of the hen, especially after Christmas, can be felt to be wider apart than those of the cock. As to plumage in general, the ground colour varies from bright chestnut to greyish and dark chestnut. Albinos are very rare, but birds with a few white feathers are not uncommon. Buff and melanistic varieties occur, and I have seen a bird which was almost lilac and brown.

Woodcock weigh: males, 9 to 12 ozs.; females, 10 to 13 ozs. Woodcock have been killed in Ireland weighing 17 ozs. and 18 ozs.

COMMON SNIPE (*Gallinago caelestis*)

Another name for the bird is the heather-bleater. This is, of course, because of the peculiar "drumming" or "bleating" sound made by the bird in the breeding season. The method by which this sound is produced is in dispute. It is indisputable that it *can* be produced by the outer feathers of the tail which are extended at right angles to the body, when, in soaring round its nest on a wide circle, up and down high in the air, the bird turns for the downward swoop. I thought I had established it for a certainty that the sound was produced in this way, by mechanical means, when I had proved that by fixing the outer tail feathers at right angles in an arrow near the feather and shooting it high into the air, the identical sound was produced by the falling arrow. But since that experiment was made a gamekeeper, known to be a trustworthy observer, wrote and told me that he had a snipe which came and fed with his poultry, and that he had watched it and heard it drum when on the ground; and we are left with the strange conclusion that the snipe's drum, like every other bird's love call, is produced vocally, though it undoubtedly may also be produced mechanically.

I have heard a snipe drum as early as 26th January in the dusk and as late as mid-August. Snipe nest in April, making a slight cup of dry grass in a tussock of grass or rushes. Four eggs are laid, varying in ground colour from olive green to light brownish-buff, richly blotched and spotted with brown; the markings often run spirally round the egg.

Snipe, like woodcock, are both migratory and resident in England. In hard winters many thousands join the home-bred birds, but in open, mild winters comparatively few visit us. Among winter visitors are the two other species of snipe, of which the Great Snipe (*Gallinago major*) is a winter straggler from Scandinavia or Siberia to Africa, but the Jack Snipe (*G. gallinula*) is a regular autumn immigrant. A Common Snipe weighs from 4 to 5 ozs., and 8 ozs. is a recorded weight. A Great Snipe weighs 8 ozs. and a Jack 2 to $2\frac{1}{2}$ ozs.

A Common Snipe has fourteen tail feathers, a Great Snipe sixteen, and a Jack twelve.

CHARACTERISTICS OF BIRDS OF PREY

GOLDEN EAGLE (*Aquila chrysaëtus*)

SOMETIMES CALLED the black eagle. Plumage, mainly rich dark brown, but with tawny streaks and paler plumes on head and neck. It is this mixture of colour which explains the names "black" and "golden." The nest is a mass of sticks lined with dry stems and tufts of heather and other plants, made as a rule on a ledge of steep rock, or more rarely in a tree. The eggs vary in colour between dull white stained with lilac-grey and brown, or blotched with red-brown lilac. Breeds only in the Scottish Highlands.

The golden eagle feeds largely on grouse and ptarmigan, mountain hares and occasionally young lambs. Will also attack roe deer fawns and red deer calves.

WHITE-TAILED EAGLE (*Haliaëtus albicilla*)

Sea eagle, Erne. The old birds are brown with a whitish head and white tail, but young birds up to five or six years have no white marks. Builds a large nest of sticks on a cliff or rock, occasionally on an island tree. Two bluish-white eggs are laid, faintly marked with brownish red. This rare eagle used to breed in the Highlands and in one or two places on the west coast of Ireland.

Food: Various birds and small animals. Will also hunt for fish in the manner of an osprey.

Peregrine Falcon (*Falco peregrinus*)

Also known as the hunting hawk and goshawk (in High-lands and Shetland). Plumage, dark-barred slate-grey above, with a white breast spotted and streaked with black. Young birds are mottled-brown above and yellowish-brown with darker streaks beneath. Breeds in rocks and cliffs and occasionally in trees, perhaps utilising a crow's old nest. Eggs, two to four, generally laid in April; resembling, but much larger than, kestrels' eggs, mottled chestnut-brown. Peregrines are not uncommon in inland mountainous districts, as well as on high sea-cliffs in south and south-east England and Wales.

Food: Grouse, partridges, rooks, gulls; will also strike down a homing pigeon.

Kite (*Milvus ictinus*)

Also known as the fork-tailed kite, glede, and puttock. This bird is on the verge of extinction. It builds a nest of sticks in trees, lined with scraps of rubbish, wool, hair, and even bits of paper. Plumage, mainly reddish-brown, with lighter breast. Eggs not unlike those of the buzzard. The kite was at one time a common object of the countryside, so much so as to be a nuisance to the villager whose washing it would carry away when hung out on hedges to dry. To-day breeds only in a few parts of Wales.

Food: Small birds, including young game and poultry chicks, small animals, and reptiles.

Common Buzzard (*Buteo vulgaris*)

Sometimes known as puttock. In colour it is as a rule a rich brown above with paler markings below, but buzzards vary a good deal in their depth of colouring. About mid-April it builds a large nest of sticks, lined with wool and dry leaves, generally on a ledge or crevice of rock, but sometimes in trees. Three or four large round eggs are laid, sometimes dull white stained with grey and brown, sometimes handsomely marked with reddish-brown and grey. Belongs to mountainous districts in Wales, the Lake District, the Highlands, the Bristol Channel, and is occasionally seen in the southern counties of England.

The buzzard is a stately flier, and floats and circles at a great height with slow beats of its broad round wings. It is too slow in flight to be a danger to grouse and other game birds, and its main diet is of young rabbits, small birds, mice, moles, reptiles, and even insects.

ROUGH-LEGGED BUZZARD (*Buteo lagopus*)

This is a rare winter visitor from Scandinavia and Northern Russia. Its legs are feathered to the toes like the golden eagle's instead of being bare as in the common buzzard. Its plumage resembles that of the common buzzard, except that it has a white patch on the tail. It has been met with in all parts of Britain, but chiefly in North-East Scotland and East England. Less than a score have been recorded from Ireland.

Food: A little larger than the common buzzard, in its winter visits to England the rough-legged buzzard preys on rabbits.

OSPREY (*Pandion haliaëtus*)

Also known as the fishing hawk. Dark brown, with a white-flecked back and tufted white-marked head. As a breeding species it is to be feared that it is extinct. Occasionally visitors are to be seen, but its fishing habits have led to its destruction by gamekeepers and others. It used to nest in North Scotland on islands such as that of Loch-an-Eileain. To-day, a rare bird of passage in spring and autumn.

Food: The bird sights its prey from above the water of lake or estuary, plunges down and emerges with the fish in its talons.

MARSH HARRIER (*Circus aeruginosus*)

Sometimes known as the moor buzzard. A typical bird of prey of the Fens, nearly as large as the buzzard, but not so heavy in build. The adult male is mostly brown, with a paler head and breast, and the female is brown nearly throughout. It builds a large nest of reeds on the marsh, and the eggs, from three to five in number, are bluish-white. Nests in Norfolk and the wilder bogs of Ireland.

Food: Small birds, young water hens and the like, also frogs and reptiles.

HEN HARRIER (*Circus cyaneus*)

Sometimes known as the dove hawk (male) and the ring-tail (female). Belongs to moor and mountain as well as marsh, and nests in parts of Scotland and Ireland, in the latter country being sometimes known as the chicken hawk. Male, mainly grey plumage with white beneath; female, chiefly brown with barred tail. Nest, usually hollowed in heathery hillside; four to six eggs are laid, bluish-white sometimes with faint reddish spots. Nests in Orkneys, Outer Hebrides, and perhaps Ireland.

Food: Small mammals, voles, rats, mice, young rabbits, birds, frogs, lizards, insects.

MONTAGU'S HARRIER (*Circus cineraceus*)

Ash-coloured harrier. Much resembles the hen harrier, but is slightly smaller in the body and with long wings and tail. A summer visitor which sometimes succeeds in nesting in the marshlands of East Anglia. The nest is built of sedge on the ground. It occasionally nests elsewhere besides the Eastern Counties, in England and Wales. Reaches the breeding grounds in April.

Food: Similar to that of the other harriers.

SPARROW-HAWK (*Accipiter nisus*)

Sometimes known as the blue hawk or pigeon hawk. The mature sparrow hawk has a blue-grey back, and its breast is barred transversely with brown. The male is considerably smaller than the female, and immature birds are a dull brown on the back instead of grey. The sparrow-hawk builds in various kinds of trees, sometimes in the old nest of a crow or woodpigeon. The five or six eggs are very pale blue in ground colour, sometimes smudged with pale brown, but sometimes very handsomely spotted and blotched with rich chestnut.

Range: All wooded parts of the British Isles.

Food: Poultry and game chicks if it can get them, wood pigeons, blackbirds, thrushes, and smaller birds.

KESTREL (*Falco tinnunculus*)

Windhover, stannel hawk; sometimes known among keepers as the red hawk. Male, reddish-brown with a few dark spots; head and tail grey. Female, larger than the male, generally a deeper brown. The underparts of both are spotted and streaked with black like the breast of a thrush. The kestrel nests in trees and among cliffs, occasionally on towers and ruins or in the hollow of a broken tree branch. Four to six eggs are laid, varying from yellowish-white to yellowish-red in ground colour, spotted with deep brown or freckled with rich red and brown.

Range: Common in most parts of Britain.

Food: The kestrel is one of the most useful birds we possess, and is a valuable friend to farmers. It preys mainly on mice, and may be seen almost stationary in the air hovering over likely parts of field and meadow. Sometimes a "rogue" kestrel will take young pheasants from the rearing-field.

MERLIN (*Falco aesalon*)

Stone falcon (from its habit of sitting watching on a rock); blue hawk (from the colour of the male). The merlin is the smallest of British hawks and belongs to the open moorlands. The upper parts of the male are slate-grey, narrowly streaked with black, and the tail has a black band towards the tip, which is white. The upper-parts of the female are dark brownish-grey, and the under-parts of both birds are white with dark spots or streaks. Immature birds are brown like the female. The eggs, three to five, are laid in May in a hollow among heather; they resemble those of the kestrel, but have darker frecklings. The bird belongs to the northern parts of England and Wales, but in winter is sometimes found farther south.

Food: Small birds of the moor, snipe, and small shore birds. It is practically harmless to grouse.

HOBBY (*Falco subbuteo*)

A rare summer visitor, much persecuted by egg-collectors. The hobby in colour is dark grey, almost black upon the head; the sides of the neck are patched with white, and the breast is white flecked with black. The cock is smaller than the hen. The immature young are mottled brown and cream colour. Hobbies breed in June, generally utilising the old nest of a crow or magpie, adding a little new material. The eggs are three or four, resembling those of the kestrel, but are much smaller.

Range: Spring immigrants reach the southern counties in May, but occasionally straggle northwards.

Food: Preys on small birds, particularly swallows on their southern flight, and starlings, but is practically harmless to game, though unfortunately is shot by gamekeepers. In the summer it feeds largely on dragon flies, butterflies, cock-chafers, and bats and beetles caught at dusk.

HONEY BUZZARD (*Pernis apivorus*)

If not extinct in England, on the verge of extinction. In plumage it is chiefly brown above, white-barred with brown beneath, except in the female, which is barred beneath by brown and yellowish-red. The heads of both birds are grey. Two or three eggs are laid, white patched with reddish-brown. It is a summer visitor arriving in May, and has nested within recent years in parts of England and southern Scotland.

Food: The honey buzzard feeds occasionally on small birds and animals, but its characteristic food is wasps, bumble bees and their grubs, for which it will scratch in the earth to carry off the combs to its nest.

Apart from the *Falconidae*, seventeen other birds may be classed as more or less predatory. Seven of them belong to the crow family, five are owls, and five are gulls. A brief description follows.

CROW FAMILY *Corvidae*

RAVEN (*Corvus corax*)

Corbie. Ravens nest usually on a ledge or in a rift in a cliff, but sometimes in a tree. The same nest is used year after year, and the birds pair for life. The eggs are small for the size of the bird, and resemble those of the carrion crow.

Range: Mainly the sea cliffs of the south and west, but also in Wales, Ireland, and Scotland.

Food: Chiefly carrion, but omnivorous.

CARRION CROW (*Corvus corone*)

Sometimes called corbie crow, and to be distinguished in appearance from the rook by the absence of a white patch at the base of the beak. Unlike the rook, the carrion crow is a solitary bird. The nest is usually in a tree, but sometimes on a ledge of rock. It is a large, solid structure of sticks thickly lined with wool and hair. Four to five eggs are laid, greenish-white in colour, blotched, spotted and speckled with various shades of greenish-brown and grey.

Range: Throughout England, Wales, Ireland, and Scotland, but less frequent in the extreme north.

Food: It is a savage bird, which eats not only carrion but eggs and birds. It will also kill a lamb or weakly sheep, beginning by pecking out the eyes.

HOODED CROW (*Corvus cornix*)

Hoodie, grey crow, Royston crow. Easily distinguished by its light grey body, the head, throat, wings, and tail being black. It is chiefly found in the north and west of Scotland and in Ireland, but also to be seen as a winter visitor in the south and east of England.

Food: This bird is no less savage than the carrion crow in its attacks on living creatures, and its diet is as varied as that of the carrion crow.

ROOK (*Corvus frugilegus*)

Rooks are abundant in England, but decrease in numbers towards the north of Scotland. The eggs are brownish or greenish white, spotted, blotched, and speckled with green, ash-grey, and dark greenish-brown.

Food: The chief food of rooks is insects injurious to agriculture, but in some districts, probably owing to drought or absence of its natural food, it has acquired bad habits in the matter of eating grain, sucking eggs, and taking chickens. See under "Rooks and Rookeries," page 52.

JACKDAW (*Corvus monedula*)

Like rooks, jackdaws are gregarious, and prefer to nest in colonies among trees with convenient holes. Sometimes, however, the difficulty of finding nesting quarters leads them to choose separate positions, in church towers and so on. The nest is large—in hollow trees it may be enormous—built of sticks and lined mainly with sheep's wool. The eggs are usually five, a good deal smaller than the rook's, pale greenish-blue, blotched and speckled with deep green and greenish-brown.

Range: Widely distributed, but not in the extreme north of Scotland.

Food: Jackdaws feed mainly on insects, worms, snails, and so on, but will take eggs and young birds in spring.

MAGPIE (*Pica rustica*)

Pyat, Mag. One of the cleverest and handsomest of native birds, mainly black and white, but with colours of shot green and purple in its long tail feathers. The nest is a large dome of sticks on a framework of sticks and clay, with the cup lined with roots and grass, and with an entrance at the side. The eggs are clear greenish-white thickly spotted with green and grey.

Range: Common in all wooded parts of the country.

Food: Magpies destroy large numbers of slugs, snails, and insects, but in spring eat the eggs and young of other birds.

JAY (*Garrulus glandarius*)

Every one knows this handsome bird with the bright blue hackle in its wing and the white tail spot which shows in flight. The nest is rather bulky, of dry twigs lined with root-fibres, generally about eight to twenty feet from the ground. The eggs are like a large variety of the blackbird's.

Range: Common throughout the country, except towards the north of Scotland.

Food: Jays destroy the nests of other birds, suck eggs, and devour nestlings. They are also a nuisance in taking green peas.

OWL FAMILY *Strigidae*

BROWN OWL (*Syrnium aluco*)

Tawny owl, wood owl, hoot owl. Every one knows the long musical hoot of the brown owl. Its plumage is mixed brown and grey, with some small white spots on the wings.

It chiefly roosts and nests in hollow trees, but will occasionally occupy old nests of magpies, crows, and woodpigeons.

Range: Common in England, but less so in Scotland.

Food: Brown owls will occasionally attack young pheasants at dusk, but this happens only during a short time in the year and for the rest of the year the brown owl is a friend to the farmer and gamekeeper alike in its destruction of mice and rats.

BARN OWL (*Strix flammea*)

White owl, screech owl, church owl. One of the most valuable of all friends to the keeper as well as the farmer. It is a fine bird, with the buff plumage of the back pencilled with brown, grey and white, while the underparts are white. It is interesting that the Latin name should reproduce the sound of the screech which is so familiar a sound of English woods by night. The barn owl makes no nest, but frequents barns, churches, and other buildings and will also nest in a hollow tree.

Range: Throughout the country, but less numerous in the north of Scotland.

Food: Chiefly mice, rats, and land voles. Quite harmless to game.

LONG-EARED OWL (*Asio otus*)

Sometimes called the horned owl. It is smaller than the brown owl, but looks taller owing to its long tail and the two remarkable tufts or plumes on its head. The plumage is much the same as that of the brown owl, except that the breast is covered more closely with dark streaks. Nesting begins in March; four to six rounded white eggs are laid in an old nest of the woodpigeon, crow, or magpie.

Range: Generally distributed, but not numerous.

Food: The long-eared owl feeds by night on mice, young rats, small birds, and beetles.

SHORT-EARED OWL (*Asio accipitrinus*)

A winter visitor, arriving about the same time as the woodcock, and for that reason, and because of its twisting method of flight, it is sometimes called the woodcock owl. Plumage, a mixture of mottled greys and browns. It is smaller than the long-eared owl, and has only short ear-like tufts on the head. There is a return migration in the spring, but a certain number remain to breed. No nest is made, but the eggs, usually six, are laid in a hollow of the heather or the sedge of marshes.

Range: Throughout the country.

Food: Largely voles. In the time of the great plague of voles in south-west Scotland during the years 1890–3, there was a great increase of short-eared owls, which destroyed enormous numbers and under the influence of the plentiful supply of food became remarkably prolific. Mr. Bell, of Castle O'er in Dumfriesshire, has described a nest found in 1892 by a shepherd, in which the hen bird was sitting on no fewer than twelve eggs as early as 29th February. Only her head was visible above the snow, and seventeen dead voles were lying round the nest.

LITTLE OWL (*Athene noctua*)

Much smaller than the other owls, and hunts by day as well as by night. It lays its eggs in hollow trees, or occasionally in rabbit holes. The little owl is a foreigner, introduced from Holland in the 'eighties and 'nineties by Lord Lilford and others.

Range: Since its introduction it has spread widely throughout the country.

Food: The little owl, no doubt, does a certain amount of good in its destruction of beetles, earwigs, and other insects, also young rats and mice; but there is conclusive evidence that it is destructive to game and poultry, and during the breeding season feeds largely on birds, chiefly starlings, blackbirds, and song thrushes. It will also kill skylarks and other birds of ground-feeding habits. The birds which it actually kills are not the only birds whose death is caused by its depredations, for it must be remembered that singing birds killed in the breeding season are also likely to have young birds in their nests.

GULLS

Harmful or Harmless ?

Gulls are birds of considerable intelligence, and of recent years have changed, and may be still changing their habits. Until the cold winters of 1890 and 1895 gulls were a rare sight above the Thames in London. In those years they discovered that the Thames was a source of food supply, and to-day they travel up all rivers inland in search of food. They are no longer merely "sea-gulls," but birds of the countryside. And this change in their habits became particularly noticeable during the war of 1914–8 and in the years immediately following. The gamekeepers of grouse moors were absent in France, Greece, Palestine, and the moors were no longer patrolled as they were. In counties with extensive seaboards—in Argyllshire, for instance, where arms of the sea run long distances inland—gulls discovered that there were sources of food supply in the eggs and chicks of grouse, and they seriously reduced the numbers of grouse in many parts of Scotland. Generally speaking, they remain enemies of grouse to-day, a position which would have seemed unlikely, say, fifty years ago, but which unfortunately must be recognised.

Six species may be listed as generally distributed:

Greater Black-backed Gull (*Larus marinus*).

The beak, very large and strong, is pale yellow; legs and toes, pale yellowish-red. Tail, white.

Lesser Black-backed Gull (*Larus fuscus*).

Beak, yellow; angle of lower part, red. Head, white; back, dark grey; wings, mainly dark grey; legs and toes, yellow.

Common Gull (*Larus canus*).

Not so plentiful as the name might imply. Beak, pale yellow tinged with grey-green near base; wing coverts, grey; primaries, first four black on outer web, first two patched with white; tail, white; legs and toes dull greenish-grey, with a tinge of dull yellowish-red.

Herring Gull (*Larus argentatus*).

The beak, pale dull yellow, with the angle of the lower mandible dark orange-red; wing coverts, grey; primaries, the two first black on the outer webs, the six greater quills crossed by a black bar; tail, white; legs and toes, pale yellowish-grey, with a tinge of light red.

Black-headed Gull (*Larus ridibundus*).

Brown-black head in breeding season; otherwise mainly grey, with white breast; legs and toes, deep vermilion red.

Kittiwake (*Larus tridactylus*).

Beak, greenish-yellow; back and wings, French grey; head, neck, breast, under surface and tail, pure white; wings tipped with black; legs, dull brown.

Of these six species a well-known naturalist, whose word carries authority, writes as follows in regard to conditions in Scotland to-day:—

"The kittiwake is purely a sea-bird, very harmless.

"Of the other five:

"(1) Greater Black-back. Most destructive, and as it is strong and powerful, attacks (in Lewis) even full-grown grouse.

"I saw one last summer in Orkney throw up a complete young fulmar.

"(2) Lesser Black-back. Less destructive, but on occasion will take eggs and young.

"(3) Common Gull. This comparatively small and inno-cent-looking bird takes both eggs and young of many birds.

"(4) Herring Gull. Another egg-stealer.

"(5) Black-headed Gull. I am convinced that this bird does much more harm to eggs and young birds than is generally realised.

"I fear, therefore, that all our gulls, with the exception of the kittiwake, are harmful in a greater or less degree."

RABBITS & HARES

The Common Hare

"AS MAD as a March hare" is a proverbial comparison, and most people, perhaps, in using the proverb, would have in mind the sight of jack hares sitting up and boxing with their fore-feet as you may see them in fields in spring. Hares at such times look as if they were showing off, or merely pretending to fight, and the round as a rule ends without damage done. But hares can, if they choose, fight savagely enough, and one may even kill another with blows of his hind feet, when he could perhaps be described as mad with rage. But hares can be mad in other ways; a jack hare, or two jacks, slowly and ceaselessly pursuing a retreating jill, or merely two jacks sitting and staring at each other. There could hardly be madness with less method.

Hares are unaccountable creatures at other times besides the courting season. If the usual pairing time is February and March in England, and March and April in Scotland, it is also the fact that in mild seasons they breed all the year round, and there is not a month in which young leverets may not be found. The female may breed at ten months to a year, but the period of gestation is not exactly known, nor are authorities agreed as to the usual number of the litter. The Rev. E. A. Woodruffe-Peacock, for instance, in *The Cultivation of the Hare*, says definitely that it is five, but J. G. Millais in *The Mammals of Great Britain and Ireland* says that "there is not the least doubt that litters of two, three, and four are quite common in the south of England, while as many as six, seven, and eight have been recorded " (*Field*, 6th September 1902). It seems that the mother hare soon after the birth of her young—which, of course, are born fully furred and able to see, not naked and blind like young rabbits—moves her family about and places them in different forms, visiting them in turn at night to suckle them. Mr. Woodruffe-Peacock says that "This regular dispersal of their young into suckling forms soon after birth is performed at night, and very rarely witnessed. I have never seen it, but was informed that 'they are carried as a cat does her kittens.' It has led to the almost universal belief that hares have only one, or, at most, two leverets at a birth. If this were the case, where mustelines are common hares would soon be extinct."

According to J. G. Millais, "when running at ease" the length of a hare's stride is about four feet, and he adds that when frightened it lengthens its stride to ten and twelve feet. But a hare need not be frightened to take long strides or rather leaps. A hare has been recorded in the *Field* as having been seen bounding along wet sand in Cornwall, with no other creature near it. The length of the stride, or rather of the leaps, was measured and found to be eleven feet three inches. A hare can jump wire-netting four feet high, as gardeners who have fenced their ground against rabbits know to their cost.

Hares can also swim well and will take to water when there is no need for them to do so. Mr. Woodruffe-Peacock writes of hares swimming the River Trent, at a place where the river is over 200 yards wide, in order to feed in a field of carrots. They were seen to enter the river at dusk and to return about dawn.

An English hare usually weighs from 7 to 9 lbs., but in Scotland the weight may be as much as 10 lbs. Millais records that in the shooting season of 1886 at Murthly in Perthshire he weighed three hares which scaled 11, 11¾, and 12 lbs. Mr. Robert Henderson at Longwitton, Northumberland, is recorded by the *Field* to have killed on 23rd October 1876, a hare weighing 13 lbs. 4 ozs., and the same paper on 1st October 1910 credits Mr. Harper of Louth, Lincolnshire, as having weighed two hares of 13 lbs. and 14 lbs. apiece.

As to the speed of hares, J. E. Harting in his monograph *The Rabbit*, in the "Fur, Feather, and Fin" series, observes that "a rabbit is said to run faster than a hare for thirty-five yards; and no one would think of comparing the two, but for the few seconds that elapse after a rabbit is pushed from its 'seat'—when it runs its fastest—and after the hare is started, uncertain, timidly cantering off, but occasionally racing away at a speed which few four-footed creatures excel."

Mr. Hugh Gladstone, in his book *Record Bags and Shooting Records*, says that "in a motor car it has been observed that at forty miles an hour the car will overtake and pass a hare, but that up to that speed the animal will usually hold its own." As to the speed of rabbits, he has been informed by a correspondent that whippets can cover 200 yards in well under thirteen seconds; that is, less than thirty-one and a half miles per hour. It cannot be supposed that a rabbit's speed can approximate that of a whippet.

Mountain or Blue Hare

This is a weaker and feebler creature altogether than the common hare, and one which, though shot for the table, cannot be said to offer a sporting mark of any kind. In the summer the general colour of the upper-parts is a brownish-grey changing to a bluish-grey in September, while in winter the whole coat is much longer and pure white, except for the tips of the ears which are always black. In these gradual changes the mountain hare's colouring much resembles that of the ptarmigan.

As regards weight, mountain hares differ considerably. Females are a little heavier than males, and weights range from $5\frac{1}{2}$ to $7\frac{1}{2}$ lbs. J. G. Millais, out of a bag of 200 made at Dunalastair on 30th October 1897, picked three which weighed $7\frac{3}{4}$ lbs., 8 lbs. 3 ozs., and $8\frac{1}{2}$ lbs.

Mountain hares belong to the hills and moorlands of the Highlands, and are to be found at any altitude over 500 feet. They are curiously foolish creatures, and a hare after bolting at top speed when first disturbed will slow down and, at a distance of eighty or a hundred yards, will perhaps stop and sit to watch its pursuer.

A sub-species of the mountain hare is the Irish hare, a slightly bigger animal, with a reddish-brown tint in its grey coat, and seldom turning more than partially white in winter. Buff varieties are not uncommon, and Irish hares usually weighing 7 or $7\frac{1}{2}$ lbs. have been known to turn the scale at 9 and $9\frac{1}{4}$ lbs.

THE RABBIT

Just as the pheasant is vaguely said to have been intro-duced into England by the Romans, so is the rabbit. But there is no proof. And just as remains of birds resembling pheasants have been found in pre-historic caves in France, so do fossil remains of rabbits exist in British formations belonging to the Pleistocene period. The rabbit, then, may be said to be indigenous to England, but it is comparatively a new arrival in Scotland. There are districts in the Highlands where a hundred years ago rabbits were unknown.

Chief among the differences between the hare and the rabbit are the facts that rabbits live below ground and produce their young hairless and blind. But rabbits can exist without burrowing, and on very wet soils where the herbage is long make tunnels and passages in the matted growth, where they breed in hollows something like the "form" of a hare. In colour rabbits are grey-brown, shading to red in the fur of the neck. But black rabbits are not uncommon, and there are districts where the local colour is grey or sandy. The tail, or scut, is black on the upper surface and white underneath, and the showing of the white scut in flight serves as a danger signal to other rabbits in the neighbourhood. But the deliberate danger signal is a stamp with the hind foot on the surface of the ground. Rabbits are naturally timid creatures, but will fight and even rout enemies in defence of their young.

For the first thirty yards of its running, when startled, a rabbit may be faster than a hare, but a hare in its stride, with its far longer hindlegs, is a different creature altogether. A rabbit scuttles, but a hare bounds. As to weight, a well-fed rabbit turns the scale at from 3 lbs. to $3\frac{1}{2}$ lbs., but rabbits have been shot weighing up to 4 lbs. 14 ozs. There may be a suspicion, with an exceptionally heavy rabbit, that there has been crossing with the so-called Belgian hare turned down to increase size. A rabbit weighing 5 lbs. 10 ozs. (paunched) has been reported in the *Field* from Tagg's Island, Middlesex, and another, unpaunched, at 6 lbs. 8 ozs., from Stratton Strawless, Norfolk.

FOUR-FOOTED ENEMIES OF GAME

IN DAYS gone by, the name for these was "vermin," a word to which the Oxford Dictionary attaches the following definition:—"Animals of a noxious or objectionable kind. Originally applied to reptiles, stealthy or slinking animals, and various wild beasts; now, except in the United States and Australia, almost entirely restricted to those animals or birds which prey upon preserved game." It is a short and comprehensive word, but has it any other recommendation?

Of enemies of game—of creatures, that is, which regard pheasants, partridges, and so on, as a desirable form of food —chief among the four-footed comes the fox. And to understand the balance of wild life, and the difference to "preserved game" in districts where there are gamekeepers and districts where there are none, an inquirer into such matters might be invited to study conditions in such a county as Surrey, for example, where over large areas building is gradually spreading, and where gamekeepers are becoming scarcer, yet where hunting is still carried on. What happens is that the only creature that is "preserved" is the fox. In districts where large areas are occupied by golf courses, and where there is added to these here and there an area belonging to or under the control of the National Trust, there are no gamekeepers to carry guns or set traps, and the result is that stoats and weasels abound, but the one poacher who goes his way absolutely without hindrance is the fox. Surrey apart from its towns is a county of commons and woodlands, in which it is not easy to get a fox away in front of hounds, and the balance of wild life is a balance very certainly in favour of the fox. Much has been written of the possibilities of preserving foxes and pheasants on the same ground, possibly in the same coverts—granted, probably, a plentiful supply of rabbits—but where rabbits are kept down by golf clubs, farmers and gardeners, and an absence of pheasants means also an absence of gamekeepers, the fox flourishes and the partridge disappears. It is in this type of countryside that the fox, protected by countryside tradition, becomes of the natural game bird of the country-side the arch-enemy.

But the fox is not the only enemy of the partridge or the pheasant, and it is not only in an unkeepered countryside that the partridge's enemies tend to multiply. Stoats and weasels—no game estate can afford free existence to either of those lithe and graceful gobblers of chicks and eggs. One virtue they possess—the weasel, perhaps, in greater measure than the stoat—they are by nature destroyers of rats. And for rats to-day, no more than in the days of the Mayor and Corporation of Hamelin, can a word of anything but execration be found. The calculation has been made—I do not guess upon what authority—that there are more rats in Great Britain than there are men, women, and children, and that each rat costs a farthing a day for board and lodging. Forty million rats at a farthing a day works out at fifteen million pounds per annum. Is it any wonder that Ministers of Agriculture have approved the institution of Rat Weeks? Is it not rather a wonder that for every farmer every week is not already a Rat Week? But the farmer, queerly enough, takes little notice. The gamekeeper, who does, is perhaps a better friend to the farmer even than to himself.

Other four-footed enemies of game are more or less inimical and more or less uncommon. Take two of the rarest first—the polecat and the pine marten. I have only once seen a pine marten that was killed on an English shooting estate. That was near Godalming in Surrey, where, in March 1932, on part of Peper Harow Park which now borders the Guildford-Milford by-pass, one was caught in a tunnel trap which had been set for stoats. Whether or not it had lived its life in that part of the countryside which, until the by-pass disturbed its quiet, was secluded and wild, will never be known; at all events it was an old animal, as could be seen from the state of its teeth. I believe that is the only record of a pine marten in Surrey since 1879, when one was seen by Mr. George Lodge near Dorking. So rare, indeed, have pine martens become that they deserve special protection by law, though whether such protection would have the effect hoped for may be questioned, since the trapping of a pine marten to-day can hardly be anything but an accident.

Polecats are not so uncommon. Indeed, I have myself known of two polecats within a few miles of Guildford during recent years, and have heard of others in different parts of the county. The two of which I had personal experience both made their appearance during the years of the war of 1914–8. One I saw quite close to me in a wood near Chilworth; I was separated from it by the barbed wire fence which at that time surrounded the powder factory, and watched it moving quietly through a carpet of dog's mercury. The other made its presence known by its attacks on rabbits in a wood near my house, of which it killed eleven in all, being seen killing the sixth by my gardener, who had strict injunctions not to shoot it. However, in killing the eleventh it was scared by a dog, and left the neighbourhood, to appear again—if it was the same animal —two years later, when I was able to watch for it myself, but never had the good fortune to see it. Each time its work was unmistakable—two rabbits near the same spot, each with the neck and lungs torn out and left lying where they were killed.

Rare though the polecat and pine marten may be, there is one four-footed enemy of game still more uncommon— so rare indeed that the late J. G. Millais, before the war of 1914, when only a few specimens were known to survive in west-central Inverness-shire, believed that nothing could save it from extinction—and that is the wild cat. The wild cat is, of course, a quite different creature from the tame cat gone wild—the poaching cat of English woodlands. The true wild cat is a different species altogether. It is not structurally different; all that can be said is that it is stronger and bigger. But the marked difference between its appearance and that of the domestic cat is the shape of the tail. The domestic cat's tail tapers to a point, the wild cat's is thicker in fur and ends abruptly. It is ringed with black, the ground colour of the fur, which is striped vertically with dark on the body, being a rusty yellow-grey.

There is no fiercer animal in Great Britain. The wild cat is absolutely untameable. That has been proved beyond any doubt by that courageous lover of animals, Miss Frances Pitt, who has reared more than one wild cat from a kitten. She has given her readers a full account of a particular kitten which grew from a tiny scrap into a full-grown savage of six years and nine months, when he was carried off by an epidemic of cat influenza. Except as an absolute baby, he could not be handled. He was intelligent, knew members of Miss Pitt's family by sight, and would take food from the hand, but spat with fury when doing so. He accepted as a spouse a tame cat named Beauty, whom he could not bear to be out of his sight, and by whom he became the father of many sons and daughters, to all of whom he was kind and gentle. But otherwise as regards body or heart he was "untouchable."

It is difficult to estimate the numbers or to define the distribution of the wild cat to-day, but according to Miss Pitt it is fairly plentiful in the birch coppices along the hillsides of west-central Inverness-shire, the north of Perthshire, and in parts of Ross-shire, while stray individuals turn up from time to time in other districts.

There remain two possible entries in the list of enemies, entries which some would include and others exclude. One is the hedgehog. There can be no doubt that hedgehogs will suck eggs; there is abundant evidence that if a hedgehog happens to come across a partridge's or pheasant's nest he will gladly make an omelette of the whole sitting, and he has indeed been known to do so and to go to sleep among the egg-shells. But that he deliberately hunts for nests or eggs there is, I think, no evidence whatever; merely he is omnivorous and if he finds eggs he finds a meal. I am afraid the case against the badger is rather more serious. He too is omnivorous, and as with the hedgehog there is no evidence that he hunts for nests; but I fear that badgers cannot be absolved from occasionally finding their way into chicken-runs with unhappy consequences. Even so, badgers before now have been accused of crimes afterwards traced to foxes; and for one badger that discovers he has a taste for poultry there are hundreds that never dine off anything more valuable than wasp grubs. My own personal experience is, of course, limited, but I have lived with badger and hedge-hog neighbours for many years and, as far as game and poultry are concerned, have never traced harm to either. Grass lawns, in which badgers dig for the grubs of cock-chafers, are a different matter.

ROOKS & ROOKERIES

A Census—Rook Shooting

IT IS a strange fact, but it is a fact, that the place of the rook in the economics of farming and the countryside in general has never been thought worthy of official study by the Board of Agriculture. Is the rook a friend or foe of the farmer? To judge by the numbers of dead rooks hung up as scarecrows in farm fields you might suppose that he was generally decided to be an enemy; that, in particular, he must be kept by any means possible from the neighbourhood of newly-sown wheat or of potatoes.

Here, for instance, is what Mr. W. M. Tod says of him in the volume devoted to *Farming* in the *Haddon Hall Library*:—

"The worst enemy of wheat is the rook. Although wheat is subject to the attacks of a multitude of different kinds of fungus and animal pests, their destruction is as a drop in a bucket compared with those of the rascally rook. He digs up the grain with his powerful beak as soon as it is sown, and continues to do so till it appears above the ground; then he ceases digging and pulls up the plants by catching hold of the shoot in his beak, because every now and then a plant comes up with the kernel still attached, which he can eat. There is nothing so annoying as to see whole rows every plant of which is pulled up and left lying on the top of the ground. It is useless to plead excuses about insects, for no possible number of insects would equal the damage of half a dozen rooks left undisturbed, and the only prevention is constantly to watch with a loaded gun."

On the other hand, there are seasons of the year when neither newly-sown wheat nor potatoes are available as food, and when the rook finds other diet in farm fields—wire-worms, grubs of beetles, leather-jackets, perhaps. What is the balance of harm or good done by a rookery? Would not a Minister of Agriculture find the question worth inquiry?

Turn to another question—the preservation of game. Here, again, is the rook a friend or an enemy? Take the evidence. In *Pheasants and Pheasant-rearing*, by W. B. Tegetmeier, four witnesses speak of the damage done not only in the matter of taking eggs, but even destroying young birds. This is the testimony of two landowners in County Sligo, Lord Clonbrock and Lord Dunsandle, as given to one of Mr. Tegetmeier's correspondents, the late Colonel Whyte of Newtown Manor. Lord Clonbrock writes that "the rooks about me have within the last year or two taken to hunt up and destroy the eggs as regularly as if they were so many magpies. I did not believe my keeper at first, but going myself to look out, I saw them regularly beating up and down a piece of rough ground where the pheasants nest, and when they found one they would rise up a few yards in the air and then pounce down upon it."

Lord Dunsandle writes of the same season: "This year the rooks have taken to destroying my pheasants' eggs, and the mischief they have done is incredible; the fields are strewn with broken eggs."

A third correspondent writes: "A few years ago, in a dry spring, with a north-east wind for many weeks, when the rooks could not bore for their accustomed food, about one hundred and fifty pheasants' eggs—*i.e.* the shells—were found under the rookery near the house, having been taken by the rooks to feed their young, other food failing them."

Mr. J. E. Harting, for many years natural history editor of the *Field*, speaks of "a rook in the act of carrying off a pheasant's egg from a copse in West Sussex. The bird was carrying the egg upon the point of the bill, and on being fired at he dropped it. There was a large and irregularly shaped hole towards the larger end."

Finally, another correspondent describes the killing by rooks of young pheasant chicks:—

"On 13th June my keeper observed about half a dozen rooks engaged amongst the coops of young pheasants, and, suspecting their object, drove them off. The next morning, having fed and watered the young birds, he went to his cottage, and, looking out about six o'clock, saw a strong detachment of rooks from a neighbouring colony in great excitement among the coops. He ran down, a distance of two hundred yards, as fast as possible, but before he arrived they had succeeded in killing and for the most part carrying off, from forty to fifty birds, two or three weeks old. As he came amongst them they flew up in all directions, their beaks full of the spoil. The dead birds not carried away had all their heads pulled off, and most of their legs and wings torn from the body. I have long known that rooks destroy partridges' nests and eat the eggs when short of other food, but have never known a raid of this description. I attribute it to the excessive drought, which has so starved the birds by depriving them of their natural insect food that they are driven to depredation."

So much for the case against the rook; unimpeachable testimony from men of life-long experience, two of them agreeing in attributing exceptional behaviour to exceptional weather conditions. On the other hand, Mr. Tegetmeier himself states that he has known many cases in which pheasants have sat and reared their young safely, almost immediately under a rookery; and if I may be allowed to cite my own experience, it is that during thirty years' residence in a particular district of Surrey, in the neighbourhood of several rookeries of considerable size, near which year after year I have reared pheasants, I have never known rooks to do any harm either to pheasants, wild and hand-reared, or to partridges.

Then what is the balance of evidence? Does it not all point to a question of food supply? When rooks can get plenty of their natural food, grubs, wire-worms and so on, they are not only harmless, but the best of friends to the farmer. When they cannot get their natural food, they get what food they can.

And again, is there not a question of numbers? The natural food supply of so many acres might suffice for so many rooks. Double the number of rooks, and you halve the natural food supply. May it not be the case, then, that where rooks do mischief either to crops or game, it is in districts where they are too many in number for the natural food supply? And if so, ought not their numbers to be reduced?

To determine these questions, obviously you need knowledge of basic facts. First, in any district, you need to know (a) the area of farm land; (b) the quality of farm land, i.e. whether arable or pasture; (c) the numbers of the rook population.

In fact, you need a census of rookeries. For such a census, taken over the country as a whole, the *Field* has argued and pleaded for many years—up to the present in vain.

A CENSUS OF ROOKERIES

Yet such a census has been taken in a single county, and by a single individual; with such valuable and interesting results that it seems incredible that it has not been followed by a survey of the rook question, if only as an agricultural question—a question of the first magnitude. In the autumn of 1922 Mr. Walker Stewart contributed to the *Scottish Naturalist* a paper describing the taking of a census of rookeries in the spring of that year, and giving statistics of acreage of farm land, moorland, and land more or less closely populated. His figures are worth study.

Lanarkshire covers an area of 879 square miles (562, 821 acres). Mr. Stewart found in the course of his explorations that this area seemed to divide itself naturally into two portions, the north-west half of the county, with Glasgow on the boundary, the Firth of Clyde; and the south-east half, which embraces the sparsely populated area of the basin of the Upper Clyde. He gives a table to illustrate some of the contrasts between these two areas:

	North-west Area.	South-east Area.
Proportion of farm land of .	90 per cent.	10 per cent.
Rookeries (125) . .	101	24
Scattered nests (33) . .	31	2
Total nests (18,882) . .	8,552	10,330
Winter Roosts—		
Deciduous . . .	1	0
Coniferous . .	0	1
Nesting Trees—		
Deciduous . . .	85 per cent.	14 per cent.
Coniferous . .	15 ,,	86 ,,
Complaints—		
Egg-stealing . .	None	90 ,,
Grain-eating . .	Very few	See below

Now, are not these figures remarkable? We notice at once that the north-west area embraces 90 per cent. of the farm land of the county and carries 80 per cent. of the number of rookeries, but produces only 40 per cent. of the stock of rooks. Mr. Stewart informs us that a large proportion of the farm land is hayfields and old pastures; and we notice that complaints from farmers are few and from gamekeepers none. But the rook must get his food from somewhere, and presumably he stalks the grass fields and plough for leather-jackets and grubs. In short, his numbers are sufficiently well proportioned to his food supply, and he behaves himself well.

It is otherwise in the south-east area. Here there is only 10 per cent. of the farm land of the whole county. But the rookeries are enormous: they are only 20 per cent. of the numbers of the whole county, but they supply 56 per cent. of the stock. And their feeding habits are most objectionable. Practically all the gamekeepers complain that they take the eggs of grouse and other game birds, and as for the farmer's side of the case, Mr. Stewart tells us from his personal observation that "immense damage is done to the crops during the whole of the six months in which these birds are in their summer residence, and the ground underneath the nests soon becomes absolutely littered with grain husks in the spring and early autumn." In short, in this south-east area the numbers of the rooks are disproportionate to their natural food supply, and they take instead to the grain and eggs. They are plainly harmful in such circumstances and their numbers need to be reduced.

But a further curious point will be noticed. The rooks of the north-west area nest mainly in deciduous trees, and have a large deciduous winter roost. The rooks of the south-east area nest mainly in conifers, and have a large coniferous winter roost. This would seem again to be a question of supply. On farm land you will get deciduous trees, on moorland you get conifers, and the rooks nest where they can. And one accompanying circumstance seems to follow. When rooks nest in deciduous trees, they are the more readily dealt with: the nests, and the young birds presumably, can be better seen and the numbers of the birds more easily reduced. In fir plantations, on the other hand, the thick foliage must to some extent prevent the birds from being shot at, and we may suppose, too, that distances would be farther for the would-be destroyer to go. At all events, it is the rooks of the Scots pine rookeries which do the most damage, and it is these rookeries, clearly, which need to be destroyed.

Here, in short, is an inquiry thoroughly carried out and involving logical conclusions. It is an inquiry privately made and concerning one county only; and if there is a single conclusion that is inevitable, it is that a similar inquiry should be instituted by public authority on a national scale. For it is surely a national question. Farmers and sportsmen are living side by side in every county in the kingdom, and in every county their industry and sport are more or less affected by the presence of rooks. What is there to hinder us from being given precise information as to the rooks' numbers?

ROOK SHOOTING

If the numbers of rooks are to be thinned, how is it best done? Mr. Walter Stewart, in his paper on the rooks of Lanarkshire, quoted elsewhere, urges that shooting is not the best way. He suggests that the birds should be left to nest undisturbed from March until the last week in April, "when, with the help of a sectional rod of some light material, such as bamboo or aluminium, every nest should be methodically put down and the young killed in a humane and expeditious manner." This remedy, he observes, may sound somewhat callous, "but really it is only the stamping out of an abnormal, predatory tendency which is developing amongst some members of a very useful species of bird." He is dealing, of course, with the type of rook which develops grain and egg-eating tendencies owing to a local deficiency in its natural food supply, and his methods are as abnormal as the sins of the birds he sets out to destroy. The chief sinners, in the districts which he has studied most closely, are those which, owing to the nature of the country-side, form rookeries in fir plantations—and there, of course, a sectional rod might be employed to poke down nests. Such a method would be very seldom possible with rookeries in deciduous trees.

But it is the rookery in deciduous trees which alone can furnish the kind of shooting which could by any stretch of the word's meaning be termed sporting. There are conditions under which young rooks are shot which make the shooting mere murder. But there are others. A rookery in high elms, with the nests in the very tops—that is a very different proposition. To try to reduce the numbers of birds in those high branches in a May breeze is to discover that you can make many mistakes with the prettiest of rook-rifles. If the leaf is at all full you will first have to find your rook; when you have found him, you have also to find where you can be sure of seeing him; and when you can see him, you must take him when the wind is not blowing or when—for there is a knack in the thing—it swings him to a particular spot. Nor is he a very big mark against a blue sky; nor will you be satisfied if you do not bring him down dead from the sky to the buttercups. There is no more discomforting sight in rook-shooting than a body with spread wings securely lodged among small twigs—unless it is the bird which tumbles back into the nest. But both are to be avoided.

WOODPIGEONS

THERE ARE three species of pigeon native to this island: the rock pigeon, *Columba livia*; the stock dove, *Columba oenas*; and the ringdove or woodpigeon, *Columba palumbus*.

Of these, the rock pigeon, sometimes called the Blue Rock, is a native of caves on the sea-coast, where it affords shooting which is difficult owing to the shooter's stance, which is the unsteady floor of a boat, and which is often unsatisfactory in that it is hard to pick birds from the tide. Blue Rocks were the birds formerly used at Hurlingham and elsewhere for pigeon-shooting from traps, a form of so-called sport now happily illegal. They are in the main the ancestors of the common pigeons of the farm.

The stock dove's numbers, like those of the ringdove, are considerably increased in winter by immigrants. It differs from the ringdove in the absence of the "ring," or the white patch on either side of the neck, which instead is glossy with metallic green. It is also a smaller bird. Stock doves, as their name implies, nest in the trunks of trees, where they choose if they can a good deep hole; failing trees, they may nest in rabbit-holes. The name *oenas*, literally vinous, refers to the breast, the colour of ripening grapes.

The ringdove or woodpigeon is the commoner bird, and there are few stretches of woodland lacking in spring and summer—or for that matter autumn, early or late—his familiar croon, *Tak' two coos, tak' two*. If he is not game, he is a sporting bird, cautious in method and a fine flier, jinking at gunshot and fast over the trees. Woodpigeon may be shot from a hide in a hedge or ditch, with painted wooden decoys or newly shot birds propped by forked sticks, set head to wind among stooks of corn; or when harvest is over, coming in to roost. Some of the biggest recorded bags are:—

On 1st December 1911, in Lord de Vesci's woods at Abbeyleix, Queen's County, by Mr. Cecil Fitzherbert, 467 woodpigeons and 6 mallard.

On 14th December 1911, at the same place, by Mr. Arnold Fitzherbert, 351 woodpigeons and 6 mallard.

On 5th December 1913, at Eynsham Hall, Oxfordshire, by Mr. J. F. Mason, 373 woodpigeons, between 9 a.m. and 3 p.m.

On 23rd December 1895, by Mr. T. G. Sowerby and his two brothers, in Hertfordshire, 445 woodpigeons, of which Mr. T. G. Sowerby shot 220.

Woodpigeons are such voracious birds that bags such as these can only be regarded as so much recorded destruction of a farmer's enemies. Harting in his *Handbook of British Birds* gives the following contents of crops which he noted in woodpigeons shot in different months, chiefly between 1st September and 1st February:—

(1) 26 acorns and nearly 100 ivy berries; (2) 33 acorns and 44 beechnuts; (3) 65 beans; (4) 76 beans; (5) 87 beans; (6) 75 acorns; (7) 139 beechnuts, a few grains of wheat and a small white slug. Even larger contents of crops have been recorded by the late W. B. Tegetmeier, who found in one crop 198 beans and a dozen small snails; while Mr. F. W. Frohawk once shot a woodpigeon whose crop held 370 grains and a great number of husks of wheat, 4 seed-pods (full) of the dog-violet, 6 peas and half a pea-pod, 9 pieces of clover-leaves, 1 seed, 1 small stone, 4 snails (*Helix caperata*) and 1 parasitical fly (*Ornithomyia avicularia*).

With such records as these it is not difficult to imagine the damage done to farm crops by flocks of migrant pigeons which occasionally visit us in such vast numbers. For whatever reason, however, there appears to be no regularity in invasions of this kind, and season after season may go by without such visitations as were recorded in the early years of the century, when Sussex, Devon, and Hampshire woods in turn were white with the feathers of roosting birds, many of them dying of what gamekeepers and farmers have called "acorn disease" or "beechmast disease." Such disease is not, of course, due to feeding; it is a form of diphtheritic roup, a disease of over-crowding, and character-ised by a thick or frothy yellow deposit in the mouth and throat. Birds affected by it mope and drop dead from the trees; if shot, or picked up, the bodies should be burned.

There may come, probably will come, other seasons when we shall be invaded by hosts of migrant woodpigeons. If so, it is to be hoped that some better means of combating their ravages will be adopted than the so-called "county shoots" of the past. The method of the "county shoot" hitherto has been to fix in advance a date or dates on which every person carrying a gun is asked to take post on his own, or by permission on someone else's land, and be prepared to shoot woodpigeons throughout the day, the idea being to keep the flocks always on the move and always under fire. I never heard of shoots organised in this way attaining marked success, or indeed any; and unquestionably a very great deal of time is wasted in waiting for the chance of a shot which may never come. If such shoots are to be organised at all, they must clearly be organised over a larger area than a single county. But it is arguable whether organisation of shooting on the largest possible scale would answer the farmer's purpose better than by protecting selected crops with a couple of boys armed with cherry-clappers.

Another point remains. When the Board of Agriculture first decided, in 1911, that these invading hordes of pigeons deserved serious attention, the date chosen for issuing a notice to farmers and others was the month of March; and when, later, county shoots were organised, it was in the spring, when the migrant flocks were about to leave us. The result was that the pigeons which were shot were more likely to be local birds thinking of nesting than foreign pigeons moving here and there in large numbers. And home-breeding pigeons shot in the spring were killed just at the time of year when they may be doing the farmer the one service of their lives in feeding on the grubs of cater-pillars. The home-breeding woodpigeon never feeds more voraciously than on the larvae of those oak-stripping pests among moths, the Dotted Border (*Hybernia marginata*), and Mottled Umber (*Hybernia defoliaria*). Incidentally, to shoot woodpigeons in April and May is to kill parent birds at season when young birds are still in the nest.

TRAINING DOGS FOR THE GUN

SETTERS

IN THE education of the young setter, the trainer should observe one guiding principle, viz. the development, to his personal advantage, of his pupil's natural instincts. The puppy will begin by hunting for his own pleasure; he should end by serving his master's.

To obtain this result he should be encouraged rather than restrained. The trainer can take everything out of a young dog, he can put little in that is not there already. Before taking a puppy out to hunt, he may be taught to drop to hand in the kennel yard, and to come up when called by name. When the puppy is old enough to gallop freely, take him out to hunt. Two or three may with advantage be run together, as they encourage one another to go. Select an open and unfenced country, if available. The trainer should walk briskly into the wind, endeavouring to keep the puppies going well out in front of him, the farther the better. At first they will chase everything they find, but in time they will begin to take less notice of larks and such like, and become seriously interested in game birds. Some puppies insist on chasing hares for several months. The best cure for a puppy that so behaves is to take him among a lot of hares until he becomes sick of chasing them. He should be shown the error of his ways only on returning tired and blown from a futile hare chase. He may never look at a hare again.

We will assume that the puppy has taken seriously to game

birds. He should henceforth be hunted alone. Running him with an old dog tends to destroy his initiative.

Sooner or later the puppy will show signs of pulling up on winding game, next he will begin to "flash point," before rushing in and chasing. On no account hurry after him at this stage. The "flash point" will soon be prolonged into a real point. When this occurs, do nothing to disturb him. His whole attention should be riveted on the game. Approach him noiselessly, almost stealthily, and from a flank, not from the rear, which will make him nervous, and inclined to look round at you—a bad fault. He may, if interfered with, even crouch down, and regard you in a deprecating manner, as if saying, "Am I doing anything wrong?"—an attitude of mind to be avoided at all costs. If you have the luck to reach him before he dashes in, hold him a second or two on his point, stroking him with the hand gently along the back, which aids in keeping him stiff; then walk in beside him and flush the birds, pressing him gently to the ground when they rise. Keep him down a short time and make much of him. Your puppy will soon be pointing staunchly, and you will thereby have acquired infinitely more control over him.

Ranging and quartering are instinctive in a well-bred setter; they can be controlled by art, but not taught. Dogs vary in the method and extent of their range. Provided that a dog is hunting his ground to the best advantage, with an eye to his trainer's position, and the direction in which he is proceeding, he should be interfered with as little as possible, unless he persists in boring straight into the wind, or ranging over ground behind that he has already traversed.

A word on the use and abuse of the whistle. It is the crux upon which many trainers break down. Speaking generally, the less it is used the better. Too much whistling makes some puppies run wild, and these are generally the best ones; others lose their initiative.

CAPTAIN GILBERT BLAINE:
In the Lonsdale Library volume
Hounds and Dogs.

RETRIEVERS

The question one is most often asked about a retriever is at what age should one start to educate a puppy. That can never be answered decisively, for it depends entirely upon the individuality of the puppy. Some are precocious and need training early; some need endless time, and then again, some show at once that they are eager to please you and be with you. Some show an independent and refractory spirit from the outset. If you can find a puppy with the wish to please combined with courage and intelligence you can count yourself lucky.

Never attempt to teach too much or too quickly. Take, for instance, retrieving. It is usual to start a puppy with some such object as a stuffed rabbit skin, a ball, tobacco pouch, or glove. A very great number retrieve naturally and from the earliest age; others at first refuse, probably because they do not understand what is required of them. If you have an old dog call him in to help and let the puppy see the old dog retrieve and receive approbation from you, and then try him and he will probably have tumbled to what you require. When he has do not in your delight overdo it and so sicken him of what he should look on as a privilege.

When you have got him proficient in retrieving dummies be very careful how you start him on game. A dead partridge is, of course, ideal, as it is light and easily carried, but never, never send him for any game that is not dead. You can try and instil tenderness in retrieving into him from the start. If he is reluctant to give up the dummy insert your fingers in his mouth with his lip between them and his teeth and say "gently" or "softly" or whatever word you decide on. Hard mouth may be hereditary, but it is in many cases caused by thoughtlessness on the part of the trainer or through some accident.

Words of command are all essential. "No" is perhaps the most useful word in the dictionary of a trainer; it is easy to use and should be used whenever the dog is doing what he should not. And so for all words of command, whether "sit" or "drop" or "stop" or "go on" or "hi on," "get over," or "hi lost," "get it," "fetch it," when they are decided on for their various purposes let the decision be final and the one that is always to be used.

When you have occasion to punish a dog think what you are doing and what punishment fits the crime and the criminal! A scolding is sufficient for some dogs, chastisement is necessary for others. Usually a good long scolding and perhaps a shaking is more effectual than chastisement. When you have once gained a dog's confidence, trust, and affection, you have gone a long way towards your journey's end. Remember that to the dog we all seek to find, once found, we become the absorbing factor in his life and on us depends his happiness and his well-being.

The majority of dogs like water—some do not. An ideal way to start a puppy to go into water is to take him in company with some water-loving dog on a hot day to a stream. If he goes in after the old dog, which he probably will, well and good. You can then throw something for him to fetch —a tennis ball is good as it shows up, is not slippery to the mouth and floats well. If he will not go in, try (if you do not mind) paddling in yourself a little way in a shallow stream or get someone to hold him whilst you go round and call him from the other bank. This may all seem troublesome, but it will repay you.

There is so much that can be done with dummies and obedience lessons in the summer months, all of which if properly carried out will prove invaluable when the shooting season starts. Never take a young dog straight into the shooting field. Make him understand discipline, so to speak, in the home circle before experimenting with him in public.

From *Primary Education of Retrievers*, by Lorna Countess Howe, an admirable chapter in the Lonsdale Library volume *Hounds and Dogs*, which ends with a tribute to a great retriever:—

"I cannot pass over the help I got from my Labrador Dual Ch. Banchory Bolo, who taught me much by his sagacious ways and showed me so often that he knew better than I and that had I left him alone and not interfered the game bag would have been heavier to carry home."

POINTERS & SETTERS

When should a puppy commence his training? A most important question and most difficult to answer. It so entirely depends on the temperament of the puppy. There is no doubt some of the oldest and best strains will almost train themselves. I had two puppies in 1913 that at four months galloped and hunted on their own with no one with them; they would point birds on the ground and back one another absolutely naturally. As a general rule one would think it advisable to take out a puppy with a well-trained dog that does not gallop too fast and that will return to the whistle or the hand. The young one is pretty sure to follow the old dog. After a few days of this, changing the ground as much as possible, the young one may be put down by himself where there is plenty of game and be allowed to find his nose. No notice need be taken of a flush or chase. The first thing to do is to get the love of hunting firmly established; one can do any necessary checking later.

Perhaps the most difficult part of a handler's work is to teach a dog to quarter his ground. This is easiest done in a field of, say, a hundred yards wide, far better than on an open moor or down, and saves the distraction of perpetually whistling, of which one hears far too much nowadays, showing to my mind very faulty training. This quartering means a lot of hard walking on the part of the handler, who should quarter the ground himself encouraging the dog to work in front of him, but it is well worth it, as it means an economy of ground, far less walking, and much better sport for the gun. If the handler can get his puppy to turn with him with a wave of his hand half the training is done.

When or whether to use a check cord is a matter for the handler's judgment, but it should only be used with a very obstinate pupil. A very important point to bear in mind is never to let your puppy get tired. Always take him up after a good performance, and not when he has done wrong. A dog, when he has had enough, invariably gets sloppy and careless, and is inclined to false point.

When the puppy has now got confidence in himself, put him down with another of the same pattern and pace, but well trained; likely enough if they are near one another when the old dog finds, the young one will stop as well and great progress has been made. With some high-couraged young ones care is necessary when to shoot. For the first time or two, it is better not to do this right on top of them as it is difficult and often impossible to cure gun-shyness.

One thing above all the handler must never do, and that is to lose temper with his dogs.

COLONEL HUBERT M. WILSON:
In the Lonsdale Library volume
Hounds and Dogs.

SPANIELS

(a) *In General*

As with all other lessons during early puppyhood, the four cardinal principles are:—

(1) Never give an order without seeing that the puppy complies with it; he has got to learn to obey you always, not sometimes.

(2) Always be absolutely gentle, both in voice and action —when you come to work in the field, you want a bold, keen dog, not a cowed listless wreck.

(3) Never give an order with which you cannot secure compliance without a display of harshness.

(4) Never persist in any lesson which is becoming a bore to the puppy.

The nearer these earliest lessons can be approximated to a game, in the puppy's eyes, the better.

See as much of your dog as you possibly can. Gain his confidence—you will do no good with a dog that is suspicious of you. Give yourself a chance of discovering any outstanding traits in his character and apply the knowledge so gained in your treatment of him—it is rarely that any two dogs can be broken in exactly the same way.

Leave no stone unturned to get a good performance as the wind-up of every lesson-time.

Do not expect your breaking to result in even progress; it is sure to have its ups and downs. One day all will go well, the next your puppy can do nothing right. He has his good days and his bad, but so have you.

Take every opportunity of getting him interested in the scent of game. Take every opportunity of developing his brains. Let him find out things for himself where possible. The world is new to him, and he must get to know it in his own way—mostly by his nose.

H. W. CARLTON:
Spaniels; their Breaking, for Sport and Field Trials.

(b) *For Covert Shooting*

Some prefer the little Cocker on account of his activity and giving tongue; others prefer the Clumber or Sussex for covert shooting. There is no keener-nosed dog than the Clumber; he is mute, a good retriever, fond of water, will face the thickest of cover, and in many cases is a very easy dog to break. It is folly to argue that the Cocker is best for covert shooting, especially where there are wild birds, for the continual "yap-yap" disturbs all game and drives it out of one end of the covert as soon as the dog enters the other. The Clumber, on the other hand, works very steadily, and his keenness of scent enables him to flush all game within reach of the guns.

A few hints on training spaniels. This must commence from puppyhood. The first lesson is to teach him to follow and to keep to heel. This can be easily done by walking him out on a lead and pulling him back when he runs forward, at the same time saying "To heel!" The next thing is to teach him to "drop." Use the word *Drop*! it is short and easy. To make the dog drop, you should hold him down with one hand and hold the other above him and use the word *Drop*! Then draw back a few paces, and should he move, go to him, carry him back to the same place and repeat loudly *Drop*! Continue this, each time going farther away, until he will stop when told and drop to command.

Now for teaching him to retrieve. When a dog is first loosed, he is most playful. This is the best time to teach him to retrieve. Make a "dummy" with a rabbit skin and throw this for him to retrieve. It is a good plan to let him see an old dog retrieve first; then try him, and then, when he is perfect in retrieving, throw the dummy and let him start to fetch it. Then shout *Drop*! and if he fails to drop, scold him and make him drop where he was told. Repeat this until he obeys the word; then pat him and let him retrieve the dummy. Now get the gun and some blank cartridges; get someone to throw the dummy, then shoot, at the same time shouting *Drop*! This will enable you to shoot over the dog with comfort.

J. H. in the Gamekeeper.

DISEASES OF GAME BIRDS

GROUSE

OF DISEASES fatal to grouse the chief are two, cocci-diosis and strongylosis.

Coccidiosis is a disease which is not peculiar to grouse. It is found in pheasants, partridges, domestic poultry, pigeons and sparrows, and probably affects most wild birds. It also occurs in rabbits. It is due to a parasite, *Eimeria* (or *Coccidium avium*), which enters into and multiplies in the alimentary canal of young grouse, destroying the membrane, preventing nutrition, and producing what is sometimes called "white diarrhoea." The young bird picks up the parasite in its food or water, and in turn as it becomes infected spreads the possibility of further infection by its droppings. These contain the spores of the parasite, and may fall into water which other birds drink, or may be dried in the sun and then disseminated afresh by the wind. An insect which largely aids in the dispersal of coccidiosis is the dung-fly, *Scatophaga stercoraria*, which is found wherever there are grouse droppings. The fly lays its eggs in droppings, which hatch out there, and the flies newly emerged from the resulting pupae proceed at once to feed on the droppings and continue the life cycle.

Coccidiosis is, so to speak, a childish disease, and full-grown grouse rarely suffer from it. They must, of course, swallow the spores in water and food in the same way as do the young birds, but their stronger constitution throws off the infection.

One of the disturbing features of coccidiosis, in the game-keeper's calculations, is that he cannot know when the young grouse are suffering from it. He can only guess, when he finds his hoped-for coveys absent in July, that the little chicks have perished earlier in the year. He will find no trace of them: he could not hope to find their tiny bodies in the heather, even if he knew where to look. Fortunately extensive losses from coccidiosis in grouse are rare. As Mr. A. S. Leslie in *The Grouse in Health and in Disease* puts it, "under normal circumstances the Providence that watches over all young things brings to maturity a large percentage of the birds that are hatched." If it were not so, the stock of grouse on the moors of these islands would vanish.

But although coccidiosis is one of the only two diseases which can be said to cause widespread mortality among grouse, what is usually understood by "grouse disease" is the other of the two, strongylosis. It is strongylosis which kills off mature grouse in the spring, and which, in "a year of disease," may empty a moor of the stock.

Strongylosis, shortly stated, is due to the presence in the intestines of a grouse of a parasite threadworm, *Tricho-strongylus pergracilis*, which causes inflammation and in extreme cases death. This threadworm, however, is not necessarily fatal. It is present in small numbers in the intestines of all grouse, even the healthiest, and normally a grouse is able to throw off any evil effects of its presence. But if the bird for any reason loses its stamina, it becomes unable to withstand the presence of the threadworm; its intestines become inflamed, it ceases to be able to digest its food, becomes weaker and lighter and dies.

The life cycle of the threadworm is most interesting. At an early stage of its existence it climbs to the tip of a green heather shoot. The grouse bites off the tip of heather and swallows the threadworm, which passes into the intestines. Here it grows to its adult stage and pairs, and the female worm then lays her eggs in the intestines. These eggs pass out in the droppings of the bird, and the larva hatches out from the egg in the dropping, and having hatched out climbs to the tip of a heather shoot, when the life cycle begins again.

But if the threadworm, *Trichostrongylus pergracilis*, is present in the intestines of practically all grouse, and yet

72

healthy grouse throw off its evil effects, what are the conditions under which infection from the threadworm becomes insistent and eventually fatal? In a word, starvation. When a grouse cannot obtain a sufficient supply of nourishing heather, it becomes weak and cannot throw off infection. What, then, causes a grouse to starve? A combination of causes. First, lack of sunshine in the summer and autumn, which prevents the seed of heather from ripening, the seed-heads of heather being an important constituent in the food supply of grouse. Second, prolonged wintry conditions which prevent the grouse from access to a supply of young green heather in spring. Third, and most important, over-crowding; too many birds on the ground. This happens after an exceptionally good—a "bumper"— season. There is not enough heather for the birds that want to eat it, and in the spring, when the process of breeding imposes an extra strain on the strength of the birds, weakness from an insufficient supply of food tells its tale.

So far as we know, "grouse disease," under the wild, natural conditions of a hundred years ago, before the days of gamekeepers and modern conditions of shooting, when eagles, peregrines, wild cats and foxes, and other so-called enemies of grouse kept down the numbers of grouse— "grouse disease" did not exist. With the increase of the numbers of grouse, it is obviously necessary to increase their supply of food, which is heather. For possibilities of increasing that supply, see "Heather Burning," page 180.

PARTRIDGES

As with grouse, so with partridges—coccidiosis and strongylosis may cause much mortality in the case of young and mature birds. But the strongyle which is fatal to partridges is not *Trichostrongylus pergracilis*; it is a smaller thread-worm, which has been named *Trichostrongylus tenuis*. It was first discovered in 1913 by the late Dr. Hammond Smith, pathologist to the *Field*, but the war of 1914–8 interrupted his investigations, and before he was able to complete them he died. In 1931, in view of the heavy losses among partridges during the winter months, *Country Life* formed a committee to investigate the causes of death, with Major M. Portal as chairman and Dr. Walter E. Collinge as pathologist. The committee in due course issued their report, which was embodied in a book, *Partridge Disease and its Causes*, edited by Major Portal and published in 1932. The editor, in briefly referring to the methods of investigation decided on by the committee, observes that in the Report of the Grouse Disease Inquiry Committee, which afterwards took shape in that remarkable monograph *The Grouse in Health and Disease*, it had been shown that the larvae of *Trichostrongylus pergracilis*, "after a brief period of development, ascend the heather and can remain hidden in the crevices of the leaves, in a quiescent, invisible, and living state for a prolonged period."

With this information—so the editor introduces his account of a discovery due to a brilliant idea—"we commenced taking washes from various grasses, weeds, and clover. In June and July 1931, a number of grasses were thus washed and large numbers of the living larvae of *Trichostrongylus tenuis* were found. These were particularly numerous on the grass *Poa trivialis*. Again in February and March 1932, still larger numbers were obtained from various species of clover, the common Salad Burnet (*Poterium sanguisorba*), Spurrey (*Spergula arvensis*), Stone Bedstraw (*Galium saxatile*) and Silverweed (*Potentilla anserina*).

"On clover the larvae were more plentiful than on any other plant examined. As bearing on this a Hampshire correspondent writes (28th February 1932): 'This year the bulk of the dead birds picked up were on thirty acres of clover ley which had been heavily sheeped and grew a heavy crop of grass aftermath. There may be nothing in this at all, but these thirty acres have had no artificials at all.'"

What happens with *Trichostrongylus tenuis*, then, is the same as with *T. pergracilis*. From eggs contained in the droppings of the partridge develop larvae, which make their way up the damp stems of various plants and secrete themselves on or between the leaves, which later are eaten by the partridge. The nematode worm is thus conveyed into the alimentary canal, where it develops, and in the intestines the strongyli pair so that the female lays her eggs, and the life cycle is thus continued. The symptoms of the disease caused by *T. tenuis* are the same as those produced by *T. pergracilis*.

Wet seasons are favourable to these parasites, and to the dissemination of disease. Prolonged drought, on the other hand, is fatal alike to eggs and larvae. Numerous wild birds were examined, but only the pheasant was found to contain the strongyle. Earthworms were found to act as carriers of the eggs and larvae.

As with grouse an insufficiency of food has much to do with the spread of the disease, and winter feeding is clearly valuable as a form of prevention.

Other diseases from which partridges suffer are common to pheasants and poultry. Coccidiosis is described under diseases of grouse. Pneumonia is inflammation of the lungs, often due to cold and wet, and with wild birds there is obviously no remedy. Diseases which are common to partridges and pheasants, and which, as regards hand-reared birds, can be met with various remedies, are described under diseases of pheasants.

PHEASANTS

Pneumonia.—The aim should be prevention. To soft food for young birds small doses of sulphate of iron should be added as a tonic, in the proportion of a quarter of a grain to half a grain according to size.

Roup, once thought to be due to a neglected cold, is now recognised as an infectious disease due to a specific parasite. A white viscid discharge fills the mouth and nostrils. In early stages the nasal passages should be syringed out with a 3 per cent. solution of boric acid. When once the disease has really taken hold the bird should be destroyed and the carcase burned.

Enteritis, characterised by severe purging, cannot be cured. The tainted ground should be disinfected with quicklime, ploughed, and sown with crop. No fresh stock should be put on the ground.

Gapes.—This disease is caused by a nematode worm, *Syngamus trachealis*, which adheres in mating pairs to the trachea, causing small tumours filled with pus. The worms can be removed with a feather, but where large numbers of young birds are affected manual treatment is impracticable, and the best remedy is powder blown into the coop so that the birds must inhale it. A powder which has been found to be effective is a mixture of powdered chalk and powdered camphor in the proportion of one ounce of chalk to half an ounce of camphor. As a preventive and remedy alike, garlic mixed with barley meal, or simpler still, onions chopped up in water, have been found effective. Garlic as a remedy for a cold in the head—doubtless the sneezing which is a symptom of gapes—was first recommended by a Roman writer, Palladius, in his *De Re Rustica*, about A.D. 300 to 400.

Scaly Leg is an objectionable disorder due to a parasite, *Sarcoptes mutans*, which burrows under the scales of the legs and the upper-part of the toes, where it sets up irritation forming white, powdery matter which raises rough crusts. The treatment is to wash the legs with carbolic soap, and to clean all coops, perches, &c., with limewash and carbolic acid. Sitting hens should be most carefully examined to guard against infection.

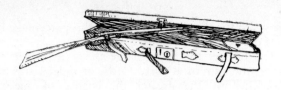

GUNS & CARTRIDGES

By Major Gerald Burrard, D.S.O.

YOUNG SHOOTERS, and some old ones too for that matter, are frequently bewildered at the mere thought of choosing a gun or guns. This is hardly surprising, as so much conflicting advice and information has been both written and spoken that it is hard to see the wood for the trees. But if we discard all frills and think only of the essentials, certain facts emerge which are beyond dispute and so provide a working basis for choice.

Briefly, these essentials are as follows:—

(1) A shot-gun is a weapon for firing a charge consisting of a considerable number of pellets of shot. These pellets vary in size, but when making comparisons we must bring everything down to one common denominator. So let us take the size known as No. 6 (which means 270 pellets to the ounce) as our starting point since it is the size which is most commonly used.

(2) For all practical purposes it can be assumed that the. different sizes of guns propel their shot charges at the same velocity.

(3) The shot charge scatters in flight, and consequently the more pellets there are to start with the closer these pellets will be to one another at any given range. In shooting parlance, "the denser the pattern." Actually the scattering, or pattern, can be controlled within certain limits by the boring of the gun, which is termed the "choke." But again we must work to a common denominator and assume a constant boring. For convenience let us take a "half choke," which throws 60 per cent. of its charge into a 30-inch circle at forty yards, which is the accepted yard stick for measuring pattern.

Here again for all practical purposes this percentage holds good for different sizes of guns.

(4) The heavier the shot charge the more pellets there will be in the pattern at forty yards, or indeed any range, and consequently the greater the chance of one pellet hitting some small vital spot in a bird.

(5) The heavier the shot charge the heavier must be the gun to fire it, as otherwise the recoil becomes excessive.

This fact is based on one of the fundamental laws of motion and is unalterable.

So much for the essentials.

Now what do you want your gun for? Most beginners will say, "Everything." Quite so. But what do you want it for most often? Wildfowling, where you will have to take long shots at big and tough birds? Or driven partridges, where most shots are under twenty yards?

These are extremes, and the average sport of the average shooter will lie between them. But it must be remembered that a gun has to be carried and that after a long day it can become surprisingly heavy. It may be very nice to know that you can kill a cock pheasant stone dead at fifty yards every time *if you hit it*, but will you be able to do your part as well as the gun does its if the gun is a bit heavy?

There can be no mistake greater than being "over-gunned." If the gun is too heavy it becomes your master, and you must always be master of your gun. For this reason it is always better to err on the side of lightness provided that lightness is not abused by being combined with too heavy a shot charge, which means unpleasant recoil, bruised cheek and headache.

The experience of many thousands of shooters who have fired many millions of cartridges since breech loaders were established has shown that a shot charge of round about 1 oz. is a very good average for the type of shooting obtained in most countries. This permits the use of a nice light gun of round about $6\frac{1}{4}$ lbs. which is quite capable of handling heavier charges on occasions when only a few shots are likely to be fired.

No mistake can be greater than thinking too much of ability to kill at very long ranges. It is the easy shots which fill the bag, and were I asked to define a first-class shot I would say the man who never misses an easy chance. On no account handicap yourself for the easy chances by the weight necessary for sixty yards. Shots at this range are possible with suitable armament, but the forward allowance necessary is so great that a kill will always include a big element of luck.

It is better to be practical and realise the limitations both of man and gun and concentrate on perfection within those limitations.

So let us take an ounce charge as our datum point.

Experience has again proved that this weight of shot is handled best by a 12-bore, that is by a gun in which the barrels are of such a size that 12 balls of lead, each exactly fitting the bore, weigh 1 lb. And the weight can be round about $6\frac{1}{4}$ lbs.

The shooter who thinks this too heavy can try a 16-bore, in which 16 balls of lead fitting the bore go to the pound, and $\frac{7}{8}$ oz. of shot. Now the weight can be 6 lbs. or a little less.

The next smaller size is a 20-bore, but these have the disadvantage that their cartridges stick in the barrel of a 12-bore if loaded accidentally sufficiently far down to permit the loading of a 12-bore cartridge behind them. Many bursts have been caused in this way, and for this reason 20-bores are a mixed blessing. Better to use a light 16-bore and fire a shot charge of $\frac{3}{4}$ oz.

The degree of choke or boring can be decided on in consultation with the gunmaker after a trial at his shooting school, which is probably *the* greatest advantage the young shooter of to-day has over his grandfather, or even father.

So far we have only thought of shot, but shot must be propelled by powder. There are many shot-gun powders, but actually there is little to choose between any of the established varieties. Personal preference is frequently without sound basis, but it is quite a good guide to follow.

It may, however, be mentioned that smokeless shot-gun

powders are generally of two main types: 33-grain and 42-grain. This only means that the bulks of the two types necessary to fill exactly the old 3-drachm measure of black powder days, weigh respectively 33 and 42 grains.

When buying guns and cartridges take your gunmaker into your confidence and trust him. If you don't trust him go to another maker whom you can.

An ejector gun, which automatically ejects a fired cartridge case on opening, is a joy, but not an essential. It is a matter of money.

Then as to barrel length. What is the best length? The answer is easy: there is no such thing as any best length. The best length of barrel for any individual shooter is that length with which he finds he can shoot best after trying various lengths. Here is another use for the shooting school.

So do not be led astray by red herrings. Stick to the essentials which have been set out, go to a gunmaker whom you trust and spend as much money on the gun as you can afford. You will not regret it.

But one word of warning. You will doubtless be tempted to buy a second-hand gun some time or other. *Never consider one which has not been Nitro-Proved, no matter how alluring the bargain.* The marks of Nitro-Proof are on the flat parts underneath the breech ends of the barrel and are unmistakable.

And if you are buying a gun from a dealer take its number and ask the original maker its age. Then there can be no doubt nor unpleasantness.

RIFLES & RIFLE SIGHTS

So much for shot-guns. But first-class sport is also to be had with a rifle. The old "rook and rabbit" rifle of thirty years and more ago has been superseded by the ·22 rim fire, which is probably the most accurate cartridge, within its range, yet made. It possesses the advantages of cheapness and what is termed "non-rusting," a wonderful boon. For this last does away with the need for cleaning since the priming composition in the cap contains ingredients which preserve the bore from rusting and this composition is no less than about one-third of the total explosive charge in the cartridge, instead of being one-hundredth as in the case of a cartridge with a central fire cap.

Shooting with a ·22 is the best basis for all rifle shooting, and the man who learns in the ·22 school will soon adapt himself to any larger and more powerful weapon.

But whatever the weapon, whether a ·22 or a heavy rifle for big game one should never, never, never think of firing a shot at a living beast without first trying the rifle on a target to make sure of the sighting.

The sight of the future, indeed, of the immediate present really, is the telescope sight. But until this fact is realised and some form of mass production enables the sight to be sold and fitted to the rifle, at a reasonable price, the majority of sportsmen must be content with the second best, which is certainly the aperture or "peep" sight. With this form of backsight all that one need do when aiming is to look *through* the aperture without bothering about trying to centre anything; place the foresight on what you want to hit and press the trigger. One centres automatically, and if you trust to instinct all will be well. But if you start trying to centre the animal or the foresight you will set up eye-strain, unconscious though it may be, and you will bungle your shot.

One last word. All those who handle firearms belong to one of two classes: those who are safe and those who are not. You can always tell to which class anyone belongs when you first see him pick up a firearm. If he opens it at once to make sure that it is not loaded he is safe. If he fails to do so he is not. Treat him accordingly if you happen to be next to him.

Proof & Nitro-Proof

NOTE.—By the Gun Barrel Proof Act of 1868 it is legally necessary for every gun to be Proved before being issued for use. Proof is carried out by the London and Birmingham Proof Houses and consists of submitting the barrel in different stages of its manufacture and the finished gun to a very severe test by firing abnormally heavy loads of special Proof Powder and shot.

About 1892 Smokeless Nitro Powders were introduced and these imposed a more severe strain on the gun than the old Black Powder. Accordingly, in 1896, a special Nitro-Proof was introduced. This was an *optional* Proof and comprised an even more severe test with special Nitro-Proof loads in addition to the ordinary Proof.

Since about 1905 most new shot-guns were submitted to Nitro-Proof by their makers before sale as it was obvious that Smokeless Nitro Powders had replaced Black Powder for general usage. But Nitro-Proof was not made legally compulsory until 1925, since which date all new guns must have passed Nitro-Proof automatically.

G. B.

On Cleaning Guns

Guns have to be cleaned in many different kinds of places. Avoid stone or brick floors.

It is easier to handle barrels when cleaning them if, when the gun is taken to pieces, the fore-end be snapped on again.

The first thing to do, in cleaning barrels, is to remove the powder fouling. This will dirty any material used. Therefore use newspaper, torn up into pieces which can be rolled up into a ball and pushed through the barrels with a jag screwed on the end of the cleaning rod. When you have pushed through two or three balls, practically all the fouling will have disappeared.

To clean the barrels thoroughly, the next step is to remove the jag and substitute a brass wire brush, dipped in oil (B.S.A. "Kleenwell" or Young's "303 Cleaner" for choice), which should be pushed through once and again. *N.B.*—Brass brushes, being of the softer metal, cannot possibly scratch steel.

Next, dry with a flannel patch wrapped on the jag and inspect. A final oiling may be given with a flannel patch. A patch is always preferable to tow, of which it is difficult to twist on exactly the right quantity.

Last, the fore-end may be removed, brushed with an old toothbrush dipped in oil, and barrels and action wiped with an oily rag.

So much for a dry day. On a wet day, barrels and action will need drying. If the gun has been left wet and there is rust, it can be removed with boiling water. (Never use emery powder.) Rub dry with flannel. Dry the spaces between barrels and rib with blotting paper.

If the gun has been used in rain, remove barrels, and shake the stock well. Shake the fore-end in the same way. Wipe dry and apply oil.

To touch triggers, &c., with oil, use the point of a bodkin or knitting needle. Do not use a feather.

It is seldom necessary to remove the locks. This is a simple process, but do not attempt it without going over the whole process with your gunmaker.

Guns should be sent to the maker at the end of every season for overhauling. This adds to the life of the gun.

GUN-CUPBOARDS

You will not find a gun-cupboard mentioned as a necessity, or even as a convenience, in every treatise of shooting. Yet who having once known the use of a cupboard, the ease with which a gun can be taken from it and replaced in it, the sense of safety which it bestows on the handler of the gun, the saving of time granted to the user of the gun day by day and week after week, the saving of space when only a gun and not a gun in a case has to be provided for—who, once having possessed a gun-cupboard, and having once known the friendliness and companionship of its niches, its arm-high floor, its welcoming glass door, could possibly contemplate a shooting season without one?

And a cupboard, of course, not for one gun only, but for two, four, six guns in a row; for more, if there are more in the house in use, or likely to be; a cupboard to set guns in side by side, guns of different owners, of various bores, a cupboard which will even house a rifle; and, too, a cupboard which shall give the owner of the gun or the guns in it that quiet pleasure of an autumn day and it may be of a winter night, in merely looking at a beloved weapon in the safety, the cleanliness, the promise for to-morrow behind the glass of the shut door. Strange, that a gun-cupboard still lacks its sacred bard!

We may find gun-cupboards—or gun-cabinets, if the name be preferred—thus described, to be made to order, in the sporting catalogues. Here is one: For six guns, with three drawers and cupboard lined cloth, 7 ft. 6 ins. high, 2 ft. 7 ins. wide, 1 ft. 2½ ins. deep; oak, walnut or mahogany; price, what shall we say? . . . This, of course, is for six guns, each put together, standing upright on their stocks, trigger-guard next the wall, barrels in loop-holed shelf; one long drawer running the width of the cabinet and two drawers below it, each running half the width; and underneath the drawers, behind doors with lock and key, space for gun-cases, cartridge magazines, cartridge bags, game bags and whatnot. It is all very complete, and costs—well, you could get quite a good gun, if not of the best London finish, for what it costs.

But the best gun-cupboard of which I have had experience did not cost as much as that. It cost—well, it cost the price of a deal-framed glass door, 4 ft. by 1 ft. 9½ ins., complete with handle, lock and key; a plain deal drawer, 17 ins. by 13 ins. by 6 ins. deep; and a wooden framework for the main part of the cupboard itself, which is of polished cedar wood, and cost nothing—at least, not to its owner. But if the frame of the glass door, and if the drawer, are of so cheap a wood as deal, why is the main part of the cupboard of polished cedar? For the reason that it was never intended for part of a gun-cupboard. It was originally part of a boat. When the owner was at Oxford, he rowed in his College Eight, and at the end of the races, the boat, being of no further use, was sawn up and its eight thwarts presented to their occupiers. And the occupier of No. 3 thwart, having sur-veyed his apparently meaningless acquisition, gave it meaning and purpose by framing it, giving it a door and a drawer, and fastening it up in the corner of a room which serves the quintuple purpose of a lobby, a lavatory, a museum, a hat-and-coat rack, and a gun-room; and there, as a gun-cupboard, it occupies a corner of two out of four walls whose other occupants are foxes' masks and brushes, golf-club bags, cases of stuffed fish, innumerable hats and coats, and a barometer—a room of which the atmosphere, whatever the weather outside may be, is invariably set fair.

In the rack of this gun-cupboard, then, may be set, and are set, guns; but not as they are set in the gun-cabinets of the sporting catalogue. They are set, not with the trigger-guard, but the top-lever, next the wall; which has the obvious advantage of enabling the heel of the stock to sit comfortably on the floor of the cupboard, and the barrels to rest comfortably upright against their niches at the back of the cupboard—niches conveniently cut in what was originally the rib of the boat. Guns, after use, could not more easily be deposited in a safe resting-place.

And under the guns, on the next floor, or deck, so to speak, is the deal drawer; which shall hold chamois leathers of different sizes, boxes to hold rook-rifle cartridges, a dozen odds and ends for the easier cleaning of guns; and among other happy appurtenances, a couple of those leather sheaths with discs blocking the sight of the left eye, so that guns in the cupboard, without the need of the use of a cross-eyed stock, can be used or left unused, by him whose right eye or whose left is the master—a convenient adjunct to a gun-cupboard at the disposal, on occasion, of members of a family. A gun-cupboard, in short, holding more than guns; holding a drawer, and the drawer containing things useful and things which have been used, things new and old, dry and oily, and, tidy or untidy, a drawer that can be shut.

P. Q.

SHOOTING SCHOOLS

To PICK up an early edition of the Badminton Library volume *Shooting: Field and Covert*, and to turn to the chapter headed "Hints for Beginners" is to realise how far we have travelled in methods of training and in general outlook on wild life in the course of two generations. Here is one of the best-known game shots of his day, giving his best advice as to first lessons in the use of gun. The "young shooter" is to go out and shoot alone "so long as he has an experienced sportsman at his side," and having been first instructed as to handling a gun, loading it with empty cartridges, pulling the trigger and so on, he comes to the real thing:—

"At first a small charge of powder only may be used, and he may be taught to fire this off at small birds, every attention being paid to his handling his gun with safety as if it were loaded. He may next be encouraged to shoot at small birds with a half-ounce of shot. If he succeeds pretty well, and is above all things careful in the way he manages his gun, he can next be permitted to fire at pigeons (with their wings slightly clipped, so as not to fly too fast) from under a flower-pot or out of a trap, at a distance of fifteen yards or so."

It all sounds oddly primitive, with the vague directions as to "small birds," and the pigeon with clipped wings under the flower-pot, but it is the philosophy of an age which produced some of the greatest figures in the world of shooting. Yet outstanding as were such game shots, for example, as Lord Ripon and Lord Walsingham, might there not have been many more of a nearly equal skill with them, had their beginnings in the shooting field been those which are open to beginners of to-day? If there is no single game shot to-day of such pre-eminence as the two or three leading shots of thirty or forty years ago, the average of good shooting is to-day unquestionably higher than when the readers of *Baily's Magazine* were invited to send to the editor lists of the best shots they knew. Those were the days of "the professionals," of men who were invited to the big days of this or that shoot weeks or months ahead of the day or days; in times when men could somehow afford to devote endless leisure to whatever sport they chose. To-day no editor who knew anything about the conditions under which sport is carried on would think of asking his readers to compile a list of best shots, so many are very good and so few pre-eminent. There are two reasons for that: one, that most men who shoot have learnt how to hit at a shooting school; and the other, that few have sufficient leisure, and that few, who have leisure, would care to spend all of it shooting.

To begin with, a shooting school makes it possible for every one to shoot with a gun that fits him. In the old days, a boy as often as not fitted himself to the gun he was given. Perhaps the gun was too long or too short in the stock, perhaps it was too straight or with too much bend; perhaps, worse still, the boy's left eye was the master, and he did not know it. In any case, if he was made to shoot with a gun that did not fit him, he could not shoot well. To-day things are different. If he is given a gun, or if a gun is to be made for him, the gunmaker sees that it fits. Placed opposite a big white iron target, the beginner finds himself with a "try-gun" in his hands—a specially constructed weapon with an adjustable stock—and is told to fire at a black mark which can be moved backwards and forwards or up and down with a pulley and string. When he fires, the charge shows a black splash on the white target. If the splash is consistently high, the stock wants more "bend"; if consistently low, it needs straightening. If it is consistently to the left, the stock needs to be "cast-off"; if consistently to the right, to be "cast-on." All this is assuming that the gunmaker has found out for certain that the shooter's right eye is the master eye, that is to say, that when aiming with both eyes open it is the right eye which takes control. If, on the other hand, he has discovered that the left eye is the master—which is frequently the case with left-handed bowlers and batsmen at cricket—he will probably suggest that the gun should be fired from the left shoulder, or—a much simpler remedy—that a disc fitted to a sheath be placed on the left barrel, so that the left eye does not see the muzzle of the gun and the right eye takes control. There is a third possibility, which is, for the shooter whose left eye is the master, to build a cross-eyed stock, so that the left eye takes charge when the gun is fired from the right shoulder, but that, though often effective as a remedy, means building an ugly gun.

We will suppose, then, that the shooter has been duly fitted with a gun, and come to the second stage of shooting school instruction, that is firing at clay pigeons thrown from a trap. His first shots will be of the simplest sort; he will be stationed in an open field, with the trap concealed by a bank of sods a few yards in front of him, and the clays will be thrown at a given signal straight away from him. When he has learnt how to time his shot and can break clay after clay thrown straight away, to the right and to the left, firing easily and quickly but without hurry, he will proceed to double rises; he will be given two clays to think about, one to the right and one to the left. With a little practice he will score a right and left; with more, several rights and lefts in succession. The time has come to adjourn from the field to "the covert."

This is a long strip of rough field with bushes and brushwood scattered through it, and with concealed traps which are to throw up clays at unexpected moments and in different directions, going away right and left, or coming back overhead, or crossing, or rising two at a time. A variety of shot is offered as the shooter walks on down the ride running through the covert, by a clay bowling fast over or across the grass—a clay that is a rabbit. When the beginner reaches the end of the covert he has been offered almost every kind of shot that would naturally come his way when actually walking up game.

He is now to be taken on, to practise shots at driven birds. He takes his stand some thirty yards from a high hedge, on the other side of which are traps which are to throw clays towards him with a flight resembling that of partridges. First come clays thrown so as to fly straight over the shooter's head, and the shooter finds that they actually do fly straight over his head untouched, until he gets into the knack of lifting his gun to cover the clay the moment he sees it and to keep the gun swinging up as he pulls the trigger. At last he finds the knack, and having found it, he is further tested with clays thrown to his right and left, when he has to learn whatever he does never to fire "down the line," that is, in the direction in which other guns may be imagined to be standing, but always at a safe angle, towards or away from the hedge. Last and hardest test of all come two clays thrown together, or one following the other, either both to his right or left, or one to the right and one to the left. If he can score a right and left at these clays more than once, he is justified in believing that he might be able to hit a driven partridge.

Now for the last test, high pheasants. He is taken to another part of the shooting school grounds where, behind three tall elms rises a wooden tower, with ladders scaling from stage to stage, and on the top stages traps to throw clays out over the shooter's head, or to the right and left, but in any case high—as high as he is ever likely to see live pheasants flying. And if he can score three or four hits running, when the clays are thrown straight over or at any angle to the right or left, he need not be afraid of standing with other guns outside a covert in the Christmas holidays, on a day in December or January when pheasants are flying as high and as fast as pheasants can.

All the morning, or all the afternoon, perhaps—for he will find that to shoot at clay pigeons through the morning

and afternoon of the same day is a task beyond the hardiest
—he has been shooting in the friendly company of a coach
who has watched hundreds of beginners with a gun, and has
taught them what to do and what not to do, how to correct
faults, how to make good weaknesses, above all, how to
handle, carry, and fire a gun with assured safety. The shooting school with such a coach gives him opportunities of
practice which even "the experienced sportsman at his
side" could never have given him in the old days. It is not
too much to say that the modern shooting school, besides
its insistence on "safety first," has imparted in an afternoon
knowledge, and with knowledge skill, which in times past
could only have been the outcome of years of experience.

And it is not only the inexperienced who benefit. Many
men who have shot for many years find that an hour or so
at clays at the beginning of the season, when muscles are
slack, gives just that zest of grip and perception of pace
which the shooter, lacking practice, knows he needs and
realises he has recovered. He will begin the first day shooting well ahead instead of—as perhaps he remembers his
coach told him he shot as a schoolboy—"behind and low."

WHICH IS THE MOST DIFFICULT SHOT?

HERE IS a question often asked, and one to which no final answer is likely to be forthcoming: none which could be hoped to represent the choice of all those who have shot under so many different conditions, at different game or wild fowl, in different parts of the country or the world at large. Yet it is interesting to notice where, in the main, the differences lie. That can be seen most plainly by comparing the answers given to the question, What is the most difficult shot? a generation ago with those which are given to-day. The question was discussed in two sporting magazines, *Baily's* and the *Badminton*, which are no longer with us, in the early days of the century. Those were great shooting days. They were days in which the name and fame of individuals—one name may stand as an example of many, the late Marquess of Ripon—were familiar in every gun-room. They were the days before the war of 1914–8; the days of the great "pheasant era"; days when bags numbered four figures—and days which we are not likely, and perhaps do not all wish, to see again. And the answer to the question, What is the most difficult shot? was found, as it might be expected, in near relation to the numbers of the bird most often fired at.

In the *Badminton Magazine* of April 1905, the editor, the

late A. E. T. Watson, put the question to a chosen gallery of recognised game shots. They were fifteen in number; they formed a historic gathering, and as such, their names deserve record:—The Marquess of Granby, Earl de Grey (Marquess of Ripon), Lord Walsingham, Lord Ashburton, Lord Westbury, Prince Victor Duleep Singh, the Hon. A. E. Gathorne-Hardy, the Hon. Harry Stonor, Major Arthur Acland-Hood, and Messrs. R. H. Rimington Wilson, F. E. R. Fryer, Reginald G. Hargreaves, T. S. Pearson Gregory, Arthur Portman, and H. W. Gilbey. And here, condensed into a few lines each, are their answers:—

Marquess of Granby.—A genuinely "tall" pheasant, "sailing" with perfectly motionless wings, "curling" and possibly dropping as well.

Earl de Grey.—A high pheasant coming down wind with a drop and a curl.

Lord Walsingham.—A bird which comes *straight* over your head at a moderate height, and which for some reason (*e.g.* empty gun, thick wood in front) cannot be shot when approaching—you must then turn round and shoot under the bird.

Lord Ashburton.—A pheasant, thirty-five to forty yards away, crossing and dropping with motionless wings.

Lord Westbury.—Cock pheasant dropping with outstretched wings and curling away from the shooter.

Prince Victor Duleep Singh.—A high dropping pheasant with a wind behind and wings practically motionless.

The Hon. A. E. Gathorne-Hardy.—A pheasant which has come straight at you too low to shoot at in front, and which you turn round to.

The Hon. Harry Stonor.—A high cock pheasant flying down the line of guns with wings outstretched and motionless.

Major Acland Hood.—A low partridge or pheasant on one's left.

Mr. R. H. Rimington Wilson.—Really high pheasants in a wind and with a curl.

Mr. F. E. R. Fryer.—A low skimming pheasant against a dark background.

Mr. R. G. Hargreaves.—The second barrel at a flock of teal well on the wing. Ptarmigan driven round the top of a hill.

Mr. T. S. Pearson Gregory.—Pheasants coming down a hillside and skimming with a curl below. Driven grouse in a hilly country flying in the same way.

Mr. Arthur Portman.—High pheasants floating off a hill with no apparent movement of the wing.

Mr. H. W. Gilbey.—A real high pheasant with a curl on.

There you have the chorus of agreement—fourteen votes out of fifteen—the most difficult shot is at a pheasant.

And now travel forward thirty-one years—into another generation—from May 1905 to the autumn of 1936. The great "pheasant era" is a thing of the past: four figure totals are no longer daily entries in game books, and the whole activity of the sport of shooting is a far simpler business. And the outlook of the shooting man, as a consequence, is much more natural. Instead of pheasants occupying his attention, to the exclusion—at all events for the latter part of the season—of almost everything else, he sees his sport and the chances it gives him, simple and difficult, in a better perspective. Pheasants are seen to offer their own problems, but other birds, too, offer problems better worth attention. The question, What is the most difficult shot? gets different answers from those of thirty years before. Here, taken from correspondence in the *Field*, are half a dozen replies, typical of others who to-day are—as they would have been thirty years ago—recognised game shots:

A, looking back over the season, compares memories of success and failure:—

"Grouse were difficult to kill by reason of their great pace and their habit of swerving suddenly. At times they were hard to see against their background. . . . Partridges were hard because often there was very little time or space to shoot in front. Their habit of scattering on sight of the guns made it difficult to concentrate on a selected bird. . . . It is not easy to dictate as to the verdict, but in my opinion the partridge will have escaped the ordinary sportsman most frequently while the pheasant will have died most often."

B. "Partridges . . . can attain to the almost impossible, offering targets that beat the quickest and most certain of shots. . . . To analyse the snipe, we will go down to an English marsh on a winter's morning. The rushes brittle with frost, and every puddle a crackle with sheet ice; the snipe are in, but wild as hawks, and rising in whisps ere ever you get within fifty yards of them. No Indian paddy-field birds these, and as different as chalk from cheese to the snipe flushed in milder, moister climes.

"Two friends of mine, shooters of great experience, have no hesitation in awarding first prize for difficulty to the driven snipe. . . . Speaking only for myself, I place the English snipe first in order of difficulty, with the driven partridge a good second."

C. "I would without a moment's hesitation choose the high and well-shown pheasant as the one bird amongst all others to which I would give my vote for presenting the most difficult shot. By 'high' I mean one that is at least thirty-five yards up in the air. . . . And the high curling pheasant is probably the most difficult bird of all to kill cleanly and surely."

D. "What bird is it that we all waste more cartridges at than at anything else; that pays least attention to our well-meant efforts to slay him? I think the woodpigeon. To the woodpigeon I would give the prize as a general practitioner, reserving for the really high curling pheasant the 'special' award."

E. "Of the many varieties of duck which I have killed flighting, none to my mind can fly faster than the pochard and tufted going down wind; many a January evening I have heard the rush of wings in the half light and watched those aerial torpedoes dive from a great height and swing sharply into the wind before skimming over the water on which they intend to settle for their evening meal. Not even teal can twist, scatter, and gain height more quickly than the 'divers' when going down wind. . . .

"Probably very few people have tried flighting snipe in the evening, and no one that I have come across has as yet succeeded in making a considerable bag. . . .

"A golden plover on the tops in August or an August grouse drive is not too difficult, but when flighted or driven after November, whether he is coming high over the gunner crouching behind a stone wall in the south of Scotland or low over the saltings at evening time, he is a very hard bird to stop. No bird, in my opinion, can show a finer turn of speed or a greater capacity for swerving, and to kill a right and left out of a small bunch under these conditions will puzzle the most experienced marksman.

"In order of difficulty, therefore, I would place golden plover one, snipe two, tufted duck three, with a certificate of merit to the partridge (driven)."

And may an old keeper, quoted by one of the foregoing, sum up the matter? To the question, "Which is the most difficult shot," his answer was, "Weel, I'm no sure, for it a' depends."

CLOTHES & KIT

IF I am to begin with the most essential part of a shooting
man's clothing, I will choose boots. For every day of
every month in the season, in England, Scotland, Ireland
and Wales, boots, waterproof leather, laced with leather
laces, thick-soled, well-nailed boots are best.

Shoes? someone objects—why not shoes? Shoes are
lighter, cooler, quicker to put on, easier to take off.

That may be granted, and if all the ground which one has
to walk over in a day's shooting were like a cricket pitch,
shoes no doubt would be preferable. But take the ground as
you find it, day after day, from the 12th of August to the
31st of January, where and when have shoes the advantage?
Begin on the 12th of August, with dry heather and walking
as easy as you please. You will find at lunch time that you
will be more comfortable when you have removed an
accumulation of dry heather which has somehow gathered
itself inside the tops of your shoes, and if you have happened
during the course of the morning or afternoon to walk over
ground where the heather has been burnt you will discover
when you come to change for dinner that your stockings
have admitted a quite considerable amount of powdered
wood ash. If, in addition, which may happen in the driest
weather, you have lighted on a patch of sphagnum in the
low ground, it is difficult to sink in ankle-deep without
filling your shoes with water.

Or begin your day in England, on a day in September
when there has been rain in the night. Stubbles have to be
walked, and stubbles are easier walking, on a morning when

the sun is full at eleven, in light gear rather than heavy. But stubbles are not all; there is clover, there is mustard, there are potatoes, which besides being tiresome to the stride, can be as slippery in wet weather as they are dusty in dry; and, above all, there are swedes. Swedes on a sunny morning after rain are delightful to the eye, providing pocketfuls of water for the skies to shine in, but when each plant tips its pocketful from the leaf on to and into shoe leather, they cease to be merely spectacular. Swedes can even soak the stockings of the wearer of boots.

And gaiters. Gaiters help in more ways than one. They prevent laces being untied by heather stems and bracken. They keep out heather tops and drippings from turnip leaves. They may be of canvas for the heats of autumn and leather for the rigours of winter. And gaiters add completeness to comfort and to looks.

As to other clothing, there can be choices of colour. Not for walking partridges or covert-shooting, when coats or caps or hats that provide startling contrasts with the landscape may surprise other guns, but will not scare game. With grouse-driving it is different. Just as drivers and flankers are provided with white or red flags to induce grouse to fly forward, or not to break out at the side, so may a tweed jacket brilliantly diverse in shade from a peat butt, or a cap or hat, or even a bald head, showing light against a dark background, may turn aside an oncoming covey. A white pocket-handkerchief used at the wrong moment may be equally effective. "Lovat mixtures" mingle satisfactorily with surroundings of ling and granite, and so, for that matter, may the loudest check. But these come in the doctrines of correct camouflage, and perhaps, if grouse shooters in a drive wore clothes resembling the quarterings of football shirts, they would escape notice against a hill background of rock and heather. Broken colours are to be preferred to plain greys or browns.

Comfort, besides colour, requires thought. Only Scots born and bred may wear the kilt—how many Southerners have envied their freedom of limb! For there is little comfort to be had from knickerbockers—an absurd name for a man's garment—and only discomfort in sun or rain to be found in "plus fours"—the worst name for any garment ever invented. Perhaps those garments described at clumsy length as knickerbocker breeches, loosely cut round the knee itself and laced so as to fit more closely just below it, best suit shooting occasions. But the need for a name which should displace the dreadful knickerbocker remains insistent.

Waterproofs remain a problem. Of well-known makers, for material, colour, lightness, and efficiency in keeping out rain, how could they be bettered? But who, with tightened sleeves and hampering thickness of an extra garment, can shoot his best? One method of using waterproof and gun may be tried in the butts, which is to use the coat as a cape without putting the arms into the sleeves; then when need arises the cape can be thrown back and the arms are free. If rain wets during those few minutes, well, it wets. The main need, after all, is to be able to shoot.

Waterproofs for the shooter are of neutral colours that do not advertise his presence in the butt. But they become useless if the shooter's loader is not equally unnoticeable. So that it is well to make sure, before adding a loader to other impediments of the moor, that his waterproof is not of that shining white which may keep off rain but will also keep off grouse.

Two items of equipment belong alike to the open moor, grouse butts, partridge shooting, and the covert-side—cartridge bags and the shooting stick. Cartridge bags may be large or small, to carry a hundred, fifty or twenty-five. A hundred cartridges weigh ten pounds, and are a heavy weight for a ghillie to start the day with. Two bags, one to carry fifty and the other to be carried with the game-cart or the pony are better. Instead of cartridge bags, there are those who prefer belts, others who fill pockets. And coat-pockets, by the way, are not the only pockets for cartridges. Three cartridges in a breeches pocket are a help.

And cartridge bags, for journeys over railways and far moors, entail cartridge magazines. Magazines to take three hundred are a useful size, and for railway journeys need

98

locks. Cartridge bags, on the other hand, which may be carried by ghillies and friends, are better without locks. But they need initials, plainly stamped in black.

As for shooting sticks, the main quality which they should possess is that of a seat. They may be sticks for convenience of carrying, and so may have comfortable handles. But for sitting on they should provide a seat of leather, the longer, the broader, and the more spacious altogether, the better.

CHEVIOT.

WATERPROOFING: CLOTHES & BOOTS

For waterproofing clothes there are variations of a recipe that has been often recommended in the *Field* as having stood the test of many years:—

(1) 3 ozs. alum, 3 ozs. sugar of lead, 2 gallons water. Leave to soak twenty-four hours, then allow to drip dry; then brush.

(2) $\frac{1}{2}$ oz. sugar of lead, $\frac{1}{2}$ oz. alum, 1 gallon rain water. Steep for twenty-four hours. Hang to dry in open air.

Boots.—There is no better leather than porpoise hide, and none more pliable nor more easy to walk in. To make boots waterproof, stand them in a bath of neatsfoot oil, which you can get from any ironmonger. Pour the oil inside as well as out, and leave the pair in the bath—a foot-bath does very well—overnight. It is remarkable the amount the leather will drink. Let the superfluous oil run off, and then lay them aside a few days. If you put them on at once you will spoil your stockings. But the leather soon absorbs the oil altogether, and boots which have been thoroughly soaked in this way will be completely waterproof. See that the welt is wide; a broad welt is a great comfort. You will want good nails, with a double row at heel and toe. Rubber soles or studs are useless; they slip on wet ground and kick out on stones.

DON'T & ALWAYS

A FATHER'S ADVICE TO HIS SON

If a sportsman true you'd be,
Listen carefully to me.

Never, never let your gun
Pointed be at any one;
That it may unloaded be
Matters not the least to me.

When a hedge or fence you cross,
Though of time it cause a loss,
From your gun the cartridge take,
For the greater safety's sake.

If 'twixt you and neighbouring gun
Birds may fly or beasts may run,
Let this maxim e'er be thine;
FOLLOW NOT ACROSS THE LINE.

Stops and beaters oft unseen
Lurk behind some leafy screen;
Calm and steady always be:
NEVER SHOOT WHERE YOU
*   CAN'T SEE.*

Keep your place and silent be:
Game can hear and game can see;
Don't be greedy, better spared
Is a pheasant than one shared.

You may kill or you may miss,
But at all times think of this:
All the pheasants ever bred
Won't repay for one man dead.

COMMANDER MARK BEAUFOY.

COMMANDER BEAUFOY'S lines to-day, it is to be hoped, are well known. They cannot be too well known. They cover, in a general way, the advice and the cautions necessary in the matter of safely handling a gun. But they may be supplemented in detail. Besides "never" there is "always" to be thought of, and there are manners to be cultivated as well as habits to avoid. "Hints to Beginners and Some Old Sinners" might be the title of a small compendium of "always" and "never" maxims dealing with various forms of shooting, partridges, grouse, pheasants, rabbits. In partridge shooting, for instance:—

Always pick your bird out of a covey; never "brown" a covey. If you brown a covey you are pointing your gun at a space between individual birds; you are aiming at nothing and you will probably hit nothing.

When walking in line, keep in line.

Watch your host for signals, so that he need do no more than signal.

DON'T TALK.

When standing in line for driven partridges, never fire down the line even at high birds. Falling shot put out eyes.

In turning to take a bird behind the line, keep your gun pointing to the sky.

Never take long shots at birds going away.

At the end of a beat always unload.

When moving to a new beat, don't talk.

GROUSE SHOOTING

When walking in line, keep in line.

On a driving day, having taken up your position in your allotted butt, do not leave the butt till the drive is over.

When the drive is over, unload. In leaving your butt to pick up birds, leave also your gun.

In picking up the grouse you have shot, let others pick up the grouse they haven't.

COVERT SHOOTING

If a gun with the beaters, never shoot at a bird going forward.

If a gun in a ride, never shoot at a rabbit crossing the ride. On a day of hard frost, don't shoot rabbits.

If standing outside a covert, never shoot a low bird coming forward, or crossing your front.

Always know where the guns are on either side of you, and be sure that they know where you are. Never move from where you are placed.

DON'T TALK to your neighbour, the lady standing with you, your loader, or your dog.

Always unload immediately the beat is over.

FERRETING RABBITS

If you are out with another gun, be sure that you know where he is, and that he knows where you are. If you and he are on opposite sides of a hedge, be exactly opposite. If a rabbit bolts, let it get well clear to the right or left.

If a rabbit looks out of a hole, but does not bolt, do not fire; the ferret may be close behind it.

If you move to pick up a ferret, put your gun at safe.

If you put down your gun, unload.

If it is a frosty day, do not stamp. When rabbits wish to warn other rabbits, rabbits stamp.

FERRETING WITH NETS

Netting rabbits has this advantage over shooting them, that netted rabbits being cleanly killed are better to cook and to sell. Many maxims apply equally to the gun and the net.

A week or so before setting out to ferret with nets, take a spade and stop some of the larger holes in the bury, using sods, not loose soil, and pressing the sods well home. You will thus need fewer nets.

Never stop a bolt hole, and be sure that you find all the bolt holes.

For carrying ferrets, use a box in preference to a bag, and line the box with hay. Boxes do not get wet in rain, are much more comfortable for the ferret, and are quicker to open and shut.

See that the collar of the line ferret fits well and is neither loose nor tight. Mark the line with a red tassel sewn in a yard from the collar, and with three or four white tassels sewn in at intervals of a yard. Never use knots to mark the line; they may catch in roots.

Use large nets of small mesh, so that a rabbit cannot push past them.

Count your nets as you place them and as you take them up.

In removing a rabbit caught in a net, stand in the empty hole.

If it is necessary to dig out a rabbit, fill in the dug-out soil.

Keep ferrets in a dry, warm, clean hutch; feed when possible with rabbit (head and neck) and provide clean water.

DISCOMFORTS

WHY HAVE CRAMP?

I REMEMBER no evening of a winter day more clearly than one on which I spent a despairing quarter of an hour in a cold wind on a lonely roadside, on the return journey from a day's shooting in Sussex. Part of the day had been spent walking up rabbits in line, which meant treading out bracken, brambles, and other under-cover, some of it thin and some of it thick, but nearly all of it necessitating lifting the foot and bending the knee, here and there for as long as ten minutes together. And that, unless you are used to such exercise, may have uncomfortable consequences. I realised this to the full when, on the drive home at six o'clock or so in the evening, my chauffeur, who had voluntarily taken a very usefully active part in the afternoon's work, suddenly with an exclamation stopped the car, and became rigidly inactive in the leg, not without groans. He had been seized with violent cramp in the muscles of the thigh and could not move. Somehow he got himself out of the car, and I, bending over an unhappy crumpling figure, strove to straighten him out and by vigorous massage to restore movement to pain-drawn muscles. It was a long and interrupted journey home, for even when he could move again the pain returned at intervals; we had twenty more miles to go, there were only the two of us there, and I, incompetent traveller that I am, cannot drive a car.

More than once, before and since that evening, I had myself suffered that agonising pain of cramp, usually in the middle hours of the night, and had known no means of dealing with it except stretching the muscles by forcible movement and by rubbing—a remedy prolonged and chilling. And it was not until years later, when shooting days had stretched over many seasons, that I came by the knowledge of a remedy which certainly has saved myself, and I hope others who knew as little of it as I did, hours of suffering. It is possible that there may be others equally ignorant to-day.

I had been invited to shoot woodcock in the far country of the south-west, and the great day having come and gone, I found myself on the day following pursuing snipe and other quarry over ground part of which was as rough and difficult as any which it has been my fortune to face in England, Scotland, Ireland or Wales. Peat-hags, separate, solid, multitudinous, stretched before me; peat-hags divided one from the next by wet peat; peat-hags, some of the lowliness of a foot-stool, some the height, it seemed to me, of a dining-room table; peat-hags stretched before me, unforgiving, unavoidable, for countless acres, and here and there from among those acres, snipe arose crying into the wind, and I arose and descended crying after them.

At the end of the afternoon I found myself walking home in the company of an Irish doctor, on whom may the benisons of St. Patrick, St. Luke, and all other saints and physicians rest. "I'm afraid of to-night," I told him. "Those peat-hags—the muscles of my legs—I'm not used to it. Cramp— that's what I'm afraid of. In the middle of the night. Cramp."

He looked on me benignly; he, I say, out of his exuberant knowledge of *materia medica* unguessed at by an English would-be snipe-shooter, surveyed me benignly over Cornish heather and peat.

"Why need ye have cramp? Quinine. In the glass of whisky-and-soda before ye go to bed. Five grains of quinine. Ye needn't have cramp."

Nor, I believe, need anyone else.

MIDGES

Worst, I think, on a warm, cloudy day in a grouse butt, perhaps after rain. Or when waiting for any kind of driven shot on an autumn day without wind, when your stand happens to be on low ground, or in the neighbourhood of trees. But intensely irritating always, and to be provided against by more or less infallible and less or more evanescent prophylactics, such as oil of lavender or oil of geranium. These be for the neck, the temples, the ears, and the neighbourhood of the ears, and for all portions of the scalp covered or uncovered, protected or not by hair or cap or hat or kerchief.

But for the legs? A simpler protective covering, yet not to be used—or I have not seen it so used—about the temples or the ears. But absolutely certain, completely efficacious; without scents or need of anointment, to be applied once and for all day long, beneath stockings, thin or thick. Just toilet paper, wound about from ankles to knees as putties are wound. A midge will find its way through the closest interstices of knitted wool, but against the thin, hard impenetrable surface of toilet paper proboscis, jaw, appetite exercise themselves in vain.

CHEVIOT.

SPLIT FINGER

All who shoot, or for that matter do anything out of doors in times of frost and east winds—especially those past middle age—know the misery of split skin near the nails of thumb and fingers. A friend advises as a cure the dabbing on of a mixture of equal parts of glycerine and lemon juice, which, if it doesn't heal the split forthwith, prevents it from spreading.

If lemon juice is hard to get, vaseline alone, put on at night under a finger-stall, is helpful.

TIPS & TIPPING

HOW MUCH ought I to give the keeper as a tip after a day's shooting? It is an ever-recurring question to which there can be no fixed answer. The following is the substance of a correspondence recently published in the *Field* following an article by a writer signing himself "Cheviot," who had been asked by *Field* readers to suggest a scale of tipping applicable to various typical situations. "Cheviot" asked for criticism, and here is his suggested scale:—

"(*a*) Walking up partridges in September, two guns, five brace—5*s*.

(*b*) Ditto, four guns, twenty-five brace—10*s*.

(*c*) Walking grouse in August, three guns, twenty brace —10*s*.

(*d*) Ten days or a fortnight's stay in a lodge in the Highlands, with five or six days' shooting; head keeper £2, second keeper £1.

(*e*) A day's grouse driving, eight guns, thirty-five brace —10*s*.

(*f*) Ditto, 100 brace—£1.

(*g*) Partridge driving, two days, forty and fifty brace— head keeper, £1, 10*s*., second keeper 10*s*.

(*h*) Covert shooting, fifty pheasants—10*s*.

(*i*) Ditto, 200 pheasants—£1.

(*k*) Ditto, three days, 300 pheasants, 100 duck, 100 hares and rabbits—head keeper £2, second keeper £1."

Criticism followed this suggested scale. "C. J." writes:— "Had I been one of two guns in September killing only five brace on a manor (no mention is made of other game than partridges) my tip would have been a very grudging 5s.

(b) (c) (d) might be even a little higher.

(e) With eight guns 5s. to head keeper and 2s. 6d. to loader, probably an under-keeper, should be ample.

(f) £1 to head keeper is too much; 10s. should be ample, and 5s. for the under-keeper if he loads for you.

(g) and (h). Half these tips ample.

(i) If said birds are high and healthy, and especially if there are fines for killing hens, the scale seems reasonable.

(k) Reasonable, except that the second keeper's tip should be only 10s."

From the United University Club, Pall Mall East, "Zulu" writes:—

"Perhaps the most satisfactory way out of the tipping difficulty is for the host to disallow tips altogether. I tried the experiment in a week-end winter shoot that I shared with some friends, and after seven years' trial I think we were all agreed, hosts, guests and keeper, that the plan was a success. For convenience sake we used to send each guest a printed card with particulars of train service, post, telegraph, &c., and we put a note as to 'no tips' on this card. Each year I gave the keeper a Christmas box which included a sum in lieu of tips calculated roughly on a basis of 5s. per guest per day. It was not a fixed sum, but varied slightly each year according to the bag, &c. Taking several years, our bag, mixed, averaged 1,031 head, and I find the Christmas box averaged £9, 16s. The total cost of running the shoot (exclusive of board and lodging) averaged £435 a year, so that for a very trifling addition to the expenditure we had the satisfaction of knowing that our guests were spared the worry and expense of tips."

"J. B. F." thinks the weather ought to be taken into consideration:—

"Take a day's grouse driving. A bad day may easily reduce a hundred brace to fifty, and so may bad shooting. Combined with this I take the number of cartridges I fire.

If you want a scale, say 5*s*. for every twenty-five cartridges for a man who is neither rich nor poor. The latter need never go beyond, and seldom as far as a pound.

"As to 'Cheviot's' scale, I should call (*a*) (*b*) and (*c*) too high; as to (*d*) five or six days' shooting is too indefinite; (*e*) (*f*) (*g*) (*h*) and (*i*) are all too high if, as I assume, he is dealing with eight guns on each occasion."

"Corvidae" gives a gamekeeper's point of view:—

"As 'Cheviot' asks for criticism, perhaps a few words from a keeper's point of view would be welcome. I think the proposed standard laid down by 'Cheviot' a very fair one taken generally, but might I suggest that if gentlemen wish to tip the keepers they do so, not taking the 'bag' into consideration, but the amount of sport derived from obtaining that bag, and taking into consideration the amount of skill employed by the keeper in obtaining those results? Tipping to a given standard is, of course, impossible, as shoots vary so much in character and composition, consequently the amount of work involved on one shoot to obtain a given bag would be more than trebled on another with quite different facilities for rearing, showing game to the guns, &c. Personally I would far rather receive half a crown, given me in the true sporting spirit, with a kindly word of praise concerning the day's sport, than a sovereign given in a manner as a bone thrown to a dog."

"Centurion" criticises the scale of tips under the typical situations chosen:—

"Personally, under these situations, I should approximately tip as follows:—(*a*) 2*s*. 6*d*.; (*b*) 5*s*.; (*c*) 5*s*.; (*d*) head keeper 30*s*., second keeper 10*s*.; (*e*) 5*s*.; (*f*) 12*s*. 6*d*., provided butts were in good order; (*g*) head keeper £1, second keeper 10*s*.; (*h*) 5*s*.; (*i*) 10*s*.; (*k*) head keeper 30*s*., second keeper 15*s*. I have always thought that, for a single day's driving, either grouse or partridges, a fair approximate basis to work on for tips is 1*s*. per brace from all guns collectively, *i.e.* for a hundred brace day to eight guns it would work out at 12*s*. 6*d*. per gun, and the keepers would get £5; if to six guns, each gun would presumably get more shooting, and I should increase the tip by 5*s*. each gun, the keeper receiving £5, 5*s*."

"Pintail's" criticism is on somewhat the same lines as "Zulu's":—

"An old friend of mine solved the question for all who shot with him by asking the keepers, when he took a shoot, how much they expected to receive in tips, and giving them himself a larger sum down than they expected to get, on the understanding that they were to accept no tips under penalty of dismissal. His argument was that he disliked his guests being worried, and also that he asked many to shoot with him who could not afford to tip as others did. At first his guests felt uncomfortable when thanking the keepers at the end of a day or visit that they could not reward them pecuniarily; but grateful thanks and a shake of the hand seemed appreciated and understood."

"Shikari" has as simple a scale as any:—

"A plan I, personally, have adopted and find to work well, is twopence a shot, hit or miss, with a minimum of 5s. and a maximum of a sovereign. How does this strike you?"

That is the substance of a correspondence extending over a number of weeks in the *Field*, which, if it were re-opened to-day, would, I think, be conducted on much the same lines and with much the same results. If there can be said to be a general conclusion among the critics, it is that "Cheviot's" suggested scale of tips is too generous. On the other hand, the correspondent signing himself "Corvidae," who is a gamekeeper, regards "Cheviot's" standard as "a very fair one taken generally," and in conclusion, the would-be tipper on "Cheviot's" scale might reflect that at least he would never be regarded as having given too little, and that by adopting the suggested reductions he would not, after all, effect a very large saving in the expenses of a shooting season.   P. Q.

ON LEAVING THE DEER-FOREST

Before the guest comes south he will want to give some trifling gift to those men his friends the foresters who have worked him so hard and spoken to him so courteously and given him so many happy memories. I think the following would please the recipients: For a week's deer-stalking, unless it has been a truly wonderful week, I suggest the bestowal of: £2 to the head stalker, £1 to the second stalker, 10s. to one ghillie, and a sum, equivalent to 5s. a head, to be divided among other ghillies than your own and the pony-men.

If you are the wealthy lessee of an expensive forest I suggest, I only suggest—lesser sums may seem to you sufficient—that you give, at the season's end, £25 to the head stalker, £10 to the second stalker, and that you divide or cause to be divided, a further £20 among the other members of the forest staff. And, quite possible, an additional gift of books, or a subscription to some such weekly, as the *Field*, will please as greatly as the more practical recompense.

PATRICK CHALMERS:
Deer-Stalking.

SHOOTING & FORESTRY

DIFFERENT INDEED must be the ideals and the methods of the scientific forester and the designer of game coverts: the one intent on tree-growing as a commercial proposition, perhaps as a national industry; the other with the shooter views of a practical man desirous, within a more or less limited period of time, of rendering this or that area of woodland attractive merely to a particular species of bird—the pheasant. The one plants thinking of timber cut in rotation, his eye ranging past his own lifetime into the centuries; the other hopes to produce his effects next summer and autumn.

And so for the first, the forester, the vision is of thickly planted, periodically thinned blocks of tall, clean stems rising from bare soil; no side branches, but all the living wood of the tree thrusting upwards to its need of light and air; and when it has fulfilled its period of growth, felled to lie side by side with its fellow-prisoners, healthy, straight and strong, stacked for the sawmill.

For the second, the sportsman and gamekeeper, the need is different. His coverts are to be sunny, with trees growing to their natural shape, and plenty of room between them; with a stream, perhaps, running its free course in sunlight and shade; with plenty of undergrowth of shrub and flower and fruit, and not on level ground everywhere, but with knolls and dells, high slopes open to the warmth of the morning, and closely branching trees for shelter at night; and separated, too, by rides east and west, north and south, broad rides east and west, narrow paths north and south; belts, clumps, outlying strips and shaws, joined some of them and separate others, but bordered and sheltered each and all of them with hedge and tangle of fruit and berry-bearing shrubs.

Here are different ideals, different objects, different effects, different results. Shall we say that the forester's are so far-sighted, so altruistic, almost so inhuman as almost to be beyond the purview of the ordinary countryman? In days of changing ownership of land and property, with income tax and other taxes almost beyond calculation from year to year, scientific forestry has become a matter less for the private individual than the State. Let us turn to the nearer prospects of treating and using woods as we find them.

MAKING A GAME COVERT

No one in these days is likely to set himself the task of planting bare soil solely for the purposes of a game covert. He is more likely to find himself the owner or tenant of a piece of woodland more or less useless from the point of view of the forester, but capable of being developed and fostered for the purposes of the woodman and the gardener, with chestnut to be cut for fencing and the stickmaker, and hazel for hurdles, bean-sticks and pea-boughs; birch-copses, perhaps, to be thinned, and various undergrowths to be felled and stacked for the pleasant purposes of wood-fires. There will be strips of woodland seemingly existing merely as strips, perhaps the shelter of days gone by, and stretches of bracken, whitethorn, blackthorn, holly and bramble which can never be thought of economically but as happy English jungle; oaks here and there, and here and there a spreading beech; carpets of primroses, anemones, bluebells. . . . Just English woods—Barnes's " Zunny wood-lands . . ."

But even so, "zunny woodlands" may be useful and productive; may contain valuable shade and shelter and fruitful undergrowth. Here, then, are some of the trees and shrubs and plants to be found and encouraged, may be planted of set purpose, in the natural surroundings of a game covert.

Of trees affording natural food, oak with its acorns first,

and beech with its mast beloved of pigeons—but under beech no plant grows. For the edges of a wood, hawthorn, for its berries and its beauty. Sycamore and ash provide seeds, and add to oak leaves decaying vegetable matter productive of insect life.

And trees for roosting pheasants? If it has not happened that others have had the forethought to provide such ever-green night shelters as pheasants love, fir and pine can be planted to-day with the hope of attracting crowing cocks to roost on evenings not too far distant. Two trees are of outstanding value:—

Norway spruce (*Picea excelsa*).—Will stand shade if not too dense, when first planted, but needs sun for growth.

Scots pine (*Pinus silvestris*).—Fast growing in its early years; slower but more handsome as it grows older.

A faster grower than either of these is the Douglas fir (*Pseudotsuga Douglasii*), but less sturdy of habit in its early stages. Pheasants also like roosting in larches, but larch does not, of course, provide the same shelter as an evergreen tree.

We come now to plants for undergrowth, and first to shrubs bearing fruit. The following are valuable as being "practically rabbit-proof," which means that they are un-likely to be attacked by rabbits when established. Nothing in the stage of the tiny young plant is safe from rabbits, and all young plants should be protected by wire-netting.

Berberis aquifolium.—Evergreen, 2–6 ft. high, yellow flowers, dark purple berries. Will grow in shade.

Berberis vulgaris.—Deciduous, 4–7 ft. high; bright yellow flowers, red-orange long-shaped berries.

Berberis Darwinii.—Evergreen, 5–10 ft. high; deep orange flowers and purple berries.

Cotoneaster Simmonsii.—Evergreen, 6 ft.; orange-red berries.

Gaultheria Shallon.—American partridge berry. Valuable shade-bearer; white flowers, purple-blue berries which pheasants like; 2–2½ ft.

Leycesteria formosa.—Himalayan honeysuckle. Deciduous, 4–10 ft.; purple berries.

Ligustrum vulgare.—Common privet, 6–10 ft.; dark purple berries.

Rosa rugosa.—Japanese rose, 4–6 ft.; large red hips.

Rubus fruticosus.—Common blackberry.

R. deliciosus.—Rocky Mountain bramble, 3–6 ft.

R. Idaeus.—Common raspberry.

Symphoricarpus racemosus.—Snowberry. Deciduous, 4–7 ft.; spreads rapidly, white berries liked by pheasants.

Viburnum opulus.—Single Guelder rose, 6–15 ft.; dark purple-red berries.

Non-fruiting plants, useful for cover.

Cytisus scoparius.—Common broom, 2–6 ft.

Spartium junceum.—Spanish broom, 6–12 ft.

Cornus sanguinea.—Dogwood or Cornel.

Hypericum Androsœmum.—Shrubby St. John's Wort; shade bearer.

Laurel. *Prunus lauro-cerasus.*— Common laurel.

  ,,   *L. nobilis. Bay.*

  ,,   *Prunus lusitanica.*— Portugal laurel.

} Valuable as shelter and for flushing points.

Rhododendron ponticum.—Valuable for shelter and for flushing points.

GAMEKEEPERS

Ancient & Modern

KEEPERS OF the old school are not to be met every-where to-day, which is, on the whole, fortunate. He whom I remember was typical of the oldest school of all. He was a middle-aged man, with his head set low between his shoulders; his face was red, his hair earthy, and his eyes a sullen blue; he had a Newgate fringe, and teeth of various shapes and colours. He wore a coat and breeches of cord of that peculiar drab brown which has clothed gamekeepers since game was first kept; his shirt was grey flannel and with-out a collar. His cottage lay among spruce firs between the carriage-drive and the road; conveniently opposite was the village public house. I do not know which could have told most of his temper, his wife or his dogs; he kicked his dogs, which was a foul thing to see. As to education, he could neither read nor write; nor had he any better acquaintance with natural history than was proper to the attainments of keepers of his period. Every creature which was not game was for that reason the enemy of game, and so was to be shot or trapped or otherwise put out of a world which should only fitly contain partridges, pheasants, hares, rabbits, and gamekeepers. His traps befouled the woods; the hazels which he hung with stoats were horrors known afar. His

nesting forays were better admired; they resulted occasionally in clutches of eggs which were sent in for inspection
on a dinner plate, and I can still pick out from a cabinet a
jay's egg or two and a clutch of sparrow-hawk's eggs, of
which the red-brown blotches seem to me almost as bright
and the blue shell as delicate as on that May morning when
they were brought in unblown from the wood.

Yet he belongs to the oldest associations—he, with his
sullen eyes and his iron-shod boots, his "Come here, old
wooden-head" to the big black retriever, and the stories
whispered of him in the village, belongs to the best remembered of all those early days. It was he who showed me the
first pheasant chick I ever saw, and he produced that not
from under a hen or the run of a coop, but from a fold of
his flannel shirt, where he had half a dozen, peeping and
cheeping in the warmth between his shirt and his body. It
was he who first expounded to me the mixing of meal for
the birds on the rearing-field, and I have never since separated from the name of keeper the smell of boiled maize and
wheat, powdery sacks thrown over the shoulder of a wet
coat, and the steam floating out from the door of a hut under
a hedge of dog-roses. He it was to whom I brought very
carefully in a basket the contents of a pheasant's nest spied
in the grass of a roadside bank, only to be greeted with a
grim chuckle and the information that they were addled and
meant for someone else passing down that road.

E. P.:
Shooting Days.

GAMEKEEPERS IN THE 'EIGHTIES

It is difficult to say what amount of "keepering" a manor
requires, as this depends upon its size, position as regards
towns, footpaths, and poachers; its amount of covert or
arable, as well as the number of head hand-reared or naturally sustained; also whether the estate is compact—and so
easily protected—or the reverse.

A good head-keeper and two under-keepers will easily

look after an estate of about 3,000 acres, if favourably situated for protection and night-watching. A bad keeper can scarcely manage with the same number of assistants half as many acres. But a really good keeper, competent to manage the shooting under his charge, is invaluable, as far as sport is concerned, and it is better to give such a man 25s. a week, or even more, than be ill served by one at 20s. It is only the best men with the best character who can obtain high wages, and the difference of 5s. per week that exists between a first-class man and an ordinary one is repaid over and over again by his better preservation of the game.

A head-keeper, as well as any intelligent assistant, should be provided with a small pair of field-glasses, such as can be bought for a couple of pounds, and taught how to use them. When the glasses are once focussed to suit the man's vision, as used on an object a few hundred yards away, they should be fixed from further movement, so as to be instantly available. . . .

As soon as a keeper gets a new situation, it is his duty to make the acquaintance of, and so be able to swear to, all the poaching characters of the locality, but on no account ever to drink with them. Doing so is the first downward step a keeper takes, and a very fatal one.

As to keepers defending themselves against night poachers by carrying guns, it is a mistake to think they do so. A poacher will much sooner shoot a keeper than a keeper a poacher, should both be armed, and so the former gets the first chance of using such a deadly means of defence. It is far better that keepers should carry revolvers.

Revolvers, however, require considerable care in their handling, or they are liable to cause accidents to their possessors. The only way to carry a revolver safely in the pocket, so that it cannot explode by a fall or jar, is to take out one cartridge and let the hammer lie on the uncharged chamber. Above all things avoid a cheap revolver, such as is sold by ironmongers for about £1.

Shooting: Field & Covert
(The Badminton Library, 1886).

TWENTIETH CENTURY

He is one of the modern school, vigorous, alert, and enterprising: perhaps not such an entertaining companion by flood and field as the veterans of other days; he may fail to amuse by quaint turn of phrase or picturesque appearance, nor will he have the time to turn and saunter along with you for half an hour's leisurely conversation when you chance to meet.

But he is the right stamp of man for all that; courteous to all and yet familiar with none, considerate of all the interests of others yet never unmindful of his master's, he has justly earned the respect of the whole countryside. Fair and just in all his dealings, his underlings know that while good work will not pass unrecognised, no slovenly or slipshod ways will be for an instant condoned. He has no slight knowledge of natural history, and moves through life with an observant eye and an open and adaptive mind, not wedded to tradition, but ever ready to consider new theories or suggestions and turn them to his purpose. In the field he never gets hustled or flurried, and is quick to make the best of unlooked-for contingencies when they arise. His books are accurately and neatly kept, and require little or no endorsement at the hands of the agent; for he is a business man with all his energies and faculties concentrated on his work, only asking of his subordinates what he freely gives himself —cheerful and ungrudging service and a whole-hearted devotion to duty.

CAPTAIN AYMER MAXWELL:
Partridges & Partridge Manors.

GAMEKEEPERS

"The First Time Through"

PREVIOUS TO the day, the whole staff should be cognizant of the various duties allotted to them, such as driving ground in and placing of stops, and each one must thoroughly understand the method to be employed in the succession of drives. It is well worth while giving a good deal of attention to these details, always with the memory of previous shoots in one's mind. Also there is a very comfortable feeling that each detail has been discussed and arrangements methodically made, and with a loyal keen staff it will be surprising if the shoot is not run smoothly and efficiently. The most satisfactory method of placing guns is by numbered stands and drawing for places, moving up either one or two places after each drive. Where stands are numbered but no draw is made, positions should always be allotted by the host, but the positions of the actual stands is certainly the keeper's job, and if he is efficient full use should be made of his knowledge and experience. The ideal is reached when owner and keeper discuss and possibly walk over the ground previous to the shoot. The former's knowledge of how birds came forward and the latter's of what happened in the drive on former occasions can be of great help in deciding proper positions.

Make sure that guns and also loaders have firm, level, and sufficient space on which to stand comfortably; a few minutes' use of a spade will often mean the difference of a gun shooting well or badly. If the foothold is uneven or on a slope, it can be most irritating to the unfortunate gun. On clay a couple of inches of ashes can be very effective and they soon grass over. It will be necessary to have a conveyance to carry game, cartridges, and other equipment. If possible, have the conveyance railed for hanging game, so that the birds keep their shape and look and sell so much better. See that instructions are given to chauffeurs, if any are out. There are many more small items that must receive due consideration, a shoot definitely can be made or marred unless these details receive proper attention. As to the stopping of a beat, this must be carefully thought out, and every possible point where birds may break should either be patrolled or netting should be put down; this can be pegged out previously so that it is only necessary to drop it. A few papers fastened at intervals along the top of the netting will be an added help. There are often points where birds are exceptionally likely to break out, and at these reliable men must be placed who are observant and keen upon the sport, men perhaps who are old in years but as keen as ever to take part in the shoot. Boys for stops are a mistake unless under constant supervision.

NORMAN SHARPE:
Organising a Pheasant Shoot.
Lonsdale Library:
The Lonsdale Keeper's Book.

GAMEKEEPERS' WOODCRAFT

Gamekeepers see more than most men of the habits of birds and beasts, game and the enemies of game. There are signs and marks by which they can detect the presence or absence of foxes, hawks, stoats, weasels, hunting dogs, poaching cats, feathered and furred game, which others without their skill would pass by. The following are a few examples of such knowledge and the use to which it may be put, gathered from the pages of that very practical monthly *The Gamekeeper* (Gilbertson & Page, Ltd., Hertford, 6*d*.).

A gamekeeper will know if a fox lies on his beat by work at earths, the short alarm crow of a cock pheasant if he sees Reynard on the move or curled up above ground (a pheasant gives the same warning if a stoat, weasel, or cat is about); by the diving flight of rooks and crows if they see him lying on an open field or on the limb of a tree, moving about or curled up in covert; by the chattering of jays or magpies, or the low clucking note a blackbird makes use of when mobbing a fox, stoat, weasel, or cat.

A gamekeeper will know if a fox works his beat by night by nests destroyed, buried game, his ballot on mole-hill, ant-hill, &c., scent of wettings, cries of green plover, springing of partridges (a cub repeatedly springs them in a vain endeavour to catch them) by their barking and tracks, by ewes with lambs bleating. He will sometimes find their homeward route by an odd feather dropped from game or poultry when passing through a fence. If none of these signs are observed foxes are scarce.

Badgers: their presence is detected by tracks to earth, evacuations along fences, young rabbits crowned out. Badgers have a cat-like habit of scratching a hole to evacuate in, and often use it several times, but unlike the cat do not cover it up. Badgers will sometimes chatter in a rather defiant manner at human intruders if at some distance; a badger will find the nests of game birds before they begin to sit; this they must do by scent, either of the bird having been to the nest in the day-time or of the eggs; it is very unlikely that they can see the run to the nest on a dark night; in this respect they are worse than foxes.

Stoats: their presence is often detected by rabbits lying out, the mobbing of blackbirds and wrens, droppings on large stones, &c., tracks in mud or snow, and game found killed.

Young rabbits seen regularly outside burrows show the absence of ground vermin, broods of small birds and pigeons hatching off and getting away denote the absence of jays or magpies.

The regular mobbing of a variety of birds shows where a pair of hawks are nesting; the tiny cry of the blue tit or wren, the chatter of jays and mistle-thrush, the almost inaudible lisping of blackbirds, the cackling croak of carrion or hooded crow, let a gamekeeper know when a hawk is near and likely to come over. Small birds will mob owls too, but in a more impertinent way, unmistakable to the gamekeeper. Partridges (usually wild) lying like stones, show that a falcon is in the neighbourhood.

If dogs are hunting mute in coverts, pheasants perched on bushes or hares going away show what is going on.

Remains of fish and tracks on banks give the otter away; heron's tracks show in the shallows; the frequent leaps of fish out of water show that pike are there, while big broods of duck, coots, and waterhens show their absence.

The whereabouts and numbers of young partridges and wild pheasants will be known by tracks to water, dusting and jugging places.

Borings in covert and disturbed cow dung in meadows near coverts reveal the presence of woodcock, the borings in ditches and around springs show where snipe frequent.

A dog hunting open ground will be noticed by sheep running and huddling together, cattle crowding along and following it.

Pigeons or rooks perched on tall trees in a covert show that no human poachers are there, while a rook or crow watched flying over and seen to suddenly swerve is reliable proof that human beings are there; jays and magpies often give poachers away by chattering.

When night-watching, the cries of birds and the behaviour of animals are very useful, the bleating of sheep, cry of peewits, springing of partridges, cry of a hare, show that dogs are running; the bark of deer, or scream of fox, or dash of pigeons from roost denote the whereabouts of human poachers. The answering neigh of a horse may show where a gang of netters have a cart waiting.

The actions of the rooks as they leave their roosting-place in the morning and fly gaily chattering overhead to the far-away stubble will generally mean a good day. Then there are the days when they, along with the starlings, fieldfares, woodpigeons, &c., will be seen feeding ravenously before the storm.

Should a newly planted covert be visited and some of the trees be found tapped, as if cut with a knife, a closer inspection should be made, and it will be found it is the work of a hare. Rabbits do the same, but they can't reach so high nor cut such strong shoots as a hare.

Should a rabbit's skin be found, very like as if it had been taken off by human hands; or a hole scratched straight down, perhaps eighteen inches, to a rabbit's nest; or the end of a burrow, or wasps' nests, scratched out; or large holes (generally about rocks) found with bracken scattered in and about them, you may be assured you have got a badger about.

If the back and hind legs only of a rabbit or hare is found, the fore-part, including skin, entirely gone; or if any kind of game is found either wholly or partly eaten, and lightly buried, it's almost certain to have been a fox.

There's no mistaking the signs of a cat being about, for if any kind of game is found partly eaten, and leaves, grass or a little soil scratched over it, it is a sure sign a cat has been there. But it must be remembered that when a cat has killed she will kill and carry home a great quantity of game, and will leave no other sign than the disappearance of the game.

A muddy gate, after a night which has been wet in the early part and dry the latter, is a very tell-tale to the practised eye. Here is the round footmark of a poaching cat, there the almost bird-like tracks of master rat, and the smaller and cleaner cut tracks of stoat or weasel. Let us examine this old turf dyke; no signs of vermin can be seen in it until we near its end. There in a small hummock is a tuft of dark green grass; examine closely, and you will find the marks of stoat or weasel. It is in fact a stoat's midden.

A couple of "hoodies" far out on the moor persistently return to the same spot hovering and wheeling, and occasionally uttering their harsh cry. There is a dead sheep there, or it may be only a hare or grouse, in any case it is worth finding.

Here is a grouse killed by a hawk and partly eaten, the

head is gone, and the breast-bone deeply cut into. No sparrow-hawk or merlin killed that bird, it is the work of a peregrine falcon. No other bird can tear the bone in that way, nor is its throat wide enough to swallow the head entire.

Grouse are some of the best tale-tellers. To hear an old cock grouse cogging is a sure sign to a moorland keeper that there is an enemy present, for instance, a fox, stoat, cat, or prowling dog. A cock grouse commences cogging and keeps increasing as his assailant gets nearer until at close quarters, when he will fly away, still telling his comrades that there is danger, and it is not until he is out of sight of the aggressor that he will cease. A fox disturbed on a moor, on a calm day, may be followed a great distance on the line he is travelling by the grouse cogging at him all along the line.

Blackbirds are exceptionally good tale-tellers, and they vary in their notes according to the different kinds of vermin; for a cat, owl, or hawk they will utter an excitable twitter, which soon attracts all their comrades in the vicinity, and then they will mob them from one part of the wood to the other; for a stoat, a blackbird utters a very low whistle, which cannot be heard many yards distant, but is a most sure sign whenever heard, being quite distinct from any other call.

FINDING A PARTRIDGE'S NEST

To some people the knack of finding partridge nests is not given, but it can very easily be acquired. If a man knows his ground well, has listened to the birds calling in the frosty dusk of evenings in February and March, and has watched his birds come out to peck on the newly sown oats at the beginning of April, he should know almost to a nicety how many pairs of birds he has, and approximately the places where they roost. The number of places where there is likely to be a nest is strictly limited, and he will, of course, look over such places carefully first. To a genuine novice the following advice may be useful—it is a simple game and can be played by one player in three minutes.

Take six feet square of sunny bank and look at it carefully for one minute. Then turn your back and write down what you have seen. No, my friend; you missed that foxglove just sprouting, the two marks of a rat's track in the mud at the bottom of the bank, a field mouse hole in the open sandy patch, and those bits of damp, dead grass under the blackberry tendril. Why should that grass be wet when you know that the sun has been on it for seven or eight hours? Well, there was rain last night, and about an hour ago a partridge scratched that grass aside and laid her third egg in a well-hidden nest, and afterwards in scratching the covering over her eggs again she turned the grass over, so that the wet side is uppermost.

Try again down the next fence, and say aloud what you see. A clump of primroses past blooming, a patch of dead oak leaves too flat and regular to conceal anything, the half-built nest of a robin (yes, it's her second nest), a shoot of wild rose, the remains of a three months' old dead blue-tit in the ditch at the bottom. Anything else? Yes, there is a tiny run through the grass. If it went straight up the bank it would probably be a rabbit, but it is diagonal. Be careful, because the hours between ten and twelve are favourite hours for a partridge to lay—after three o'clock you would be quite safe. Quite right, it is a partridge's nest, seven eggs, and quite invisible except for the run.

RICHARD PAGE:
New Ways with Partridges.

GAMEKEEPERS & FOXES

I" AM not going to beat about the bush as regards foxes, for I know that partridges and foxes do not go well together." So writes a very practical and very successful gamekeeper, the author of *The Management of a Partridge Beat*. And, indeed, the last thing that any candid well-wisher of either of the two great national sports, hunting and shooting, could desire, is that there should be any beating about the bush whatever. All of us who know anything about both sports know the best and the worst there is to be said about either. We shall all begin by granting the first great premise in any discussion or argument on the two sports, that hunting is the greater. It is the greater by tradition, by the catholicity of its appeal, by the breadth of its purposes and the simplicity of its processes, by the qualities of mind and body which it needs and exercises—by a hundred differences, great and small, counted and accounted.

And yet, even because of its very pre-eminence, does not hunting, of the two sports, expect—perhaps demand—rather too much of the other? Can it be put this way, that the one sport takes and the other gives? Can it be held otherwise—can it be contended that hunting gives anything to shooting, or that shooting gives nothing to hunting? Let an acknowledged authority, either on the sport of shooting or the customs of a countryside—the late Captain Aymer Maxwell—be *arbiter pugnæ*, and put the case for each side in turn. Here, then, is the follower of the gun making answer, or protest, to the fox-hunter imagined as claiming first consideration:—

"I am all for fair play all round, but don't quite see where I come in at all in your scheme of things as they should be. I am decent member of society, possibly deserving quite as well of my country as you, and entitled to equal consideration. I happen to prefer shooting to hunting, and one way and another I pay heavily enough already for my sport, without the extra tax levied by your foxes. The labouring class benefit far more by my presence than they do by yours, and further, your very sport is almost entirely dependent on me, for without the game and rabbits that I preserve, your foxes— now more numerous than ever before—could never be tolerated in any agricultural community. If I preserve your foxes religiously, it can only be at the hazard of my own interests, and devilish little thanks I seem to get for it: if I raise a hand to protect my own, I am at once written down as a hardened offender, a selfish brute, and an outrage on civilisation."

And here is the imagined reply of the hunting authority —or rather, let it be claimed and admitted, the right kind of hunting authority:—

"We do not seek to deny that our sport is largely dependent on your good will; we frankly admit that our foxes don't make things any easier for you, and may at times be a serious evil. We cannot deny that the law allows you to refuse us your coverts, nor could we be surprised— were legal rights and your own interests the sole consider- ations to be taken into account—if harbourage and access were denied to the fox and his hunters. Whether this would be worth your while in other ways we will not pause to consider; we would rather appeal directly to your generosity as brethren of the great fellowship of sport, who should surely all unite in furthering the interests of sport generally, even though it may involve some personal inconvenience. Do this for us, and you will not find us ungrateful or oblivious of your sacrifice, which we will endeavour to repay by every consideration of your game and your ground."

There it is then—a Penelope's web of an argument, never finished and always beginning again where it left off. So let us leave it there, and come to the practical business of the man who after all is the principal agent concerned—the man who can get things done, or prevent them being done—the gamekeeper.

To begin with, granted that the staple food of the fox is the rabbit, somehow rabbits must be provided for food. On large estates, it will somehow be contrived that rabbits shall abound as far as possible from fields which may be designed, this year, next year, or the year after, for rearing-fields. But rearing-fields, in any case, must be protected from foxes who may not be satisfied with rabbits, and the gamekeeper who knows his business will not be content with a wire fence of less than eight feet for his rearing-field, with the top two feet turned outwards, and a foot at the bottom buried underground. Later, when the time comes to turn his young birds into covert, he will somehow contrive, by placing the coops of foster-mothers on platforms among the lower branches of roosting-trees, or other devices, to induce would-be roosters on the ground to sleep out of harm's way on the higher branches. If he has succeeded in getting his young birds up to roost, he has brought them safely through the main time of anxiety. He can trust the rabbits for the rest.

But not all shooting estates, again, are chiefly concerned with pheasants. With some, partridges may come first, and then the problem is not the care of young birds, but eggs. Let us turn again to *The Management of a Partridge Beat*.

"Of course, if your employer is a hunting gentleman, naturally he likes to see a fox or two about, so one has to take the best precautions one can for the nests. The chief trouble where there are foxes is to get the nests hatched. The Euston system is the best method to work on, but I have saved many a nest by a simple and cheap method, which is just to mix a little Condy's fluid with paraffin oil, and just sprinkle a little around the nests once or twice a week. It takes the smell of the birds away, and I do not remember Reynard ever touching a nest treated in this manner. I used to do the same thing with nests beside a road or footpath; the smell is unpleasant, and dogs do not like it, and give it a wide berth. A quart bottle will go a long way and is cheap enough."

GAMEKEEPERS

Grouse & Sheep

HERE IS a problem to which there is no universal answer. What of sheep stock on grouse ground? This much may be granted; that on newly burned ground, where there is any tendency to revert from heather, sheep must somehow, by fencing or otherwise, be prevented from rooting up young heather growing from old roots or from seed, in their eager search for the sweet young grasses which follow burning. Otherwise, the old maxim holds; that if a moor is well burned for grouse, it is well burned for sheep, and that if there is plenty of young heather, sheep will do a grouse moor no harm.

"On those moors which are covered with heather, and which show no tendency to revert from grass, a sheep stock is distinctly beneficial to grouse, and several moor-owners have informed the Committee that in order to maintain the full stock of birds they have found it advisable to re-stock cleared ground with sheep. The reason for this is not far to seek. The paths and small spaces made by sheep form excellent drying ground for young birds. The hollows that sheep scoop out for themselves, in dry banks facing the sun, form admirable dusting places for coveys, and often add to the grit supplies of a moor. The heather growth is improved (1) by the sheep eating down the young heather, and so causing it to grow short and thick and form a close dense canopy which helps to resist the ravages of frost in spring; (2) by their eating down the grass; and (3) by their treading the surface of the ground, thus hardening it and preventing the growth of moss. It is also possible that sheep droppings may increase the number of flies and beetles on which the grouse chicks feed so largely. The very fact that sheep and shepherds are on the moor is apt to be an incentive to extensive heather burning, while their presence acts as a deterrent to poachers."

The Grouse in Health & in Disease.

GAME ON THE FARM

Neither the hare nor the rabbit can be argued to be a friend to the farmer; but that the partridge is, and that the pheasant may be, is demonstrable.

Times change, and we with them; never more markedly, perhaps, than in the status of the pheasant in the shooting world, and the attitude of the shooting world towards the pheasant. In the opening years of the last century—witness the diaries of Colonel Peter Hawker—the preservation of the pheasant in any considerable numbers on a country estate was unusual. Hawker himself never bred pheasants, and in the last thirty-five of his fifty-one shooting seasons did not average three in the bag—in some years he never shot one. Then came the invention of the breech-loader and with it an immense impetus to shooting in general, heralding in the 'sixties and 'seventies what has been called the "pheasant era." The best illustration of the "pheasant era," perhaps, is the published record of the personal bags of the late Lord Ripon, who in the years 1867–1913 killed to his own gun 222,976 pheasants, an average of 4,774 per year for forty-seven seasons. These were mostly hand-reared birds, and the consequent addition to the numbers of our bird population, depending if only partly on the supply of natural food in the countryside, was obviously enormous. No wonder that Captain Aymer Maxwell, writing in 1913 (*Pheasants & Covert Shooting*), refers, in judicial but plain terms, to the damage done under certain conditions by hand-reared pheasants to farm crops:

"Except perhaps in the case of winter wheat, which remains as a standing temptation, the bulk of the mischief is usually done in a short time. Fields of new sown or new sprouting wheat and barley, and grain between the ripening and the reaping, are only at the mercy of the wandering pheasant for at most few weeks of the year. Besides these cereals, among which at these critical periods of their growth a horde of pheasants can play havoc in a few days, patches of potatoes, standing crops of beans, and growing turnips are at times the subject of appreciable damage. This completes the tale of misdeeds which agriculture may impute to the pheasant, for few farmers could be hard-hearted enough to grudge him place among the gleaners on the stubbles."

That may be taken as the verdict on the pheasant as the result of rearing in the last half of the nineteenth century and the few years that followed. Then, in 1914, came four years and a half of war, and with war and among its consequences the end of the "pheasant era." Never since 1915 have pheasants been reared throughout the country on the scale familiar to pheasant shooters in the early days of the century. The days have gone by when on big shooting estates four-figure bags were the order of the day for "the first time through" and when it was possible, as a well-known game shot put it to the writer, to come home at the end of a long day's pheasant shooting and be puzzled to remember a dozen of the hundreds of shots he had fired.

There was a return to the days of pheasant-rearing after the war of 1914-8, but never to the lavish and wasteful scale of pre-war days. And in consequence, the status of the pheasant, and the light in which the pheasant was regarded by the farmer, radically changed. He had always been a guest, but there were times and places where he was counted a little expensive; now, in lessened numbers, he became even welcome. And a new interest was taken in the bill of fare which he provided for himself. People began to analyse more closely the exact nature of the food of the pheasant when left to his natural resources. Of the bird of the "pheasant era" Lord Lilford (who died in 1896) had already written, in *The Birds of Northamptonshire*, that "the pheasant, where not preserved in unreasonable numbers, is a good friend to the farmer, from the enormous number of wireworms and other noxious insects which it devours, to say nothing of its liking for the roots of various weeds; but it would be absurd to deny that grain forms its favourite food, and a field of standing beans, as is well known, draws pheasants for miles."

On this the evidence of post-war observers provided an interesting comment. For instance, the *Field* of 17th January 1920 contained a letter from Mr. H. Martin, head keeper to the Duke of Wellington, stating that on 1st January, shooting at Strathfieldsaye, he examined the crop of a pheasant which contained nothing but grubs, "leather jackets" (the larvæ of the daddy-long-legs), 702 in number. Mr. Martin forwarded a photograph, hoping it would interest readers, "especially the farmers, as we have the consolation of knowing that at least one pheasant has started the new year by doing some good for the crops." This letter was followed in December of the same year by a letter from the editor of the *Gamekeeper*, enclosing a photograph "which should prove of interest to readers who are concerned in any form of agriculture." The photograph was life-size, of a group of leather-jackets, measuring some seven inches by three, numbering in all 1,083. "The bird was found 'trespassing' upon some market gardens near Uckfield, Sussex." It may be supposed that other such "trespassers" would be welcomed by other farmers and market gardeners in Sussex and elsewhere.

May we not, then, greet the pheasant as the farmer's friend when left to fend for himself? What of the partridge? In *Partridge Diseases and its Causes*, the report of the Committee set up by *Country Life*, in 1931, edited by the Committee's Chairman, Major Maurice Portal, an analysis is given of the food-contents of the crops of large numbers of partridges examined by the Committee's pathologist, Dr. W. E. Collinge, Keeper of the Yorkshire Museum. The examination gave the following results:—

Animal Food.—Of the total bulk of food consumed, 40·5 per cent. was animal matter, 23 per cent. of it consisting of injurious insects, 3 per cent. of beneficial species, 4 per cent. of neutral species, 6·5 per cent. of earthworms, and 4 per cent. of slugs.

Vegetable Food.—Vegetable matter was present to the extent of 59·5 per cent., of which 53·5 per cent. consisted of leaves, fruits, and seeds of weeds, grass and clover, 3·5 per cent. of grain, mostly obtained in the stubbles, and 2·5 per cent. of miscellaneous vegetable matter.

Of the insect food, far the larger proportion consisted of beetles, but earwigs also were present, and the grubs of destructive moths such as the Yellow Underwing and the Turnip Moth. Of the vegetable food, there were seeds and leaves of Common Sorrel, Sheep Sorrel, Spurrey, Buttercup, Clover, Lady's Mantle, Heath Bedstraw, Ribwort, Broad-leaved Plantain, Curled Dock, Knotgrass, Tufted Hair-grass, and Rough Meadow-grass.

A farmer would have little hesitation in deciding, with these lists before him, whether the partridge were friend or foe. But, indeed, the question is never in dispute. It is an axiom of bird life in relation to farming that the partridge follows the plough. Perhaps no better testimony to that long-established truth could be found than an extract from the *Gamekeeper* of January 1940, dealing with conditions of farming consequent on the granting of the Government subsidy of £2 an acre for land ploughed up for sowing corn:—

"No keeper regrets to see land come under the plough, for increased cultivation means more food for his game, but I fancy a season or two may elapse before this newly tilled soil produces satisfactory crops. It must be in good heart after so long a rest from intensive cultivation, but un-fortunately with the cessation from tillage comes a vast increase of insect pests harmful to crops, among which the destructive wireworm always predominates. Till these are got rid of the outlook is not exactly encouraging, and the keepers may have something to do with making it better.

"It is easy to see that the freshly broken soil is teeming with insect life, if only by the rooks which flock to it. For the first time for many years these birds have available un-limited supplies of their legitimate food, and seem inclined to take full advantage of it. With these changed conditions there is hope for the rook, hope that it may relinquish its evil egg-stealing ways, and become a real help to the farmer. The rook now has its chance of reformation, to re-establish itself in the good opinion of all.

"In addition to rooks every partridge from a wide surrounding area is to be seen on these freshly turned fields, all busily engaged in searching for insects, wireworm for preference. At this good work partridges far excel rooks, their efforts being more concentrated and continuous. When shooting of late it was useless to look for partridges in the roots and on the stubbles; they were only to be found on the new ploughings, and it seemed a pity that they should be interfered with when at their good work."

So much, then, for the partridge as the farmer's friend. What of the partridge's keeper? Of the relations which may and should exist between the gamekeeper and the farmer to whose fields he has access nothing better has been written than the chapter on the subject by Mr. Walter Hipgrave, author of *The Management of a Partridge Beat*—a book, it may be recalled, written more than twenty years ago from the trenches in France.

Of the farmer himself, first:—

"You will need to be friends with the farmers in any case, whether your master owns the land or not. In my own case, my beat was split up into three farms, and my master rented the shooting. Always have a civil tongue in your head, and every time you meet the farmers on your round have a chat with them about the crops. You will find you will get nearly as interested in the crops as the farmer is himself. You will like to know what this or that field is going to be sown with, especially if it happens to be a good field for the birds. I do not mean to say by having a chat that you should be hanging about an hour or two at a time, but with just a five or ten minutes' talk you will find that farmers will soon become friendly with you, especially if your talk concerns farming. Do not upset yourself in front of the farmers if they happen to be doing something on the farm that you do not like, but keep it to yourself. I know I often used to find something being done that I thought would not do me much good on the beat, but I used to swallow it and not go and make an enemy of the farmer. I admit I used to say something to myself, but I always used to get over such troubles, and I always found the farmers willing to help me in most things.

"You may have a few rabbits on some part of the beat, for instance, and the farmer tells you they are eating his crops, and will perhaps ask you if you will kill some of them. Oblige him at once, and do what he asks you to do even if it goes against the grain. Then, again, there may be a few rats getting into the corn ricks, and he may ask you to catch them. It was very rarely, I might say, that a farmer had to remind me of these customers for I was always a bitter enemy of the rat."

Next, of the farm hands:—

"Many keepers, to tell the truth I think the majority of them, are very mistrustful of farm labourers, and often there is not the need for it. I will mention a case that happened to myself. I was told by a keeper whom I succeeded on a certain beat that a certain man on the beat was a 'wrong 'un,' and that I should need to keep my eye on him. Well, I did keep my eye on him, but I was careful enough not to let the man know it, and every time I passed him I used to give him a civil 'good morning' or pass the time of day. And in the end, instead of there being any reason to suspect him, I found out that he was one of the straightest men on the beat."

Of shepherds:—

"Shepherds can do you a lot of harm if they choose. Always keep in with the shepherd, and when your birds are nesting just quietly ask him if he will kindly keep his dog in. Do not go and say to him, 'Shepherd, you will have to keep your dog in,' or anything of that kind, or you will most likely find him letting his dog run about all the more. Try to win him over; he may have been in the farmer's employ half his life, and be a valuable servant, so it would be of no use to expect any sympathy from the farmer if things went wrong."

All hands together:—

"You can win all of the farm hands over if you only go

to work the right way. I myself have been fortunate, for all the fellows on my beat would do anything for me, and I would do the same for them if it lay in my power to do so. But if, on the other hand, you are at loggerheads with the farmers and men, you might as well pack up and clear out. You cannot expect to be successful when things are in that state. Win the farmer's favour first, and you will find that he will help you in a good many ways to win the men over too. To take an instance as regards the men, when the corn is being cut, go and knock a few rabbits over for them; they will appreciate your doing that.

"Help them in any way you can, and you will find they will do the same for you."

The Steel Gin: For & Against

Under Section (6) of the Ground Game Act, 1880, it is laid down that:

"No person having a right of killing ground game under this Act or otherwise shall . . . for the purpose of killing ground game, employ spring traps except in rabbit holes . . . and any person acting in contravention of this section shall, on summary conviction, be liable to a penalty not exceeding two pounds."

This at first sight looks plain enough. But the Courts have laid down that this section applies only to tenants, and not to landowners. Even this would not matter much, for experience shows that landowners have no particular inducement to break the law, and do not, as a fact, except in a small number of cases and to a negligible extent—e.g. in trapping rabbits which are a nuisance in gardens, and cannot easily be caught or killed otherwise—employ spring traps for catching rabbits. The real transgressor against the law, as is well known, is the professional rabbit trapper, who uses the steel gin to catch rabbits for the market, and who, in certain counties in Wales and the west of England, where this trapping for commercial purposes is practised on a large scale, sets spring traps in the open without any hindrance from officers of the law, magistrates, or the police. The law at present is openly defied, and in rabbit trapping districts is a dead letter.

And what are the consequences? Rabbit-trapping by means of the steel gin has become a trade, none the less firmly established because it is carried out under illegal conditions. So firmly is it established that the steel gin is openly and generally regarded, in the rabbit-trapping counties of the west, as a means of making money, rather than what is its ostensible purpose, to get rid of an animal which is a nuisance and a hindrance to agriculture. The result is that far from there being an organised attempt to get rid of a recognised pest, there is an organised scheme by which a large number of rabbits are trapped and sold year after year, these numbers being so regulated and controlled as to ensure a constant fresh supply for trapping and marketing in the years succeeding.

Other consequences follow. With trapping on so large a scale, not only rabbits, but the rabbits' natural enemies, stoats and weasels are caught, with the result that nature's balance is upset, and rabbits multiply. So much so, that in rabbit-trapping districts serious agriculture becomes impossible, and plain practical farming—except rabbit farming—ceases to exist.

And not only the rabbits' enemies—foxes, stoats, and weasels—are caught by the steel gin. Dogs and cats are caught by the score; it is not an uncommon sight to see sheep and lambs going on three legs; even cows are caught by the tongue. Besides animals, birds suffer; pheasants, partridges, and woodcock are found in the traps, and can be seen hanging in poulterers' shops minus legs and feet.

We come last—but we also come first and all the time—to the main, enduring, dominating fact in regard to the steel gin—its undenied, undeniable cruelty. Every year and during part of the year every day—hundreds and thousands of creatures, often after a period of many hours, die in pain by means of the steel gin.

Why should such a thing be? Because by no other means can the numbers of rabbits be reduced? But as we have seen, the steel gin is used to increase, not to reduce, the numbers of rabbits. And it is unquestionable that if it is desired to exterminate rabbits in any given district, it can be done and is done by shooting, ferreting, netting, snaring, and by gassing the rabbits in their burrows. No one would think of exterminating rabbits by means of the gin.

There remains the last argument—and it is a strong one from a single point of view, the gamekeeper's view—for the retention of the steel gin as an effective trap. The gamekeeper needs it for the trapping of stoats, weasels, and rats. *But*— the gamekeeper does not need it for use in the open. He sets it in run-through traps, which can only catch stoats, weasels, and rats. And these it kills instantaneously.

What is the balance of evidence, as regards the use or necessity for the steel gin? For or against? Surely there can be but one answer.

GAME FARMS

THERE ARE many successful game farmers, and there are different principles on which they conduct their farms. Perhaps Kipling's couplet, written of other methods, best sums up the situation:—

> *"There are nine and thirty ways of constructing tribal lays*
> *And every single one of them is right!"*

Preferences as to the proper methods of rearing pheasants differ widely. Sometimes it seems to be "the custom of the country" to do this or that; here and there the methods of an original mind have been imported from one country to another. Opinions vary as to methods of penning, choice of strain of pheasants, ways of pinioning or tying wings, the best food or way of feeding, the right size of this or that enclosure, the proper number of hens to put with a cock.

To take pens first. Generally speaking, there are two schools—those of the open pen and those of the movable pen. But there are subdivisions of these divisions. Movable pens may be of different sizes and materials. The principle, of course, is the same; you put a cock with his hens in a pen varying from 30 ft. by 6 ft. to 18 ft. by 9 ft., or even 15 ft. by 6 ft., and you shift the pen at short intervals on to fresh ground. The pen may be of wood, with a wire top, or with sides of corrugated iron, and may have sloping or perpendicular sides. The advantage of the sloping sides—the pen being narrower at the top than at the bottom—is claimed to be that in wind or rain from any quarter the birds can always get shelter. Methods, too, differ with the wire covering at the top. Some stretch the wire with ordinary tautness, others like it baggy and loose, so that if the birds fly up they do not damage their heads in the same way, though if birds begin dashing about in a small pen it is impossible that they should not knock their feathers about to some extent. But this risk can be lessened, too, by brushing the roofing wire with branches of fir, or some other tree such as beech cut with the leaf on—which means, of course, cutting beforehand in the summer. Pheasants do not fly up against a dark or solid roof; with only wire, of course, there can be little difference, so far as they can see, from open sky above them.

But the main difference of opinion among game farmers lies in the question of movable as against open pens. There is no room for half-and-half theories here; you are either an out-and-out movable pen man, so to speak, or an open pen man without any doubt on the matter at all. With the open pen you have two alternatives: either you pen a cock with his hens in an enclosure measuring from, say, 16 ft. square to 24 ft. square; or you run a hundred hens, say, with twenty cocks in an enclosure of an acre. The last plan gives the birds more room to move, but it entails, of course—as does any pen which is not covered at the top—either brailing the birds' wings or pinioning them. Brailing means tying a wing with tape or strapping it, and this entails a good deal of labour when you are dealing with hundreds of birds, for you have to shift the tape or strap from one wing to the other at intervals, to prevent the wing from becoming stiff. Pinioning, on the other hand, saves labour; the modern method is to remove the first joint of the wing when the chick is a day old; but this, too, has its disadvantages, for after the laying season you cannot sell your bird for shooting, but can only use it for the kitchen.

With a movable pen there is no need to pinion or to brail a wing. But there is always a danger, or let us say a risk, of damage to birds which you do not get with the open pen. That is in moving the pens to fresh ground. If you have careful, conscientious men working under you, or can spare the time to superintend the shifting of every pen, no doubt it may all be done carefully and gently, and without catching the birds' legs or wings. But if you have so many hundreds of pens to be moved in a certain time, and the men know that the sooner they move them the sooner they will have done with a tiresome job, it stands to reason that now and then a pen will be moved roughly and carelessly and a bird or two will be damaged. Such casualties, in a season, mount up.

Another point. With movable pens you get more eggs; that seems to be generally admitted. But with open pens, it is claimed, you get better eggs. When you pen twenty cocks with, say, one hundred hens, it is the strongest cocks only that get the hens. Out of twenty you will get so many masters—eight or nine perhaps. These will drive off the weaker cocks and not let them come near the hens: the weaker ones may get a chance towards the end of the season, perhaps, but all through the important early time the strongest cocks will have it all their own way with the hens, and, presumably, you thus get a stronger stock in the progeny.

On the number of hens to be penned with a cock opinions differ. Five, a few say; six, most; one or two give their cocks seven hens, and will tell you that if you give fewer than that the cocks treat the hens unmercifully and you get damaged birds that have to be put into hospital. And, of course, if a cock in an open pen can manage twelve or even twenty hens, he can do so in a closed pen; but obviously it is only the stronger birds with which you can be certain of such vigour; the average cannot be so high.

As to breeds, there are preferences among game farmers for this or that species, and likes and dislikes are apt to be strong. Some prefer the old-fashioned black-neck, and breed, or try to breed, no other; others like the Chinese pheasant (*Torquatus*: Ring-neck), which is a beautiful bird and a fine layer; some would choose the Mongolian, though not such a prolific layer as the Chinese; others like any and all crosses, only making sure of a change of blood by buying or exchanging from a distance. Of one bird you will hear no good, and that is Versicolor, the Japanese, and of another, the Prince of Wales's pheasant, much praise. But the Prince of Wales's, of course, is a rare bird.

Some arguments of the advocate of the open pen and the champion of the movable pen system may perhaps be developed a little more in detail. In regard to the question of quality and quantity of eggs, for instance, opinions differ widely. It is the contention of the open pen advocate that with cocks and hens running loose in a big enclosure with, say, twenty cocks and one hundred and twenty hens, or whatever proportion you prefer, you are nearer to wild conditions than when you pen one cock with five or six or seven hens; the argument being that when you have rivalry among the cocks, only the strongest and lustiest cocks get the hens, and so you are most likely to get strong and lusty chicks from the resulting eggs. Whereas, if you pen six or seven hens with a cock, he may manage his hens all right, or he may not, but in any case you cannot say that all the hens have been put to the strongest cocks. Further—the contention runs—with open pens you get fewer misshapen and badly shelled eggs, and finally, when birds run loose, you do not risk damaging them, which it is difficult to avoid when you have to move so many pens so many times in so many days.

And against all this the advocate of movable pens replies that, generally speaking, it is not so; that not only do the birds in movable pens do better throughout the season by being continually moved on to fresh soil, but you get distinct and undeniable advantages in feeding and in collecting eggs. You know that when you feed your birds they get all the food, and that all of them are fed, whereas when you throw down food in open pens you cannot be sure that every bird gets all that it wants, and you do not know how much food the birds have had and how much has been picked up by sparrows and finches. And as to collecting eggs, you know that you get them all, and you know for certain the day on which they were laid; whereas in open pens, with grass and rough herbage springing up you are bound some day to overlook some of them, and you cannot always be certain, when you find them, of the date of laying; or you may overlook them altogether—in which case, where is your advantage?

Or take, for other possibilities of argument, the question of egg-eating. With movable pens, which are easily and quickly inspected, their advocate contends that you can stop it at once; it is nearly always the cock, and you can either take him out or use some other means of preventing him from pecking an egg again. To which the other man replies that with open pens, generally speaking, you don't get egg-eating, or at all events, not so frequently as with movable pens; that egg-eating is the result partly of curiosity and partly of boredom, that birds get bored in a small place where they can see nothing going on, but that they don't get bored in big, open spaces; and that as regards curiosity, a cock pheasant will often given an egg a peck merely in an inquiring sort of way, seeing a new object lying in the pen, but he seldom breaks the egg; and that in movable pens, because of the greater likelihood of soft-shelled eggs, you are more likely to get eggs broken, and so tempt the cock into bad habits.

Are we likely to get agreement here? Not more likely on this than on other points. Indeed, what is remarkable in the whole controversy is the vigour with which advocates of one system or the other hold their opinions against all contrary argument whatever. The movable pen man has little that is good to say of the open pen; the advocate of the open pen, on the other hand, is convinced of the bad points of the movable pen. Neither will convince the other, and who is to say that either of them is wrong?

FACTS & RECORDS

Pace of Birds

IN ATTEMPTING to obtain something like a working answer to a question which must largely depend upon hypothesis; we may from the start limit inquiry into the case of birds which come into the experience of the ordinary game shot, and may leave out of reckoning the possible speeds attained by such birds as the Malay spine-tailed swift, which are probably astonishing, but do not concern the average holder of a gun or game licence.

We may take into consideration, therefore, the speed attained by birds under three different sets of conditions:—

(1) The speed attained by a bird under normal, everyday conditions.

(2) Such speed accelerated by the bird's own will either for purposes of self-protection or pursuit.

(3) Speed attained under either foregoing conditions accelerated by wind.

In regard to (1):—The late Mr. R. W. S. Griffith, in 1887, experimenting on behalf of the *Field*, organised a series of trials to ascertain the speed of birds "rising to the gun" and not aided by wind. These trials took place in the covered gallery of the Schultze Gunpowder Company in the New Forest, and the birds which were the subject of the experiment were made to fly down the gallery so that at a distance of forty yards they passed through two screens of grey cotton so thin as to be practically invisible, set two and a quarter yards apart. The time taken by the birds to cover this distance was taken by electric chronograph and converted into yards per second or miles per hour. The flights of twelve "blue rocks" worked out at—fastest, 33·8 miles per hour; slowest, 26·1 miles per hour: of pheasants— fastest, 33·8 miles per hour; slowest, 24·4 miles per hour: and of partridges—fastest, 28·4 miles per hour; slowest, 23·7 miles per hour. This was in 1887, and there does not appear to be any record of similar experiments under more up-to-date conditions.

Now for (2):—Ordinary, everyday speed accelerated by the bird's own will. Since Mr. Griffith's trials took place in a covered gallery, we may presumably take it that the birds could hardly have been flying at their fastest pace under what may be called "normal everyday conditions." Let us proceed to apply a formula as regards speed of flight formed by that very well-known scientific ornithologist, Colonel R. Meinertzhagen (*Ibis*, 1921, pp. 228–238):—

"Birds have two speeds—a normal rate which is used for everyday purposes and also for migration, and an accelerated speed which is used for protection or pursuit and which in some cases nearly doubles the rate of their normal speed."

And what may we take to be their normal speed? Colonel Meinertzhagen, "after eliminating abnormal conditions and observations based on meagre evidence," estimates the normal and migratory rate of flight in miles per hour as follows:—

"Corvidae, 31/45; starlings, 38/49; smaller passeres, 20/37; falcons, 40/48; geese, 42/55; ducks, 44/59; tame pigeons, 30/36; sand grouse, 43/47; waders, 34/51; but mostly from 40/51."

Now to take the case of birds which may be supposed likely to "nearly double" the rate of their normal speed. These would obviously be the hawks and their potential prey, who would do so either for pursuit or protection. If, then, we may take Colonel Meinertzhagen's falcons to represent the hawk family and the sand grouse to be a parallel case with our grouse and perhaps partridges, we may calculate that both falcons and grouse may be capable at will of speeds approximately to between eighty and ninety miles an hour—and that, be it noted, in windless conditions.

And if we add to these speeds the strength of the wind, it must be remembered that the wind is to be thought of as a current, and that a bird flying down or up or across wind is to be thought of as a man swimming downstream, or against the stream, or across the stream. Then if the bird flies down wind, we must add the force of the wind to the pace of the bird. A grouse, therefore, flying down wind at a normal speed of forty miles an hour in a thirty-mile wind is flying at the rate of seventy miles an hour, which, under Colonel Meinertzhagen's calculations, it could increase to one hundred and ten miles an hour.

Obviously, such a pace could be imagined capable of an even further increase. Wind *can* blow in England at fifty miles an hour or more. But it seldom does; and to be practical, let us remember that birds much dislike flying in a very high wind, and never do so unless they must.

Perhaps we may best sum up the problem of tremendous pace, under conditions we can at least understand, by a question once put in the *Field:* "The speed which birds can attain with the wind is, of course, just the point which we want to get at. A duck in a gale—that is what we should like to time. But how to measure the distance and the gale?"

WEIGHTS OF BIRDS

Capercaillie.—Cock capercaillie, when mature, weigh from 9 to 12 lbs.; hens weigh from 4 to 7 lbs., and young birds a good deal less. Continental birds are considerably heavier.

Blackgame.—Blackcock weigh from 3 lbs. 8 ozs. to 4 lbs. 4 ozs.; greyhens from 2 lbs. 4 ozs. to 3 lbs. In *Birds of Northumberland and the Eastern Borders*, by George Bolam, it is recorded that a blackcock of nearly 5 lbs. was shot on the Harehope Moors on 21st October 1893.

Red Grouse.—Cocks and hens vary in weight according to the time of year. A cock will lose weight during the early part of breeding season and picks up later, while a broody hen is fat and sluggish, but loses weight during her period of sitting. In August the average weight of a cock is 24 ozs., and of a hen 21 ozs. Generally speaking, Yorkshire grouse are heavier than Scottish, and Irish grouse lighter. A cock grouse weighing 30 ozs. is a great rarity, but birds of 2 lbs. have been recorded both from Yorkshire (Pately Bridge) and Wales, while in the *Field* of 30th December 1922 details were given of a cock grouse which was shot on the Glenfiddich moors early in September of that year, and which, on being weighed by a game dealer of Dufftown, scaled 35 ozs.

Ptarmigan.—Lighter than grouse; probably few exceed 20 ozs. Norwegian rype are heavier than ptarmigan, and in the *Field* of 15th April 1922 a correspondent mentions that in September 1921 he shot two weighing 26 ozs. each, and that his record for an old cock was 28 ozs.

Partridge.—Fourteen ounces is an average weight, cocks being heavier than hens. A bird weighing over 1 lb. is uncommon, but the *Field* has recorded one (31st October 1903) which weighed 1 lb. 7 ozs.

Red-legged or French Partridge.—Heavier than the common partridge. Cocks 1 lb. to 1 lb. 2 ozs.; hens rather less. In January 1930, at Lower Harford, near Cheltenham, a cock was shot which weighed 1 lb. 6½ ozs. A cock of 1 lb. 7 ozs. was killed in Essex in 1881, and in the same season one of 1 lb. 9 ozs. at Hanworth, Norfolk.

Quail.—Mr. H. S. Gladstone, in *Record Bags and Shooting Records*, gives the weight as 3½ ozs.

Pheasant.—It is difficult to lay down any standard as regards the weight of pheasants, as so much depends on the quantity and quality of food available. Obviously birds plentifully supplied with maize in addition to any natural food to be found in the coverts will weigh heavier than wild birds. The normal weight of a cock pheasant varies from 3 lbs. to 3½ lbs. and of a hen 2½ lbs., but birds fed on maize may weigh over 5 lbs.

Woodcock.—The average weight is 12 ozs., but there are records of birds weighing as much as 16 ozs. The heaviest on record is a bird shot at Ramsay, Isle of Man. It was very carefully weighed by Mr. D. H. Greenwood, of Glendaff, Ramsay, and scaled 17½ ozs.

Snipe.—See under separate article among "Game Birds." Of great snipe J. E. Harting, in his *Handbook of British Birds*, notes records of three which weighed 10 ozs. (average weight 7½ to 8 ozs.), and one shot at Pickering in Yorkshire 10¼ ozs.

Of a common snipe the average weight is from 4 to 4½ ozs. and perhaps one in a hundred will pull down the scale at 5 ozs. Harting records that on 14th December 1891, he received three from Dingwall, Lerwick, which had been shot a few days previously, and had probably lost something of their original weight. As it was, they weighed 5¾ ozs., 6¼ ozs., and 6¾ ozs.

A jack snipe's weight is from 2¼ to 2½ ozs.

Mallard and Wild Duck.—Mallard is the proper name for the drake, the derivation being "male" and "ard," *i.e.* the very masculine bird—analogous formations of names being coward, drunkard, braggart, and so on. Average weight of mallard, 3 lbs.; of wild duck, 2½ lbs. On 23rd November 1929, Mr. C. W. Walker wrote to the *Field* from Lundie Castle, Edzell, Angus, recording that on that evening he had shot a mallard weighing 3½ lbs. and a duck weighing 3 lbs. "These were carefully taken weights and exceeded our previous records."

Teal.—Average weight, 12 to 14 ozs.

Gadwall.—From 2 lbs. to 2 lbs. 6 ozs.

Shoveller.—1 lb. 8 ozs. to 1 lb. 12 ozs.

Pintail.—Drake, 2 lbs. 8 ozs. to 2 lbs. 12 ozs.; duck, 2 lbs.

Wigeon.—The spelling "wigeon" is found as early as 1570, and there is no more justification for the spelling "widgeon" than there would be for "pidgeon." A "cock" wigeon weighs from 1 lb. 12 ozs. to 2 lbs.; a "hen," 1 lb. 2 ozs. to 1 lb. 4 ozs.

Pochard.—Varies according to age from 2 lbs. to 2 lbs. 6 ozs.

White-eyed Pochard or Ferruginous Duck.—1 lb. 6 ozs. (A spring visitant.)

Scaup-Duck.—So called from the beds of mussels, called *scalp* or *scaup*, on which it feeds. Male, 2 lbs. 7 ozs.; female, 2 lbs.

Tufted Duck.—A winter visitant, but a certain number breed annually. Weight, 1 lb. 10 ozs. to 1 lb. 14 ozs.

Golden-eye.—A winter visitant; 2 lbs. to 2 lbs. 6 ozs.

Long-tailed Duck.—A winter visitant; 1 lb. 8 ozs. to 1 lb. 10 ozs.

Scoter.—The name is probably a variant of *Scouter* and *Scout* from its habit of appearing in straggling parties as winter visitants before the arrival of the main body of wild fowl. Young male, 2 lbs. 5 ozs.; adult male, 2 lbs. 10 ozs.; female, 1 lb. 12 ozs.

Velvet Scoter.—Mainly a winter visitant to Scotland; 2 lbs. 8 ozs.

Eider Duck.—(Welsh *ydyr*, downy) 5 to 5½ lbs.

Smew.—Winter visitant, not numerous; 1 lb. 8 ozs.

SOME RECORDS OF BAGS

Questions of numbers come up in conversation. The following may be useful for reference:—

GROUSE DRIVING

England.

Date.	Moor.	Bag.	Guns.
12 Aug. 1915.	Littledale and Abbeystead (Lancs).	2,929	8
27 ,, 1913.	Broomhead (Yorks).	2,843	9
24 ,, 1904.	Broomhead (Yorks).	2,748	9
30 ,, 1893.	Broomhead (Yorks).	2,648	9
30 ,, 1888.	Blubberhouses (Yorks).	1,070	Lord Walsingham.

Scotland.

30 Aug. 1911.	Roan Fell (Dumfries).	2,523	8

Wales.

18 Aug. 1904.	Ruabon Mountain (Denbigh).	1,562	8

PTARMIGAN

25 Aug. 1866.	Achnashellac (Ross-shire).	122	Hon. Geoffrey Hill.

PARTRIDGES

England.

	Beat.		
7 Nov. 1905.	Warham, Holkham (Norfolk).	1,671	8

Date.	Beat.	Bag.	Guns.
10 Oct. 1906.	Berry Hill (Notts).	1,504	8
Oct. 1906.	Welbeck Abbey (Notts).	1,467	8

WOODCOCK

Ireland.

28 Jan. 1910.	Ballykine (Co. Galway).	228	6
Christmas 1802.	Donaweale (Co. Cavan).	102	Lord Clermont.

England.

21 Dec. 1910.	Lanarth (Cornwall).	106	7
Dec. 1872.	Swanton Wood (Norfolk).	105	–

SNIPE

Scotland.

29 Oct. 1906.	Tiree, Inner Hebrides.	249	Lord Elphinstone and Mr. J. D. Cobbold.
30 Jan. 1915.	Tiree, Inner Hebrides.	151	Mr. J. D. Cobbold.

Ireland.

2 Feb. 1867.	Dingle (Co. Kerry).	105	Hon. E. de Moleyns
11 Dec. 1871.	Dingle (Co. Kerry).	102	Col. J. Peyton.

England.

28 Nov. 1927.	Norfolk (on less than 50 acres).	210	3
20 Dec. 1927.	Crown Point, nr. Norwich.	227	5

WOODPIGEON

Ireland.   *Place.*

1 Dec. 1911.	Abbeyleix (Queen's Co.).	467	Mr. Cecil Fitzherbert.
14 Dec. 1911.	Abbeyleix (Queen's Co.).	351	Mr. Arnold Fitzherber..

England.

5 Dec. 1918.	Eynsham Hall (Oxon).	373	Mr. J. F. Mason.

HARES

19 Dec. 1877.	Holkham (Norfolk).	1,215	(Not recorded).

RABBITS

17 Oct. 1898.	Blenheim (Oxon).	6,943	5

Extract from a Diary.—"D. this afternoon took a gun and went out shooting by himself. He came back when it was dark, evidently having enjoyed himself immensely. What sort of a day had he had? I asked him. 'Wonderful—one of the very best days I ever had in my life.' 'And what did you shoot?' 'Shoot! Oh, nothing.'"

DEER STALKING

What is a Good Head?

BEFORE ATTEMPTING to discuss in any detail the question, What is a good red deer head? it may be worth giving the measurements of five heads selected by the late J. G. Millais as heads killed before the year 1850, and as being "far ahead" of anything killed since that date. As Mr. Millais begins by pointing out, in the early part of the last century, a stag's head, no matter how large or beautiful, was considered of no value either as an ornament or a sportsman's trophy. He doubts whether there exist to-day thirty good examples of old Scottish heads. Better heads than those which have survived, then, may have been destroyed without a thought for their size or beauty. However that may be, the five selected are better than any heads killed in modern days in Scotland, and the two seventeen-pointers in Gordon Castle "are easily the best British stags' heads killed in our islands since the Pleistocene Age; and are such that even a good continental forest would be proud of them to-day." Here is the table giving details of measurement—*i.e.* length, girth, or beam, that is measurement of circumference between bez and trez points; outside spread; inside span; and number of points:—

[TABLE

153

SCOTTISH WILD STAGS' HEADS OBTAINED PRIOR TO 1850

Length.	Beam.	Spread over all.	Inside span.	Points.	Locality.	Owner.	Remarks and by whom measured.
41	7	—	35	7×7	Inverness-shire.	Col. W. H. Walker.	Killed in 1794 (R. W.).
38	6½	—	—	9×8	Glenfiddich.	Duke of Richmond.	Killed on 24th September 1831; 37 st. 7 lbs. as it fell (Owner)
36	7¾	42	36	6×7	Monymusk.	Sir A. Grant, Bart.	Killed in 1795 (J. G. M.).
36	—	—	—	8×8	Glen Moriston.	J. Grant.	Killed in 1796 (Owner).
35½	4⅔	38½	27	5×5	Kinlochewe.	Sir K. Mackenzie, Bart.	Killed in 1814. A head of remarkable beauty. (F. Wallace).
33	5¼	—	—	8×9	Gordon Castle.	Duke of Richmond.	Killed in 1826 (Owner).

With regard to the Glenfiddich head, the following particulars were sent to Mr. J. G. Millais by the late Duke of Richmond:—

"The Glenfiddich head was shot by the head forester in the Blackwater Forest, which is part of Glenfiddich. He killed it in the burn at the back of the lodge, and there is a cairn to mark the spot. The Duke of Gordon of that time (1831) sent word to his head forester to kill a stag, as he wished to send a haunch to his sister the Duchess of Bedford, who at that time was staying at Kinrara. The forester, in spying the ground, found what he thought was a dead birch tree, and as he knew there were no birches in that part of the forest, he made further investigation. The result was that he found the seventeen-point stag and shot it."

No complete records of the measurements of Scottish heads exist. But to get something near an answer to the question, what is a good head? it may be useful to compare the records of a recent stalking season, 1936, which was a year of wonderful weather, but not above the average as regards the quality of heads. It may be premised that the ideal head is not merely one with great length of antler or of tines, or of exceptional beam, or of great width over all or of inside span, or even exceptional in the number of points. It must in addition be a head of beauty and symmetry. Here, then, are some of the measurements of some of the best heads of the stalking season of 1936:—

HEADS OBTAINED IN THE STALKING SEASON OF 1936.

Length.	Beam.	Span.	Points.	Locality.	Owner.
39	$5\frac{1}{2}$	$32\frac{3}{4}$	4×6	Carse.	Mr. Ian Coats.
$37\frac{1}{4}$	5	$29\frac{1}{4}$	5×5	Glenkinglas.	Miss V. Hermon Hodge.
$37\frac{1}{4}$	$5\frac{1}{5}$	$22\frac{3}{4}$	7×8	Barrisdale.	Major Bell Irving.
37	$4\frac{1}{2}$	$28\frac{5}{8}$	4×4	Strathrannoch.	Mr. S. L. Bibby.
$35\frac{3}{4}$	$4\frac{3}{4}$	$26\frac{3}{8}$	7×6	Ardverikie.	Lieut.-Colonel Horlick.
$35\frac{1}{2}$	$5\frac{1}{4}$	$26\frac{1}{4}$	4×6	Dalness.	Hon. Lovell Coke.
35	5	$30\frac{3}{4}$	4×6	Dalnessie.	Mr. J. Hemingway.
35	$5\frac{1}{2}$	24	4×4	Guisachan.	Mr. C. Prior.
34	$5\frac{1}{4}$	$30\frac{5}{8}$	6×6	Knoydart.	Lord Brocket.
32	$4\frac{5}{8}$	$24\frac{3}{8}$	7×7	Glenkingie.	Lord Belper.

We may now compare with these, the heads of a single season, some of the best heads listed by Mr. J. G. Millais as having been obtained during the years 1850–1912:—

SCOTTISH WILD STAGS' HEADS OBTAINED 1850–1912

Length.	Beam.	Spread over all.	Inside span.	Points.	Locality.	Owner.	Remarks and by whom measured.
41	—	—	—	—	Strathglass.	J. Sargent.	(J. G. M.).
40	$6\frac{1}{2}$	40	—	6×6	Aberfeldy.	—	(J. G M.).
40	6	—	30	5×5	Glentilt.	Duke of Atholl.	(J. G. M.).
—	—	42	—	—	Ardverikie.	Earl of Tankerville.	The widest modern head.
39	$7\frac{1}{4}$	$39\frac{1}{2}$	—	6×6	Guisachan.	Lord Tweedmouth.	Weight 21 st. 7 lbs. (J. G. M.).
39	—	—	34	5×5	Kinveachy.	Major Porteous.	Killed in 1912 (Spicer & Sons).
$38\frac{1}{2}$	$5\frac{1}{2}$	39	$30\frac{1}{4}$	5×6	Strath Vaich.	J. C. Williams.	Killed in 1908; weight 19 st. (Owner).
$38\frac{5}{8}$	$5\frac{1}{2}$	$33\frac{3}{4}$	$29\frac{1}{4}$	6×6	Meoble.	Walter Jones.	(R. W.).
$38\frac{1}{2}$	$4\frac{3}{4}$	—	26	11	Isle of Rum.	Sir G. Bullough.	(Owner).
38	$4\frac{3}{4}$	—	$25\frac{1}{4}$	10	Strathconan.	Capt. Combe.	Killed in 1912 (F. Wallace).
38	$6\frac{1}{2}$	$35\frac{1}{4}$	29	6×9	Mamore.	Col. Cholmondeley.	The best head of 1911 (Spicer & Sons).
$37\frac{1}{2}$	—	—	$29\frac{1}{2}$	6×6	Strath Vaich.	P. D. Williams.	The best head ever killed at Strath Vaich.

It will be seen, therefore, from a survey of the records o measurements of Scottish heads, ancient and modern, that 40 inches is near the limit of length of antler; that anything over $5\frac{1}{2}$ inches is an exceptional measurement as regards beam; that a spread over all of 40 inches and a measurement of inside span of 30 inches are equally exceptional; and that as regards points, few heads of fourteen points or more are obtained in a season's stalking. We are left, then, with the question of symmetry. Mr. Millais has left it on record, with a sketch in illustration (*The Gun at Home and Abroad*) that the best Scottish head he ever saw and measured "was obtained by a farmer in his cornfield near Aberfeldy, in September 1889. It is a perfect royal with long points, and 40 inches long and 40 inches wide." He adds to this note the remark that "practically equal is the big Guisachan royal killed by the late Lord Tweedmouth." Either head might be described as the trophy of a stalker's dream.

Hornless stags, or hummels, are not uncommon. A stag with two single horns is known as a "switch." With brow, bez, trez, and "three on top" he is a royal, and he cannot be more. That is to say, a stag with thirteen or more points is a royal of thirteen points, and not—a name which has no place in the tradition of the forest—an "imperial."

List of Deer Forests

Particulars of some of the forests mentioned in the foregoing lists, and of other forests of importance, are given in a table with the county in which the forest is situated, its approximate area in acres, and its highest altitude.

Forest.	County.	Area.	Altitude.
Coignafearn . .	Inverness.	29,500	2,652
Ardgour . . .	Argyll.	30,000	—
Ardnamurchan . .	Argyll.	18,850	—
Ardverikie . .	Inverness.	30,000	3,569
Atholl . . .	Perth.	36,000	3,671
Barrisdale . .	Inverness.	20,000	—
Benalder . . .	Inverness.	30,000	3,757
Ben Wyvis . .	Ross and Cromarty.	20,000	3,429
Blackmount . .	Argyll.	90,000	3,602
Braemore . . .	Ross and Cromarty.	37,000	3,547
Braulen and Glen Strathfarrer . .	Inverness.	30,000	3,773
Caenlochan . .	Forfar.	9,160	3,502
Coignafearn . .	Inverness.	29,500	2,652
Corrour . . .	Inverness.	56,250	3,611

Forest.	County.	Area.	Altitude.
Craiganour . .	Perth.	15,000	2,500
Dalness . . .	Argyll.	8,000	3,766
Deanich . . .	Ross and Cromarty.	16,000	1,000
Dunrobin . . .	Sutherland.	13,800	1,706
Eriboll . . .	Sutherland.	36,000	—
Eskadale . . .	Inverness.	12,000	—
Fannich . . .	Ross and Cromarty.	20,000	3,637
Fasnakyle . . .	Inverness.	25,000	2,884
Fealar . . .	Perth.	14,000	3,424
Gaick . . .	Inverness.	26,200	3,000
Glenartney . .	Perth.	6,857	3,224
Glenbruar . .	Perth.	12,000	3,200
Glenfeshie . .	Inverness.	35,900	4,149
Glenfiddich . .	Banff.	25,000	2,583
Glen Kingie . .	Inverness.	16,580	3,290
Glenquoich . .	Inverness.	46,300	3,395
Glentana . .	Aberdeen.	26,030	3,077
Guisachan . .	Inverness.	20,000	2,991
Invercauld . .	Aberdeen.	20,020	3,586
Kildalton . . .	Argyll.	28,000	—
Killilan and Faddoch .	Ross and Cromarty.	18,000	—
Kinlochewe . .	Ross and Cromarty.	32,000	3,000
Kintail . . .	Ross and Cromarty.	25,000	3,500
Kinveachy . .	Inverness.	11,000	3,337
Knoydart and Carnach (including Barrisdale)	Inverness.	38,000	3,410
Langwell and Braemore	Caithness.	38,500	2,312
Mamore . . .	Inverness.	36,000	3,700
Mar	Aberdeen.	80,100	4,296
Meoble . . .	Inverness.	20,000	3,130
Morar . . .	Inverness.	13,000	2,818
Rannoch . . .	Perth.	11,000	3,000
Reay . . .	Sutherland.	56,000	2,980
Rhidorroch . .	Ross and Cromarty.	39,000	1,800
Rum . . .	Argyll.	27,000	3,000
Strathconan . .	Ross and Cromarty.	59,000	3,550
Strath Vaich . .	Ross and Cromarty.	26,000	3,547

THE SHOOTERS' LANDSCAPE

MARSHLAND AT DUSK

JANUARY.—The marsh is a stark place in these days. Set in the angle formed by the union of the two trout streams, it is fruitful of life in many forms during the summer. But, searched through and through by a January east wind, it is the most inhospitable place. Snipe, full and half alike, leave it during the frost, though rough and rainy weather brings them thither. Its peewit population, inspired by the very spirit of wild song and dance in spring and early summer, has left to a bird by autumn. That wayward, far-flighted, green sandpiper—"martin-snipe" of the river villagers—has not come yet. The field-fares will gather in little parties on the oaks that lie about the edge of the marsh, but there is no food to tempt them to the dry or wet parts of the marsh. A covey or two of partridges, and here and there a reed-bunting, its plaintive shrill cry going well with the east wind, seem to be the only living creatures on the marsh.

But the marsh can grow far less crude and harsh in look as the winter night begins to touch it. It then wears colours of a grand simplicity. Sometimes in January, during sharp frost, when the sun has gone under the low hills beyond the river, the scene will glow with warm colour. At one spot, just above the marsh, where the river runs darkly and highly burnished, the stars are reflected and magnified in it; and here, at the right time and spot, one may see the seven stars of the Plough, snow-white and sparkling in the water. But at the point where it slides under the road bridge, the stream increases its pace again, and its surface is broken rather than burnished. It enters upon the marsh, to flow away into the velvet of night.

The rich night black of its banks in the foreground; the less determinable shade of dark farther away on the flat expanse; beyond, the grey hill line; above this, the great curtain of purple cloud; finally, the blue vault, with Aquila, the eagle, still aloft; there is nothing forbidding in this scene at the marsh. So one can see it on many winter evenings; and so I watched it once early in January, when a lonely star of the Southern Fish was quivering on the horizon to the south, one of the shy jewels of our English horizon.

GEORGE A. B. DEWAR:
The Faery Year.

ON AN ESSEX ESTUARY

February.—In the level sunshine of mid-February the distances over the saltmarsh change and deceive. The low light of early morning lifts to a mellow radiance which dims edges and sets angles in a haze. The long slope of plough-land above the marsh stretches an acreage not to be guessed as you would guess it in sharper sunlight; the furrows recede into vaporous, immeasurable planes in which vision wanders and fails. On the saltings and over the estuary water the same mist of light fuses outlines and draws distance nearer.

A solitary redshank flits up the river bank, and except for the faster wing-beat, you might doubt whether it was not a curlew. High on the farthest horizon the grey tower of a church rises above red tiles and the masts of ocean-going yachts; the map sets the little town three miles away, but in that strange lustre her tower lifts beyond a single field, her masts must be only at the turn of the river. A tiny farm, with its stacks and barns dotted about a hill on the far bank, lies in a plane neither near nor far; the yellow rays illumine the straw thatch and light jewels in the low windows; the whole group colours like a picture hung unframed in open air. In the farthest distance of all, out towards the sea, the horizon is a thin strip of grey. A narrowing spit of pasture-land runs into the breadth of sea-water, and along it stand grey trees; there is an air about them of something exotic, as if they were palm-trees on the horizon of a desert.

PLOVER OVER SNOW-WATER

March.—The golden plover's mating-call is the wildest and truest of all cries of melting snow. In the upland levels, where the snows warm to steam and water first on the bare slopes that front the noon sunlight, the water urges its own small river-courses from the highest plateaux of the hill through snow-banks which it carves and widens for itself. The clear stream ripples and tumbles to a roar in the valley, running on the higher ground over grass passages that through all the summer will never feel the pull of water at the grass-bents and ragged heather. The streams go the easiest way down the hill, that is all; much as the shepherds or the sheep always find their way down by the quickest and gentlest road.

And by that easy course of cold water the golden plover walk and fly and call. They separate into pairs more distinctly than the green plover, and they mark the change more clearly, showing their deep black splashes on cheek and breast—the mark of the mating months that will alter back to the chequered olive of autumn and winter. They change their call, too, from the high, ringing whistle of winter to the most delicate note of complaining; sometimes a double note of some sweet inquiry which always bring its own answer; sometimes a triumphant, bubbling cry which quickens with a quickened beat of wings. The golden plover's wings keep time to his cries and his silences; he and his mate poise and counterpoise to each other in curves and slopes of buoyant flight; his silence is on level, unshaken wings, his inquiring call on a slow beat, and his chuckling joy on a double beat that changes again to level quiet, to settling again by the racing snow-water.

On the Rim of the Moor

April.—Even from the high road that skirts the Dee from Aberdeen to Balmoral you may sight ten or a dozen birds which you might look for in vain along fifty miles of a road in the southern counties. The dipper, of course, and his sweet, sudden pipings and skimming flight belong to all mountain streams and wet rocky places, and so does the grey wagtail, with his yellow under-feathers and dainty balancings and bowings; and of commoner inland water-birds, the coot and mallard and moorhen are interesting to watch, but nothing particularly rare in the south. Still, they are tame enough to take very little notice of highway traffic. The really fascinating thing is to find them intermixed with birds which belong exclusively to wildness and to the north. You will not see the capercaillie from the road; he belongs to the wood; but on the rough heather-ground and among the birch-copses on the road you can watch the cock grouse fluttering and flaunting himself before his coy partner; curlew flit and cry from wayside pools; three or four blackcock solemnly stalk a stubble; a pair of hooded crows forage savagely and lonelily at distant corners of the same field; black-headed gulls walk with rooks and jackdaws; and, most brilliant group of all, you round a corner in the road, and come upon fifty or a hundred oyster-catchers feeding with plovers on a fallow. Those black and white shining bodies and bright red bills strike an almost un-natural note of distinction; and so, in the evening, does the quiet, bat-like flitting of a woodcock over the pine trees. Woodcock in an English winter associate themselves with covert-shooting and cartridges. By the Dee in April they grace their name as they should.

Gorse Coverts

May–June.—Seen from close at hand, gorse-bushes are a curious blend of radiant flowering life and dead waste. The

161

gorse blooms on only the last ten or fifteen inches of its stem, and the rest of the stringy, writhen wood is either covered with dead spines and prickles and the husks of last year's seed-pods, or has shed even these and twists down to the root of the bush as bare as a cable. A large clump of gorse, however superbly brilliant with blossom it may be on the outside, within is a cavern of strange and unlovely nakedness. The spines and shards of last year have crumbled and rotted into a dull, grey-brown floor on which no seed will root and no creeper will run. You peer through the twisted, thwarted stems into dusky darknesses and recesses of decay. From a dozen yards away, the bushes shine as if they should be palaces for all elfland, to blow their faint horns and ride on rabbits about the woody pillars that hold up those roofs and domes of blossom. But moth and mustard seed would never dance over the prickles. Puck would wear moccasins. The one woodland creature whom the thickest and hollowest gorse clumps suit is the fox. He likes gorse which horses and cattle and sheep have eaten down close year after year, so that it has bunched and thickened where they have bitten, and at last has closed together to make a solid roof and walls, with a door where he pleases. Then he can creep in full-fed and curl up and sleep comfortably. Rain cannot wet him, and wind cannot chill him, and if the hounds come that way he can see all round him to dodge and run.

SCOTLAND IN THE DISTANCE

July.—We are beginning to think of a scene in the distance. Here on our English hills the bell-heather has already spread its acres of crimson, the cross-leaved heath, *Erica tetralix*, has touched the lower, wetter slopes with pink, and over the stretches which yesterday were dull green we get the promise of the full purples of the ling. And with those colours coming back to the horizon we think of other, wilder slopes; of a Forfarshire road that, it may be, runs from a grey, granite-built railway station to the welcome vision of the sweet-peas of the lodge garden; of the harebells —the bluebells of Scotland—that line the wayside; of rough pasture dotted with ragwort—"stunking Wullie," as the ghillie calls it; of the boulder-strewn hillside beyond the larch wood, the heather of the moor beyond that, and, farthest of all, the blue rim of hills that stand, we know, between us and the sea. Heather, the hills, wind from the sea—who that has known these does not think in July of the Highlands in August?

WATER MEADOWS

August.—I walked for the first time to-day some English water meadows. For me water meadows have always a singular fascination; they go in my mind with cuckoos calling and snipe drumming, and dabchicks diving all over bubbles through carriers, and May flies cocked on ripples, and the mauve fins and the faint scent of grayling, and scythes swishing through falling grass, and great red Devons lying as if they could never get up. But I had never walked water meadows in summer before with the precise purpose of this August morning, which was to shoot snipe and duck. I believe that earlier in the year, with the snipe swooping zigzags in the blue air above me, I should have thought it impossible to contemplate carrying a gun through these fields; and, as a matter of fact, I have never, in England, shot duck in August. But I found myself walking with a new and complete enjoyment; the reeds, the rushes, the wet ground, the soaking grass in the sunlight, all had fresh possibilities and opportunities in them, and I wanted nothing more than to hear the familiar chatter of duck before they get on wing, or to see again the flash of a snipe's breast turned to the wind.

As it happened, the morning was not a success as regards shooting; the duck were not where it was hoped they would be, and the snipe, for some reason or other, although they had not previously been shot at, were extraordinarily wild, and got up all over the place at distances at which it was impossible to fire. But I shall always remember the hour in which we walked those meadows; the untrodden, springing grass grey with rain, the bending reeds, the water mint in flower, the brooklime and water avens, the green-veined and small white butterflies which flickered over blossom after blossom, the poplars along the bank of the river. . . . There was an odd fascination in the morning, and I did not fire a shot.

SEPTEMBER MORNING

September.—There is a morning in the year which could belong to one month only. It breaks silently, as all September mornings break; but there is a mist floating in the valley which blurs the smaller trees and bushes, and out of which rise the top branches only of the taller trees. With the strength of the sunlight the mist dissolves, leaving the hay-fields and lawns drenched white with dew—a dew which changes from white into sparkling clearness just as a tumbler of ice-cold water clears into transparence on a warm table-cloth. The sky immediately above you deepens into a ring of blue heat, but towards the horizon the blue fades, and there hangs over the level line of distant trees an atmosphere of the most delicate amethystine grey. Once the faintest breath of cold air stirs as you turn the corner of the drive, only to drop away again.

It will be one of the hottest days of the year; one of those days on which only the youngest and keenest of shooters is anxious to tramp turnip fields after lunch, and when, to tire the tramper even more, the partridges themselves run into hedges and undergrowth, not to be pushed out again except by the most energetic encouragement of thirsty dogs. To some minds, perhaps, it is by one of these hot days of early partridge-shooting that the month marks herself in the memory most clearly; when the day's work begins with two or three wheels of the line of beaters and guns through a four-acre patch of potatoes, where the thwarting green stems and high, crumbling ridges make it difficult not to stumble, and difficult too, to get a firm footing when the covey whirrs into the sunlight, and even a couple of shots make the gun-barrels stinging hot to the shooter's left hand.

On such a day men like to know that their neighbours are good enough shots to kill dead at any reasonably easy chance, for the birds which alone will be included in the bag are those which have dropped without a flutter. The best dog in the world can do very little with a "runner" when no scent will lie on that dusty soil and dry leaves. The walking up of partridges is, indeed, one of the real old-fashioned sports of September that the changes of a hundred years have barely touched. The stubbles are not so high as they were when the corn was reaped with the sickle; and dogs, except retrievers, are very little used. But it is not true, as some writers would have you believe, that the only sport to be had with partridges is to drive them; and there is a certain satisfaction of sentiment in walking through the quiet fields of clover and mangolds with the scent of mustard and wet turnip leaves coming down wind and the broad leaves of the swedes tipping little pools of the night's rain over your boots, and with the brown coveys whirring up before you just as they whirred up before your father, and his father before him.

CHANGE ON THE HILL

October.—There are other distant days, but always the memory of Tweed and the Border seems to be of afternoon and evening. Or of twilight; Hawick station before dawn and silent gulls flitting over a grey town; Melrose asleep, as I drive to the hotel. But of late sunlight and dusk oftenest; the road by Yarrow, rippling under trees, and a bunch of wigeon fleeting down-stream; Eildon as Andrew Lang saw it, "three crests against the saffron sky," and Tweed as he sang of it, and as I think of it:—

> *Like a loved ghost thy fabled flood*
> *Fleets through the dusky land;*
> *Where Scott, come home to die, has stood,*
> *My feet returning stand.*

And if October in the Border country is evening, in Perthshire, Forfarshire, Ross-shire it is as surely morning. It is morning on Strathtay; we have left on the hill below us the beeches glowing through the mist; we have climbed the rough roads and grass tracks to the rim of the heather, and we are looking with clear air about us down to the white wraiths sheeted over the river. How the moor has changed! We saw it last in August, when there were roses and sweet peas in the lodge garden, and over the hill the heather hummed with bees. And now the ling has turned brown and to seed, and the crimson bell-heather is dulled by frost, and the bracken crackles dry; and even before we take our places in the butts for the grouse drive we know that the grouse, and we too, have changed. There is a cold wind, we shall move the more briskly because of the strength and spirit of it; and something of the raw cold air has touched the veins and sinews of the grouse, with their dark bodies and rushing wings. But here, too, in their new autumn plumage, are blackgame in the drive with the grouse. That slow wing beat; how many blackcock owe their lives to its deceit! We look out from our butt to the horizon of heather in front of us, and here come the grouse, whose pace we recognise at once; they are sailing towards us, plainly flying as fast as birds can, with that characteristic rocking motion from side to side which somehow emphasizes the sense of their speed, like a rocking train. And with them or above them, high and steady and straight, flies a bigger bird, seeming to go slower than the grouse; we decide to take him, and suddenly discover that we must be quick about it; he falls a noble trophy, blue and black and white, far behind the line. It is only in October that he comes to that strength and beauty; and it is not until October that the full vigour of the year hurls the coveys towards the butts—those challenging birds in the wind, heavier, blacker, and faster than any grouse of August, that swing up to us, rise over us, and are gone.

DISROBING TREES

November.—Elms and birches, of trees which stand out apart from lowlier neighbours, disrobe themselves with their own distinction. Elms, as the massed leaves thin from deep bottle-green to mellow chromes and ochres, day after day add an emphasis to shape rather than to colour. The lessening leaves group themselves exactly where they best grace the piled and branching boughs. Birches, and weeping birches more than all, drape themselves in veils; the veils grow more lucent, the sky gleams bluer between the twigs, the tree stands slender and bare—it is the most delicate procession of undressing.

But the November pageant is not yet over. The colour leaves the tall trees of the field and wood, but the hedgerows still glow into December. The dog-rose jewels itself with coral, and under the dog-rose in the hedge the thrushes sprinkle the half of the red berries that they take from the tree. The hawthorn can be even brighter than the rose—brighter, where it grows with greatest vigour, even than the clustering berries of the holly. The deepest crimson of all English wild fruits belongs to the hawthorn set against the blue of an autumn sky; perhaps with the white floss and feathers of the clematis climbing near it, to set an extra light in the picture.

But for sheer contrasted colour you may still come back to the beech-leaf carpet. When the November sun glows on fallen beech leaves, and a flock of wood-pigeons settles on the carpet to pick the mast, the dove-colour set on the copper shines into pure blue. But wood-pigeons unluckily are the shyest sitters, and, if they can help it, will not let a painter look.

Winter Sunlight

December.—December holds a day of lustrous quiet which belongs to deep and mild winter alone. From dawn to dusk no ray of open sunshine falls on any space of ploughland or lawn. No wind stirs the lightest leaf; no moving air dries yesterday's dew from the broader, greyer blades of the hedgerow grass. Over all, high and withdrawn like the roof of a tent, lies a curtain of cloud, and through the cloud filters a diffused luminousness which lights the garden and the woods as though you saw them in sunshine through dark glass. The caverned shadows in the yews and cypresses take the softness of hollows among unplucked grapes; there is a bloom set on the cedars beyond the lawn like the flush on

167

fruit; beyond the cedars the slighter undergrowth merges into the greyness of cobwebs. The air has no warmth of sun in it, but its mellow temper sets the gnats dancing above the wet grass; you may walk into the little swarm of drab-winged ephemerals, and the whole cotillion flits up twenty feet to dance down again as you pass and return.

It is the most tranquil afternoon of simple waiting; the light on the countryside is the quiet of the eyes of deer. The afternoon waits for the evening, and in the evening the grey veil lifts. A rough, cool air leaps up from the south-west, tears a rent of thrush-egg blue in the grey, and drives the chimney smoke across the rent. The whole sky lights and clears like a dawn; in the far west a belt of tawny vapour tarnishes to dark again, and across the higher starlight a cloud rides up on a new wind.

How Not to Leave Guns during Lunch

LUNCH, LARDER & KITCHEN

From a Shooting Diary

SEPTEMBER 16.—What is the best shooting lunch? This was the topic of our conversation to-day while, as we were all agreed in the presence of our hostess, we were eating it. But she, as a hostess may, even though she is an acknowledged mistress of all arts of the kitchen, would not accept our compliments. Ours was a lunch sent out to us from the kitchen. A shooting lunch proper should be more, and less, than that. It should be a lunch to be carried in the pocket; no dishes, no knives, no forks; just a packet as light and small as is compatible with a sufficiency of food.

We looked at the lunch before us. Curry, with an admirable admixture of peas, beans, and other vegetables; cold grouse, lettuce salad, tomato salad, strawberry jam puffs, apples, cheese. What must we forgo? What should we choose or substitute?

"Sandwiches," reflected O, who has inspirations of the obvious. "But of what?"

"Not at all," contradicted P. "Slices. Of chicken, packed side by side with bread and butter. Far better. Or half a partridge."

"Why half?" asked S. "A whole partridge quartered; bread and butter salted—most important, because you either lose salt, or forget it, or it blows away in the wind. And a slice of cold plum pudding. And two apples."

"Pears."

"*No*. Because the skins rub off."

"But sandwiches are really better than slices, because they

169

don't dry so easily. Brown sandwiches are good, with mustard and pepper."

K raised a hand, and we were silent for the gourmet.

"Brown sandwiches are good, if accompanied by cucumber. But better than brawn are bacon sandwiches. Take your bacon from the frying-pan and lay it reverently between slices of buttered bread—well-buttered bread. These, with cucumber sandwiches, are sufficient.

But there are possible suggestions for other sandwiches. Here is Mrs. Elsie Turner, writing in the *Field*:—

"A delicious sandwich can be made with cold duck. Butter two pieces of bread and on one piece spread a thin coating of stiff apple sauce and on the other a thin coating of the sage and onion stuffing out of the duck. Then place very thin slices of cold roast duck between the apple and stuffing, and you have an uncommon and delicious sandwich; it can be equally successful between a finger roll if a little of the bread inside the roll is removed. Smoked salmon sandwiches, too, are unusual, and when a little lemon juice is squeezed on the smoked salmon they do not make one thirsty.

"Potted hare makes an excellent sandwich, and so do skinned and boned sardines with cress between toast; the bread is cut fairly thick and toasted a nice light brown, then split, buttered on both sides and the sardines laid carefully between.

"Sausage rolls, hot or cold, are always popular, but great care should be taken with seasoning the sausage meat; plenty of pepper, a little salt, and finely chopped sage and thyme. Never have them made with sausages in their skins. I knew a Scottish cook who ordered half a pound of sausages to make sausage rolls for eight guns. We had an uninteresting game at lunch called 'Hunt the Sausage,' as she had cut each sausage into four pieces, skin and all.

"A delicious variation can be made, for cold days, by currying the sausage."

And now for some recipes old and new, proper to the Highland lodge, but not less acceptable farther south.

"P. R. C."—initials as familiar to south country gun-rooms as to Highland lodges—advises:—

"As to the blue hare, he is a meagre creature and can never be compared, as a *plat*, to the brown meadow hare. Yet of him, as of old game birds, even of the old capercailzie, a Scottish housewife can make a homely but excellent 'cock-brue,' or a thick brown soup, a plateful of which, eaten with a mealy potato, is a dinner in itself. Since the blue hare is, as a rule, vastly and unfairly neglected, I give two recipes for him; each may be both new and useful in many kitchens.

"The little white Scots hare, therefore, and two ways of cooking him: (1) Take him, the same day as shot, and skin and joint him. Wash in warm water and dry. Score and slash the joints well and lay in the following marinade: one wineglass Madeira, one of olive oil, and one of brown wine vinegar. A finely minced shallot, two cloves of garlic, a spoonful of mixed herbs, and salt-spoonful of black pepper. Cover and put in cool place. Turn the joints every day, rubbing marinade well in each time; leave six to seven days. Remove joints and drain; take half a pound of belly pork, cut into dice and brown in pan. Place on one side. Add joints of hare to pan and start frying on good brisk heat, turning frequently until well browned on all sides. Drain off all fat from pan, place little dice of pork on top of joints of hare. Add a wineglass of Madeira and a good spoonful of crab-apple jelly, one pound of chestnuts (with jackets and waist-coats removed). Braise very gently for half an hour and serve piping hot, with little force-meat balls and creamed potatoes flavoured with a little juice and grated rind of orange, browned with salamande.

"(2) The following is a way of using up the remains. Remove all flesh from bones of the cooked hare and place in mortar along with sufficient fresh-ground black pepper and a teaspoonful each of the following: Freshly-minced parsley, finely chopped chives, finely chopped tarragon and grated lemon rind, a *very* little salt and a *very* little dried herbs. Pound all well together with pestle in mortar, add a suffi-ciency of fresh butter to make a nice spreadable consistency.

Rub through sieve and add some coarsely chopped truffle. Press into little china pots and cover with clarified butter. Cover and store in cool dry place. Will keep for twelve months and makes a very savoury on hot buttered toast with a blob of quince jelly; also a good filling for patty or *vol-au-vent* cases.

"As for venison proper, the haunch of the hart of grease, so much has been written of it, and of its cookery and etiquette that, when I have referred the student to its principal masters and *cordon-bleux*—Scrope, Goldsmith, Sir Walter and Shand, most especially to Alexander Innes Shand —I am left with little to say. But I will first make three minor remarks and a statement.

"First, on reaching the larder at the lodge, the stag should be skinned and cut up as soon as possible. When cut up the joints should hang for three days, prior to despatch. Secondly, when this complimentary haunch reaches its destination, it will smell as rankly as goat-flesh. Let not the accustomed Sassenach housewife, or cook, exclaim that it must be taken down the garden and buried. Sponge it over with vinegar, dust it with pepper or ginger, and it will become as fresh as daisies in a few minutes. And subsequently it will, with care and an occasional dusting of ginger, 'keep' longer than any other meat you may name. Thirdly, I will say that crab-apple jelly is better 'kitchen' than is the habitual red-currant confection. Lastly, I will add, and cry the pity of it, that though every stag you shoot may be estimated to cost you (or someone else) anything between £20 and £50, his value at the game-dealers', at the poulterers', is nil, or a bagatelle. The red stag, as an item in the national commissariat, is negligible."

So much for shooting lunches and dinners in the earlier part of the season. What of mid-winter tables, in the house or the keeper's cottage? Here are two recipes suggested by Mrs. Turner:—

For *Partridge Pudding*, take two brace of old partridges and cut them into neat joints, season with two teaspoonfuls of salt and a teaspoonful of pepper, some chopped parsley and herbs, and add a few mushrooms if you have them. Line a greased pudding basin holding two quarts with a thick suet crust, and lay a thin slice of rump steak weighing about a quarter pound at the bottom, then a layer of partridges and seasoning up to the top; place another slice of rump steak rather larger but quite thin over this. Have ready about two pints of good stock (flavouring it with two glasses of claret is an improvement but not essential), and pour this over your partridges in the basin. Cover carefully with your suet crust and pinch the edges together. Tie a pudding cloth over the basin, place in boiling water and keep boiling for quite three hours till ready. This pudding is big enough for eight guns.

Bakewell Tart is a celebrated Derbyshire dish and here is a good old recipe. Line a baking tin about eight inches across and one and a quarter inches high with rich pastry, cover the bottom with a layer of strawberry jam—no other jam can possibly be used according to Derbyshire tradition! Put a quarter pound of butter into a pan and let it boil up, skim carefully, and while still boiling add a teaspoonful of ground almonds, the yolks of four eggs and the whites of three, and a quarter pound of castor sugar which must previously have been beaten well together; again beat together with the hot butter and pour over the jam. There should be about a quarter pound of jam and one inch of this mixture to fill the pastry case. Bake till a nice brown and serve hot or cold.

THE LAW

Game Act, 1831

THE GAME ACT, 1831, abolished all property qualification for entitling persons to kill game in England, and since that date anyone may kill it who pays the requisite duty to the Inland Revenue, provided he has permission to go on land in search of it.

In Scotland and Ireland, however, the property qualification still obtains, but this is neutralised by usage, through the ability of the qualified owner to grant permission to shoot to qualified persons, who may lawfully keep the game which they have killed.

Meaning of Game

For the purposes of the Game Act, 1831, the following are game: Hares, pheasants, partridges, grouse, heath or moor game, blackgame and bustards. The following complete the list of game to kill which a licence is necessary: Woodcock, snipe, quail, landrail, conies, and deer.

Bustards are extinct. Heath or moor game are mysterious, and a delusion of the legal draughtsman's brain. Conies mean rabbits.

ANIMALS & BIRDS WHICH ARE NOT GAME

Birds.—Swan, wild duck, teal, wigeon are not game. Teal, woodcock, and snipe have to come for protection under the provisions of the Wild Birds Protection Acts.

Animals.—Deer, although not game, require a licence before they can be taken or killed, under the Game Licences Act, 1860, otherwise than by hunting with hounds, except in enclosed lands, when they may be killed by the owner or occupier or his licensee. They are, however, included with "Game" under the Agricultural Holdings Act in questions of compensation for damage. Hares, though "Game" are included with rabbits, which are not game, in the term "Ground Game" in the Act which goes by that name, with which we will deal later. Although not game rabbits are included in the Excise Licence to kill game and are not included in the enactments as to close seasons for killing game.

It will be seen, therefore, that it is very possible to get confused on the question of what is or is not game, and that exact knowledge can only be obtained by struggling along a technical and thorny path, along which some might say it is unnecessary for the ordinary man to wander.

WHO MAY SHOOT

Licences.—No one, with unimportant exceptions, can shoot game without a game licence which can be obtained at most Post Offices and for which the prices are:—

£3 from 31st July to 31st July.
£2 „ 31st July to 31st January.
£2 „ 31st January to 31st July.
£1 for a fortnight.

A licence is not retrospective and must, therefore, be obtained *before* any act requiring its possession is done. It is available throughout the United Kingdom and entitles the holder to sell game to a licensed dealer in game.

A gamekeeper's licence costs £2.

Before anyone, with unimportant exceptions, other than the holder of a game licence, can carry a gun at all, he must procure a gun licence, except actually "in a dwelling-house or the curtilage thereof." The "curtilage" is a very restricted area, and does not mean the "grounds." Even an air-gun requires a licence. The price is 10s. per annum. Any Inland Revenue officer or constable who sees a person using a gun can enter the land in question and demand the licence.

In addition to the foregoing, the sportsman will require a dog licence, costing 7s. 6d. per annum, for every dog over six months of age. This licence expires on 31st December in each year. He will also require for his gamekeeper, if regularly employed, the usual licence for a man-servant, costing 15s. per annum.

(a) *Owners.*—An owner is allowed by law to shoot game on his own land. If an owner grants the right to shoot to another, but himself still occupies his land, he has a concurrent right to shoot ground game.

(b) *Occupiers.*—If the owner lets his land to a tenant, and grants the right of shooting to the latter, or fails to reserve the right to himself, then the tenant will enjoy the shooting. Land-owners should bear this in mind, and also that a reservation in a deed is construed with strict precision against the person in whose favour it is made. If, therefore, the owner merely reserved the right to "game" he would strictly only have the right to "game" and not to rabbits, woodcock, snipe, quail, and landrail. If, however, he reserved the right of shooting and sporting, this would cover everything.

The occupier has an inalienable right to kill the ground game on the land in his occupation, and if he ceases to occupy by sub-letting, the right passes to the sub-lessee. The right can only be exercised by himself or those persons whom he has authorised in writing. These must be members of his household resident on the land in his occupation, or persons in his ordinary or regular service on the land, or any other person *bona fide* employed by him for reward in taking the ground game. Only one other person besides himself may be authorised to kill by means of firearms. If, however, apart from the Ground Game Acts, the occupier has *full power* to kill rabbits (*i.e.* if he has not entered into an agreement to the contrary), he can invite any number of persons to shoot.

(c) *Shooting Tenants.*—The right to shoot is called in law a *profit à pendre*, *i.e.* an incorporeal hereditament of the same genus as a right of way, or a right to dig gravel, and requires to be dealt with by writing under seal to make it legally effective.

A right of shooting is only a right over the land as it exists at the time, and does not prevent the owner from developing his estate, even to the prejudice of the shooting tenant. A shooting tenant may, of course, acquire his right either from the owner or from a tenant to whom the owner has transferred his right, either expressly or by lack of reservation.

The lessee of shooting rights must use them reasonably, *e.g.* he must not walk over standing corn or work a field of roots so frequently as to injure the crop.

CLOSE SEASONS

If anyone kills hares, pheasants, partridges, grouse, heath or moor game, or blackgame on Sunday or Christmas Day, he is liable to a fine not exceeding £5.

Partridges must not be killed *between* 1st February and 1st September.

Pheasants between 1st February and 1st October.

Blackgame (except in Somerset, Devon, or the New Forest) between 10th December and 20th August.

Grouse between 10th December and 12th August.

Duck and geese between 1st February and 11th August.

The penalty is not exceeding £1 for every head of game.

Under the Wild Birds Protection Acts, for the birds

scheduled thereunder, the close time is between 1st March and 1st August, but this may be varied by order.

The text-books state that hares or *game* may not be killed at night by means of a gun. It may be doubted how far this statement holds good, but it is wise to act upon it; persons who are authorised under the Ground Game Act to kill ground game may not use firearms to do so at night.

It is useful to note that under the Protection of Animals Act, 1911, fines up to £5 are imposed for setting spring traps to catch hares or rabbits, without inspecting such traps once a day between sunrise and sunset.

Protection of Sporting Rights

The protection is twofold, both civil and criminal remedies are provided. But both must not be used by the same person for the same offence, at any rate in connection with the pursuit of game by day; he must elect which remedy he wishes to pursue.

(a) *Civil Remedy*.—The breaking of another man's close gives a right of action at Common Law in which an injunction can be asked for to restrain further trespass and damages.

The trespasser may be removed if he refuses to leave the land, and sufficient force for the purpose may be used. By the law of Scotland an "interdict" may be obtained promptly from the local Sheriff's Court.

(b) *Criminal Remedy*.—Poaching by Day.—The criminal remedy, in the case of a trespasser by day in pursuit of game, can be used both by the actual occupier of the land and by a shooting tenant; whereas in the case of the civil remedy the shooting tenant would have to join the occupier as a party in bringing the action.

Any trespasser by day in pursuit of game can be fined £2, and fine or more trespassers together £5 each, for merely entering or being on the land with that object.

If such a trespasser refuses to quit and to give his name and address he can be arrested and conveyed before a Justice and fined up to £5 costs. The offender must be brought before the Justice within twelve hours, failing which he can be proceeded against by summons or warrant.

If five or more such trespassers together, any of them being armed with a gun, use violence to prevent an authorised person from approaching them to warn them off, they can each be fined £5 and costs.

Poaching by Night.—Between the first hour after sunset and the last hour before sunrise, the Night Poaching Acts provide that any person unlawfully taking any game or rabbits on any land, public road or path, or at the outlets from such land, or unlawfully entering land with a gun or other instrument to take game, is liable, on conviction before two Justices, to three months' hard labour, and, if he then fail to find sureties, to six months' hard labour, with an ascending scale for subsequent offences. There are further penalties for assault with violence, and for the case of three or more poachers entering by night on land, any one of whom has a gun.

By the Poaching Prevention Act the police are given powers of search over persons suspected of poaching and found by them in a highway, street or public place.

Boundary Questions connected with Law of Trespass.—A sportsman who enters on his neighbour's land to gather bird or beast which, before he shot at it was in or rising from such neighbour's land, commits a trespass.

If, however, the day after the shoot he were to go on to his neighbour's land to pick up birds killed at the shoot, it would not be a trespass within the section.

If a bird rose on his own land and he shot it in the air over his neighbour's land, he could go and pick it up, provided it was dead and not merely wounded. Moreover, if it was unable to escape, he could pick it up without committing trespass.

Should a sportsman take his stand on his neighbour's land, to shoot game beaten out of a boundary hedge by a beater on his own land, he will be committing a trespass.

The law is extremely technical. It is far better on these boundary questions to have a friendly working arrangement with your neighbour.

Except in a place where a right of free warren exists, you can only shoot a dog in self-protection or to protect your property in the *bona fide* belief that there was no other way of doing so. You cannot shoot a dog merely for trespassing.

Unlawful Taking of Eggs.—By Section 24 of the Game Act, any person who has not got the right to kill game on any land, who takes from the nest the eggs of any bird of game or any swan, wild duck, teal, or wigeon, or has their eggs in his house or shop, shall, on conviction before two Justices, pay a penalty not exceeding 5s. for each egg.

The powers of search given to policemen under the Poaching Prevention Act cover also the eggs of pheasants and partridges, grouse, and blackgame. The penalty for each egg taken is not exceeding £1.

RATING OF SHOOTING RIGHTS

The rights of sporting, *i.e.* fowling, shooting, or taking game or rabbits, or fishing, are assessed to poor rate, whether exercised by landlord, tenant, or shooting tenant. They are taken into account in arriving at the gross value of land for rating purposes. If the landlord on letting reserves the rights, the tenant will pay and deduct from his rent any increase by which the gross value of the land is swollen by reason of the inclusion of the sporting rights.

Where the rights are let separately from the land, either the person entitled to receive the rent or the shooting tenant may be rated at the will of the persons who make the rate.

LEASES OR AGREEMENTS AS TO SHOOTING RIGHTS

In a yearly tenancy of sporting rights, reasonable notice only is necessary, and apart therefore from special provision, a six months' notice to quit cannot be claimed.

It is well to remember that in a lease for a short period it is desirable to give a game limit, *e.g.* two hundred brace of grouse per annum.

It may be necessary to insert a clause that the tenant is to keep down rabbits, or keep up the stock of partridges in some defined manner; or to provide that the lessor, if he cut timber or undergrowth in a manner prejudicial to the shooting, shall reduce the amount of rent payable.

The tenant may, in suitable cases, be made to covenant not to kill hen pheasants after a certain date, or to preserve foxes and permit hunting, to indemnify the lessor against damage by game under the Agricultural Holdings Act, or to keep down vermin, or not to assign or underlet his rights without the consent of the lessor.

DAMAGE DONE BY GAME

Under the Agricultural Holdings Acts, the last of which was passed in 1923, an agricultural tenant is entitled to compensation for damage to his crops by game (which means for this purpose deer, pheasants, partridges, grouse, and blackgame) in cases where the right to kill the game is not vested in the tenant or anybody claiming under him, other than the landlord, and he has not permission in writing to kill it.

The damage must exceed 1s. per acre of the area over which it extends; the amount may be determined by arbitration, failing agreement, but notice in writing must be given by the tenant without delay.

When the right to kill is vested in some person other than the landlord, the landlord is entitled to be indemnified by such person against all claims for compensation. The arbitrator may also make an allowance where, by a tenancy agreement made before 1909, compensation was payable by the landlord.

In addition to the above provisions there is the Ground Game Act already mentioned, which gives the tenant an inalienable right to kill ground game on his land.

GAMEKEEPERS AND THEIR POWERS

Apart from special powers possessed by gamekeepers appointed by Lords of Manors, with which we have not space to deal, the law gives certain powers to keepers in general, among which may be mentioned:

(1) A right to require anyone doing any act on his employer's land, for which a game licence is necessary, to produce such licence and, on refusal, to give name and address and place of issue of licence.

(2) Power to require a trespasser on his master's land in pursuit of game by day, to quit such land and give name and address, and on refusal to do either of these things, to apprehend him and take him before a Justice.

(3) Power to demand from anyone whom he finds on his master's land by day or night in possession of recently killed game, the delivery up of such game, or, on refusal, to seize it. He must apparently see the game actually in the man's possession and not merely search him on suspicion.

(4) Power to arrest and hand over to the police anyone found on his master's land at night for the purpose of taking or destroying game or rabbits. This power of arrest is only given to keepers of owners or occupiers, not to those whose masters have only the shooting rights.

WILDFOWLING

By J. Inge

"The falling leaves and the fading tree,
The long white line of a sullen sea."

AUTUMN BRINGS to many a "wildfowler" memories of past seasons and the anticipation of others to come. I have composed the following notes in order to initiate the "would-be" wildfowler into the joys and thrills that go hand in hand with long waits and lone nights on mud-flat and tideway.

Large bags are very much the exception; the wildfowler must be content with small returns, and resigned to none.

There is no rule of thumb for wildfowling, the best laid plans go awry. The knowledge expounded in books is of infinitesimal value, when it comes to the whys and wherefores of this sport, but from every season's experience we learn something new.

For those who are unacquainted with the more common species of wildfowl to be found on the marshes and adjoining inland fields (permission to go to them is, in most cases, willingly given), I have given a brief account of their habitats and migration periods. The list of wildfowl is, of course, very incomplete, but I have purposely only dealt with the kinds that the "fowler" will commonly meet in the course of his wanderings. The smaller varieties such as the stint, &c., I have, owing to lack of space, been forced to omit.

SPECIFICATION OF WILDFOWL

GEESE

Note.—The description of colouring in these notes applies only to the adult birds. The varieties of colouring of the young birds are enormous.

Grey Lag Goose.—The nearest relative to our farmyard goose, the grey lag is easily the largest of the wild geese. His weight may be anything up to 10 or 11 lbs. The head, neck, and breast are ashy brown and the stomach is of the same colour with broken bars of a darker brown. The shoulders, rump, and lower back are almost lilac. The bill, legs, and feet are of a pinkish tinge. The tail has a white fringe. This species is the only kind that nests with us, the other four being only foreign visitors. Its nest is found in the North of Scotland and the Hebridean Islands. The foreign visitors of the same species migrate to our shores towards the end of September. Like that of all wildfowl the period of migration extends over several weeks.

White-fronted Goose.—Abundant on the West Coast, in Ireland, also in fair quantities round the Wash. It is easily distinguished by the white patch on its forehead. In general colouring very like the grey lag, but with darker and less broken bars on the stomach and these bars also extend up the chest. The smallest of the grey geese, about 5 lbs. Migrants reach our shore during October, but they are to be found at full strength in December and January.

Pink-foot Goose.—In form like the grey lag but smaller, about 6 to 7 lbs. The bill is black with a pink band where it joins the face. The rump is brown and the upper breast is fawn with no suggestion of grey. The upper tail, coverts and shoulders are of a dark bluish-grey. The feet and legs are of a distinct pink. It nests in Iceland and islands in the locality. The migration period extends from the end of September to the beginning of November. It is abundant on the East Coast; only odd ones have been seen in Ireland. The emigration period, like that of all other wildfowl, takes place in March and April.

Barnacle Goose.—Head, neck, throat, and chest black, except for white forehead, chin, and sides of the head. The back is lilac grey, heavily striped with black and narrow white. The under-parts are grey fading into white below. The wings and tail are dusky brown. The bill, legs, and feet are black. Weight about 4 to 5 lbs. It nests in the Arctic, Spitzbergen being a famous breeding ground. Parties reach us towards the end of September, but are seldom seen in great numbers before the beginning of November. It is plentiful in the North and in West Ireland and the West of Scotland.

Brent Goose.—The smallest of all the geese. Black bill, head, neck, legs, and feet with a small white half-collar on the front of the neck. Breast and under-parts browny slate, white area under tail. Weight between 3 and 4 lbs. The only variety that never goes inland. It nests on the fringe of the Arctic. Migration to its feeding grounds takes place in October. It is very plentiful on the East Coast. Small packs are, however, found all round our shores and in Ireland.

DUCK

Mallard.—Bottle-green head, white ring round neck. Chestnut breast. Dark bottle-green curled-up tail feathers. Primary wing coverts, both sexes, white fringe on edge. Lower parts brown mottled grey. The wild duck is a broken dark brown all over with a bright blue band on the wing. The nearest relative to our farmyard bird. It nests throughout the British Isles in fair numbers. During October two separate migrations take place; our own residents move south, thus making way for the vast flocks of foreign invaders who take possession of our shores and inland marshes.

Wigeon.—Chestnut head with gold crest. Silver grey body. White-edged green patch on wing. Nest plentifully in the North of Scotland. During the month of October wigeon arrive in great companies. Being a salt-water bird, it is never found anywhere (in numbers) except on tidal waters. Small lots or single birds will visit inland ponds and the advent of flooded meadows will also attract them.

Teal.—Head warm brown with a buff-edged green band enclosing the eye and running back to the nape of the neck. Grey black speckled breast and a silver back. By far the smallest of the duck tribe, it is a common resident in the British Isles. In the same way as the mallard, our residents give way to foreign visitors during the months of August and September. It is not really true to say that all the birds nesting with us leave in the afore-mentioned months, because by the process of ringing it has been discovered that many remain here for the winter.

Golden-Eye.—Dark green head and back. Bright golden eye, white breast. A fresh- and salt-water duck that is given to solitude. It nests in the Arctic circle (Scandinavia). The normal migration period is October, though there are early exceptions. The bird makes a peculiar whistling sound with its wings.

Pintail.—Rusty-brown head, browny-grey back, white breast, long narrow tail. This duck nests practically all over Europe, but does not reach our shores in very great numbers. It is a common visitor to the Dee and Mersey, where it arrives about the beginning of October. Elsewhere in the British Isles distribution is uneven.

Pochard.—Dark reddy-brown head, slate-blue bill, greyish-brown back and wings, white under-parts. A fresh-water duck. It breeds in most parts of the British Isles, but never goes far north. Immigration from Northern Temperate regions takes place about the end of September. The bird is very fond of flooded meadows, especially those between the Old and New Bedford rivers.

Tufted Duck.—Drake small black and white with long crest feathers, blue-grey bill. Duck brown and white, no crest. This bird is now a permanent resident in all parts of the British Isles. Migrants reach us in October, and being fresh-water duck will be found on lakes and flooded meadows. Ireland has her full quota of tufted duck, and I have in mind one lough in Northern Ireland that in December is black with them.

WADERS

Knot.—Winter plumage ashen grey with darker streaks, under-parts white with grey lines; there is a bar of white on the wings. Longish grey legs. Breeding plumage; the knot has a circumpolar breeding range as far north as Greenland. The migration period extends from August to October; throughout the winter vast flocks haunt the sands or mud-flats of the East Coast. They migrate to their northern breeding places during the month of April.

Redshank.—Upper-parts and head mottled brown and buff. Under-parts brown barred white. Long bright red legs. This bird is a resident, but at the same time great numbers migrate to our shores from overseas. They are found mostly on the saltings; some, however, spend the day in the inland fields, returning late in the afternoon. April and May show a general movement northwards. In August the young birds appear on the shore, and by September many of them have moved south.

Grey Plover.—Grey with dark speckling. Large black eye. This bird breeds in districts round the Arctic: in the autumn migratory birds reach our shores. They are more often seen on the East Coast than on the West. Summer plumage: the grey plover differs from the golden plover, apart from colouring, in that it possesses a hind toe which does not seem to be of much use to the bird. It finds food on the saltings, though occasionally it ventures inland.

Curlew.—Upper-parts buff, speckled with brown, lower parts white streaked with pale brown. Beak curved and from 6 to 8 ins. long. It is an abundant resident in the British Isles, and nests amongst other places on northern moors. Migrants make their first appearance in August. Night-time seems to be the time they prefer for their immigration. Curlew are found practically everywhere round our coasts. Their mournful and plaintive cry lends an air of entrancing solitude to the waste marshes so dear to the heart of every "fowler."

Snipe.—Buff speckled with brown and dark brown, under-parts light buff speckled with light brown, breast streaked with brown. Brown cap on head, white cheeks, brown band on each side running from base through the eye to the nape of the neck. Long straight head shaded from black at base to buff at top. Three varieties visit our shores. Two are regular visitors, namely the common, or full, and the jack snipe. The great snipe is only very occasionally met with. Immigration takes place from about the middle of October onwards. Apart from our own residents the common snipe breeds all over Europe. The jack snipe never nests in the British Isles, though odd birds stay here during the summer, usually pricked (birds). It immigrates at about the same time as the common snipe. When put up the "jack" seldom flies for more than 80 yards before pitching. The flight of the great snipe is very similar to that of the woodcock, and the bird has many times been confused with the latter. The great snipe has sixteen tail feathers, the common fourteen, and the jack twelve.

Woodcock.—Large liquid black eye. Brown-barred head. Brown narrow crinkled bars on light-brown chest. Darkish-brown back. Long straight brown beak. This bird breeds only sparsely in the south of England, but in Scotland and a few favoured counties farther north, such as Norfolk, it nests frequently. Migratory birds breed in Norway and other districts in that latitude. Visitors reach our shores about the beginning of November (a favoured time is the first new moon in November). The bird is sometimes skin and bone on arrival, but three days' feeding restores it to a normal condition. After that it moves inland and over to Ireland, where it is most abundant.

Golden Plover.—Buff with dark speckling. Large black eye. It has a black bib and head in its breeding plumage. It nests in parts of the British Isles, Wales being a very favoured locality. Elsewhere it nests in Northern and Central Europe. Migration takes place in the autumn. During the winter large flocks will be found on inland fields near the saltings. These birds are abundant in Scotland, the North of England, Lincolnshire, and South Wales.

THE SHOOTING COAT & SOME POSSIBLE METHODS
OF APPROACHING WILDFOWL

A poacher's pocket is preferable to a game bag. The kind of pocket that I have had made for my coat will hold as much as, if not more than the average game bag, and does not lessen the speed of bringing the gun to the ready. This pocket is made as follows:—Procure a piece of mackintosh just short of the width of the coat when spread out, and about 1 ft. 8 ins. deep. Take half the depth of the mackintosh and sew it into the lining of the coat, then fold the other half up so that it lies as near as possible on top of the first half and sew the two ends together. The pocket now is in the form of a large bag that goes right round you; sew three or four buttons on the inside, and your pocket game bag is complete. When carrying the gun on the shoulder, I find a hole is worn by the cross-bolt; this is very easily remedied by sewing a piece of kid glove on to the place where the breech usually rests against the shoulder. For the distribution of cartridges many people use a cartridge belt, but where a belt is not included among the accessories, the manner of distributing thirty or so cartridges about one's person needs every consideration. Personally, I prefer to carry about a dozen or so in the two side-pockets of my coat, and the rest evenly distributed between the side- and hip-pockets of my trousers. If by chance it should come on to rain, those cartridges in your pockets will be kept dry by your coat overlapping them, whereas if you had put them in your coat pockets, apart from being an extra strain on the shoulders, they would all become damp and useless.

To make a start, let us suppose you have arrived at a small village situated, say, on the East Coast. The scene depicted the morning after your arrival is one of entrancing solitude. Sandhills stretch in an endless line north and south. A small river banked by faggots threads its way through the sandhills to the sea, and is known as the "Haven." North of the Haven is a vast expanse of sand and mud-flats, and south of it a large salt-marsh, cut here and there by numerous small channels. Sandhills divide the salt-marsh from the inland marshes or the low-lying fields, which are bounded by dykes. A talk over a pint of beer with the local inhabitants reveals the fact that curlew are going to the inland marshes to feed every morning about seven o'clock and returning to the mud-flats about six o'clock in the evening. There are a few duck and snipe in the dykes: a small bunch of teal is usually to be found where the Haven joins the sea: redshank are plentiful: there are a few grey plover, godwits, and knots: two or three bunches of golden plover haunt the inland marshes.

Possessed with such information, our first step is to get permission from the farmers who own the fields comprising the inland marshes. Permission to shoot duck, snipe, golden plover, and curlew over their land is in nearly every case willingly granted: the one unfailing stipulation is, naturally, that no game must be shot. So be sure, when discussing this subject with the farmer, to emphasise your enthusiasm for the shooting of wildfowl alone.

There is now only one more important piece of information to be sought, namely, the movements of the tides. High tides occur when the moon is new and when it is at the full. It is, however, with the new moon that they reach their highest point. Tides come up roughly an hour later each day, and when the high tides occur from six p.m. onwards, it is the time for the wildfowler to be on the alert. Between the new moon and the full moon the tides are fairly low, and curlew and other waders at eventide remain in comparative security on the sea edge. The only chance of a shot at curlew is to lie hidden in the sandhills and catch them as they come back in the evening from the fields. The high tides, however, bring about quite a different state of affairs, for instead of resting secure till the following morning, the fowl are gradually driven nearer and nearer the shore. The closer they get, the more restless they become, and eventually are forced to take wing. This panorama of birds, unable to settle, flying up and down the coast, is a wonderful sight. Duck also join in the general confusion. During the afternoon, while the tide is out, a place for concealment must be sought. On the salt-marsh, you notice a piece of ground a little higher than the rest: closer inspection shows that the last tide left this part dry. Marsh weed being the only cover available, a pit must be dug, and before doing this you must decide in which direction you are going to shoot. Having satisfied yourself on this point, the next thing to decide is whether a lying or a sitting position is the most convenient. A pit for lying full length is made as follows:—

Dig a "grave" about 6 ft. long, $1\frac{1}{2}$ ft. wide, and between 6 and 10 ins. deep, so that, on lying down, your feet point due east. Place the loose sand along the south side of the pit so that the south wall rises perpendicularly another 6 ins. Smooth down the sand gradually till it reaches the normal level.

You will be quite invisible to birds passing north up the coast.

In order to shoot in a sitting position, I recommend the following, especially on the edge of a marsh or sand-hills:—

Dig a hole about 2 to 3 ft. deep and about 2 ft. square. Cut out of the sides three seats facing the directions best suited. Place the loose sand on the side of the pit where there is no seat, and stick in plenty of marsh weed or marram grass, whichever the case may be. You are now in the position to take birds coming from three directions.

The tide is coming in, and hundreds of waders have gathered on the tide line. An incessant piping can be heard all along the shore. Knot and redshank can be seen flying restlessly up and down the coast. A bunch of curlew have just come over from the inland marshes, and are now hunting the mud for delicate morsels. The tide is coming in rapidly now, and with it must the waders assuredly retreat. The glasses pick out a spring of teal, directly opposite the hide. They are quite unconscious of nearby danger; will they come into shot? Perhaps they do, and if so, presumably, good sport will be obtained. Such are the joys of fowling with the high tide in September. One more point—before isolating yourself on a small island in the marsh, be sure to notice that your line of retreat is not cut off; neglect on this score may, if nothing worse, force you to swim for it, and as you have your gun to think about, that's no joke!

During the day, when the tide is out, you may glean quite good sport by a tramp round the reedy inland dykes. A few snipe will be there, and possibly a duck or two. When walking along dykes remember the golden rule: Never walk along the edge, but always in a line parallel with it about 6 yards or so out. If you walk along the edge, you can be seen all the way up the dyke, and duck won't wait!

Invariably snipe, when put up out of a dyke, will give the impression of a hasty exit to the next parish; but a flushed snipe in a dyke-ridden district will, if watched carefully, be seen to fly round in a large circle, and then suddenly dive down and alight in a dyke, probably not more than two or three hundred yards away. Mark the spot as nearly as you can by a bush or any cattle that may be near by, and walk straight there.

Patience on the part of a gunner plays a great part in his chances of a shot at golden plover. By nature golden plover are amazingly conservative, for they will be found day after day in one particular field, no matter how much they are disturbed. That field will usually be a large one, and plough land or grass meadows are frequently favoured. Through the glasses a flock of golden plover may be seen to settle in a field, and a plan of campaign must now of necessity be thought out. The direction of the wind is of foremost importance (golden plover usually fly up wind if possible), followed by a careful survey of the locality. Is there any possibility of coming on terms with them by stalking? The art of approaching birds unseen by them can only be learnt by experience, and apprenticeship in this art, fostered by many failures, is the only way to succeed. The field is surrounded by dykes, and a stalk up one of these would bring us no closer than 70 or 80 yards to the nearest bird, so that method can be ruled out. Apart from a long tedious wait in the hopes that they may leave the field via your hiding place, there is only one plan left to exploit.

Creep into a ditch, say two fields away, upwind to the

plover. Lay a single cartridge on the bank close at hand, and fire off one barrel into the air, then push your spare cartridge quickly in the vacant chamber, and wait. The plover rise immediately, seeming not to know from which direction the shot has come and, flying low over the ground upwind, may present a fairly respectable target. Many times have I managed to get good results by this method.

Golden plover, passing over out of range, can sometimes be brought well within gunshot, thus: As they approach, fire a shot into the air ahead of them; the effect is to make them dive to earth and pass quickly low over the ground, presenting a hurried shot before climbing speedily heavenwards. The impetus given to their flight by such a descent will often cause the gunner to miss a bunch of a dozen or so birds entirely; so don't be afraid to give a liberal forward allowance. An interesting point about golden plover is that you can whistle a single bird over you, whereas you can whistle a flock until you are blue in the face, and they won't deviate from their course one inch. The reason is simple enough. The single bird is looking for his companions, and the "flock" are intent on finding good feeding pasture. If you can make a noise like a nutritious field, then the flock is yours.

Curlew, in the early part of the season, are very good table birds. I say the early part of the season, and advisedly. From December onwards they seem to grow fleshy armour-plating. The saying goes, "Cook the bird with a brick, and when the brick is done, so is the bird."

In September the young curlew are not wise to the guiles of "fowlers," and here are one or two ways of coming to terms with them. Soon after dawn, and in the early part of the evening, curlew flight to and from the inland fields. These journeys to and fro render it compulsory for them to pass over the sandhills, and by the process of eliminating parts of the dunes not favoured for their transit, a suitable hide can be made for the purpose of interception.

During the day-time, whether in the salt-marsh or in the fresh marshes, curlew are constantly changing their feeding grounds, and if you keep well under cover, your patience will certainly not go unrewarded. Young curlew are by nature inquisitive, and I have constantly tricked these birds passing to one side out of range into easy shooting distance by playing on their inquisitiveness. I have allowed a little white terrier to run about near my "hide," and immediate investigation by any nearby curlew will be the result, perhaps fatal! Another method to be employed on sighting your quarry is to imitate their feeding call, a low-toned trill, and at the same time to raise your hat into the air (in full view of the bird) and give it a shake, but be sure to withdraw it at once out of sight. The curlew will gain the impression that another of its species has found a succulent morsel and is just settling. Round he will come to have a look, and the rest is left to you.

On some parts of the coast the shore is infested with cockle-pickers. Fowl, I have noticed, take little notice of these stooping figures, as they search here and there over the mud-flats. By emulating these cockle-pickers, I have frequently come well within easy range of curlew. But be careful not to look direct at your quarry, for any movements contrary to the roving trade will make them suspicious, and when this happens, I very much doubt the success of the ruse.

A WILD GOOSE CHASE

Permission to pursue barnacle geese on private land included the loan of a keeper (an Irishman with a great sense of humour). He took us along the road, telling us to drop out at intervals of about 60 yards. This manœuvre brought us facing a large open field of turnips, in which about five hundred geese were feeding. In the way of cover we had a high thorn hedge, behind which we hid with the kind of hopes that emulate a pensioned barometer. In the meantime the keeper worked his way round to the back of the geese, with the intention of driving them over our hiding-places.

But something went wrong. The geese rose beautifully at the appearance of the keeper, but instead of coming over us they veered round and took a semi-circular course well to our right, completely out of range. Sadly we watched them cross the sandhills until they became mere specks descending to the island out in the bay. After invoking deities, interspersed with remarks concerning the keeper's past and future, we held a council of war and decided to go to the sandhills to await the return of the geese to their feeding ground. On arriving at the sandhills, we spread out at intervals of 40 yards, and prepared ourselves for their return.

In the distance we heard the faint honking of the geese as they talked over their latest disturbance. A low haze hung over the glassy sea. Not a cloud or a breath of wind disturbed the serenity of the day; sounds there were in plenty, but of a kind that lent a still more peaceful air to these so natural surroundings. All along the shore we could hear the weird call of the curlew, mingled with the shrill piping of the oyster-catchers.

Then came another sound that chased away all else, the sudden far-off clamouring of geese. Some of them must be on wing now. Yes, there they are, a small bunch heading for our hiding-place. We do not worry about these; they are the scouts, sent out to see where the danger (if any) lies. Slowly they pass over, about six of them, talking quietly to themselves; then they wing round, and return as slowly to their flock to make their report. This is evidently satisfactory. A period of silence intervenes, broken only by the waves on the shore. Then the air is suddenly rent by the full-throated cry of the geese. They are all on wing. We grip our guns tighter and settle ourselves into an easier position. Here they come, flying low over the sea in a long line straight for us. An unforgettable panorama is now displayed: the geese are splitting up into groups, and therefore taking the formation of perfect V's and W's. What a sight! We are held enthralled, and almost forget the more serious business in hand. Two-thirds of the geese are a little too high. Suddenly I spot a small bunch lower than the rest, coming straight for me. Nearer and nearer they come, nothing suspecting. Now they are over me. Up I jump. Bang! Bang! A clean miss with the right barrel, but a bull's-eye with the left. The goose falls quite 50 yards behind us. Out of the corner of my eye I see another goose hurtling to earth. The next gun is also in favour with the gods.

It is all over. The geese have gone, honking their grievances to the sky. They will not return.

Pub Lore

The village inn situated in the vicinity of a 'fowling centre is frequently the centre of 'fowling wisdom. Here one learns the movements of birds, and the nature of the tides, whether they be "making" or otherwise. In the evenings, habitués of the local pub come and honour the God Bacchus. During the day they have either been toiling in the fields or watching the marshes; some, after working all day, hurry down to the marshes on the chance of getting a duck at the evening flight. But whatever they have been doing, they will be found seated in the bar-parlour when night comes, "swopping lies" and joking with the landlord. As their tankards are refilled, so their stories reach the "pinch-of-salt" stage. Many an enjoyable evening have I spent in their company, trying to believe the impossible, for unbelief would bring offence where none is meant. First and foremost they are "philosophers," and a kinder-hearted crowd you could not meet anywhere. Rumours of wars and another sixpence on the income-tax do not trouble them at all, but "No beer in the 'ouse to-day, gentlemen," would produce mental and verbal chaos.

I will do my poor best to reproduce one or two of the stories that I have heard. Before I go on, I should like to say that they are unconscious liars, in that their stories, like those of all sportsmen, have an essence of truth in them, but, by constant narration, have grown beyond recognition.

He sat in his favourite corner by the fireside within arms-reach of the bar counter. I came in and sat opposite him. After an exchange of greetings, we started chatting about the scarcity of 'fowl that winter. "Times are not as they were," he said. "Why, I bide the time when the shore 'as been black with duck. Did I ever tell you about the bunch of curlew?" I shook my head; then he started. "I was down on the 'fetties' one day, when I sees a big bunch o' curlew feeding close under a bank; so I says to meself, 'them's yours, George, if you're careful.' So off I goes home and gets me old muzzle-loader and loads 'er right up to the top wi' shot, and a good amount of powder I 'ad in 'er, I may tell you. Then I goes down and creeps along under the bank. Just when I gets into range, up they all get. Bang! Bang!" Here my narrator stood up and took hold of his walking-stick, and pointing it as if it were a gun, proceeded to move the stick about in a circular fashion, as if he were washing the wheels of a car with a hose in a great hurry, at the same time making a swishing sound with his mouth. "Got the 'ole bloomin' lot!" Then he sat down and looked hopefully for another pint. He had it, and deserved it.

On another occasion, I had been on the marshes all day and had returned tired and thirsty to the local inn. Inside an habitué was just about to "hold the floor" with a yarn, which, if my memory proves correct, went something like this: "I were down on the sand-'ills waitin' for the evening flight. In front of me stretched the marshes, and about 30 yards out was a piece of marsh 'igher than the rest. I don't take no notice, but as the tide is comin' in, so this mound becomes an island, which gets smaller and smaller. Suddenly out of the grasses on the mound I sees a pair o' ears pop up; I ses, 'that's funny, it must be an old 'are,' and so it is. Well, the island soon becomes awash, so I waits for the old 'are to come to shore, but 'er doesn't, 'er goes seawards. Now there was biggish waves acomin' in. Well, I lets fly at 'er when I could see 'er, but at the moment I fires a wave comes up and 'ides the 'are; well, I lets fly several more shots whenever I sees 'er, but it's no good. So I does the opposite, and fires when I can't see 'er, with the result I shoots 'er dead; and that's as true as I sit 'ere."

I gave a clap, but it passed quite unnoticed by the admiring group of listeners!

In a little inn on the West Coast of Ireland I had an experience which I shall never forget. The landlord's mother, a dear old soul, "did" for me, and at the same time did herself extraordinarily well with the bottle. She was, unfortunately, a dipsomaniac.

I had been shooting all day and, being very tired, went to bed early. Asleep one minute, awake the next; something had woken me up—the door creaked; a faint light showed and then became brighter. Someone was creeping into my room: by the light of the candle she was holding I recognised the ample form of my hostess. I closed my eyes tight and tried to give the appearance of deep sleep, putting in one or two snores to complete the picture. The light became very bright, and I gathered that she was bending over me to see if I was properly asleep; then the light lost its brilliance. Peeping out, I saw her lean over the bottom of my bed, gently pull up the mattress, and to my amazement produce three bottles of "porter," which she tucked in her dress. Then giving a glance round she made for the door. I "woke up" and asked her what she wanted. She replied, "To see if yer honour were comfortable; good night, sir." I have thought often of my sleep on three bottles of porter (outside, not in); may she be forgiven!

A bitterly cold day—snowflakes swirling, creeks frozen—with numbed fingers and feet you return from the snow-covered wastes to the shelter of the inn. A large fire burns brightly in the bar-parlour. You are chilled to the marrow, and you want something to warm you all over. Mulled ale is the answer (No, it is not an advertisement!). Some inns have cone-shaped brass canisters hung on the walls: take one of these, and have it filled to the top with beer and place therein ginger and some brown sugar. Place the canister in the fire for about two minutes, then pass the warm ale into a tankard, and if the contents have not brought your circulation back to normal, then—have another. But, seriously speaking, it is an infallible beverage for circulating the blood into its proper channels.

Early to bed is the secret of withstanding cold and dreary waits on marsh and mud-flat. Late bed means tiredness later on the next day; when tired you are far more susceptible to cold.

FLIGHTING

Flighting is a word that is used for shooting birds at night and in early morning. What birds are you going to shoot at? or rather what birds are you going to see between sunset and dark or dawn and daylight? First and foremost are the duck. These will have spent the day out at sea sleeping and cruising about, then when darkness creeps on apace they will fly inland or on to the saltings in search of food. Secondly, geese, who feed inland during the day and flight out to some sandbank about an hour before the duck come in. Duck and geese are most regular in their times of arrival and departure, except when influenced by the moon. I will mention this later. At dusk, plover (green and golden) fly here and there with no particular destination in mind; also you will hear, rather than see, snipe landing from dizzy heights on to the fresh and salt-marshes—a rush of wings, a thud—and silence. There seems little doubt that persecution has caused duck to flight in at night and return at dawn, or even before it is light. Many centuries ago they fed during the day like any other fowl, but when fire-arms came into use, they became marked birds, and for security rather than choice they fed under the concealment of darkness. The question must then arise, "Why don't the geese do the same?" The answer is because the expression "silly goose" is quite erroneous; there is no bird able to look after itself so capably as a wild goose, and all wildfowlers are unanimous on that point. Apart from moonlit nights, the period allotted for flighting lasts little more than a quarter of an hour, and if the dusky curtain could be raised for a second, the spectacle of thousands of duck leaving their daylight sanctuary for the feeding-grounds would be a wonderful sight; but all we hear is the swish of wings, with perhaps a fleeting glimpse of a shape like a mangel-wurzel.

SUITABLE PLACES

Let us take first the sanctuary geese. Two well-known sanctuaries are in Norfolk and Gloucestershire. The day is spent on strictly private land, where they can be seen but *not* touched. About an hour before dusk they fly out to some sandbar conspicuous from their point of view, and sleep in security till just after dawn, when they make their way at a tantalizing height to their forbidden feeding-grounds. The only chance you will have of coming on terms with them is when they have a strong—and it must be strong—head-on wind against them, or better still a snowstorm. I remember one bitter morning before dawn lying in a "grave" on the foreshore; snow was driving towards the place where we hoped the geese might be. To cut a long story short, the geese came over not more than 2 yards high (a professional wildfowler in Norfolk will remember this occasion), and our fingers were so numbed we couldn't pull the triggers! But such is wildfowling.

Secondly comes the wild goose that has no sanctuary. On certain parts of the coast there are geese that have no undisturbed feeding-ground, their existence is a precarious one, fortified by cunning observation. Let us take first the example of geese coming into a large open field to feed. Here they come—flying well out of gun-shot till they are over the centre of the field; after flying round two or three times in narrow circles (never within range of the boundary hedges or ditches) they land right in the middle. Through the glasses you see sentries posted while the rest feed. A strong prevailing wind seems to be the only occasion when you may get a shot, but, strange to relate, this method is often unproductive, even though, like most birds, they must rise against the wind; somehow they always scent danger in hedges and ditches, and consequently pass over just out of shot. Short of stalking, which in such open conditions is absolutely useless, there seems only one thing left and that is to dig a pit (when the geese have gone to their night quarters) in the middle of the field, remembering to cart away all the turned up earth. Then place a layer of sticks over the pit and on top of them the vegetation of the field. You must be artistic or—no geese. The next morning at dawn, creep into your pit and cover over your entrance; the rest should need very little imagination. When cattle are feeding in the same field as the geese, it is sometimes possible to get a shot by walking alongside one of these animals: the theatrical cow has even been used, but both methods are pure chance.

Thirdly, there are the geese who feed on a salt-marsh, usually a thousand or so acres in extent. You will probably notice that they frequent a certain area more regularly than another. In order to get a shot you need observation, coupled with a strong element of luck. The following suggestion might come in useful some time. If you can get three more friends so much the better. Supposing you can, dig four pits that occupy the four corners of a rectangle, the pits at the ends of the two longer sides being about half a mile apart, and those at the ends of the shorter sides about 300 yards apart. Patience is what you now require, and to be prepared for a good stay, because marsh geese are not particular about punctuality. If they settle in the rectangle well out of range, a drive might be attempted. If you are by yourself luck plays an even greater part, though a great deal depends on your observation and the way you have camouflaged your pit. Don't make the pit too large in circumference. If it is inclined to fill with water, try sinking a barrel, and if the weather is cold put some straw in the bottom of it, because warm feet will keep your circulation normal, which is a matter of great importance in wildfowling.

"DUCK FLIGHTING"

Duck flighting is divided up into two groups: marsh and inland flighting. By far the most numerous of the duck species that feed on the saltings are the wigeon. Their call of "whee-ew" may be heard any night during the winter, echoing over the mud-flats. They are usually the last to come in to feed and the first to leave, and, unless they have been very much shot at or the weather hard, do not indulge in a preliminary fly round to see if the coast is clear, but swoop in with a roar of wings to their dinner-table. Picture a marsh criss-crossed by creeks that allow the tide water to run out into the sea in front of you. Heavy rains or a high tide very often leave small pools on parts of the marsh where the ditches are not close together. Go to these in the day-time and spend an hour or so in nature study. These pools very often tell a tale; there may be feathers about, or the print of webbed feet on the sides of the pool. Whichever it is, you have learnt something to your advantage. I have noticed on many occasions that if a flock of wigeon have found a particularly good feeding-ground, they will come in there without making a single call and remain in silence for some considerable time. After all, it is quite natural to keep something special to yourself and not make a song about it. As regards concealing yourself preparatory to the evening flight, I never think it matters a brass button whether you lie on a piece of sacking or stand, but what does matter is moving about; when you have decided on your "stand," stay there, and concentrate with eyes and ears. Like any other sport, the secret of wildfowling is to banish worries or anything else entirely from your mind; think only of the duck that may presently arrive, and leave the morrow to take care of itself.

What of the duck that prefer to feed on inland pools and flooded meadows? The most common varieties are the mallard, teal, pochard, and tufted duck. The two latter kinds are usually inland residents, except when severe cold drives them to the coast. These inland duck "flight in" a little earlier than the marsh duck—partly because they have farther to go and partly for scouting purposes. When there is no moon, they are amazingly punctual in the time of their arrival. Night after night I have heard the soft quacking of the drake mallard and the whistle of wings at exactly the same hour. As regards the pools, you can only find out if duck are coming there by the signs, and then make your plans. If there are flooded meadows, you may see quantities of duck on the water and hear them at night, but it is no use going after them until the flood water has gone down, leaving a dabble about two or three inches deep: *then* is the time to lie in wait. Duck, especially shovellers, like to find their food when it lies *just under* the surface.

Now, what of the morning flight? I have purposely left

this item to the last. The ducks have, so to speak, stuffed themselves throughout the night. As the dawn casts its first glimmer over the sky, so the duck rise from their dinner and flight seawards. In the meantime the prospective gunner leaves his warm bed and threads his way sleepily over stiles or sandbanks to a chosen hide, and there awaits the duck. Quite definitely it is no use going out, if (1) the wind is in the ducks' favour, (2) there are no clouds, and (3) there is no strong prevailing wind against them. Personally speaking, I have never found the morning flight satisfactory—an opinion justified by the experience that duck go out before the light is suitable for approximate shooting.

HINTS

Here are a few do's and don'ts with reference to flighting. Always face down wind, as duck travel up wind to settle. Do not look at the sky in search of the 'fowl, your eyes will become watery and duck will pass close overhead, to be heard but not seen—always look at the ground, and *not* skywards until you hear the whistle of wings. Choose a cloudy night in preference to a star-lit one: clouds, especially the fleecy sort, make an excellent background, while stars have the reverse effect. If the night is dark I find it is a great help to fashion a *mud* foresight on the gun. Never forget that in order to shoot properly you must keep warm, but at the same time remember to leave your arms free for raising the gun easily. It is best to have a hat that is turned up at the back and down at the front; use it like this during the day, but turn it back to front at night; your scope of vision will be considerably increased, especially vertically. All this seems very obvious, but I have seen men who ought to know better, entirely disregard these "obvious" rules, with disastrous results. Don't give up waiting until the shooting light has really gone; odd duck often come in after the main flocks. A very great friend of mine always chooses to sing out something about going home, just at the moment when the flight really starts. How often have I thought the flight over, when really the duck that had come in were only a prelude to many more. If you have the time it is always worth while seeing it out. Always make a gunning pit so that you can face, under cover, in any direction. A short while ago I was staying in a locality strange to me; however, I met a well-wisher who insisted that I should come with him to a small pond about half a mile from the sea, the inland side of some sandhills; where he predicted numbers of mallard. On our arrival I found he had previously dug two pits of the ancient chariot type on the side of the pond farthest away from the sea. (Facing the pond you were hidden, but completely exposed *a tergo*.) He then explained that the duck came straight into the pond from the sea, and well they might do if there was a land breeze blowing, but unfortunately that particular night the duck had a wind straight off the sea. What I expected to happen did happen; the duck flew high and fast over the pond, and after travelling a short distance turned and came lower up-wind. Of course they spotted us and passed well to one side, out of range. This latter remark sounds at variance with what I said about concealment at flighting time, but as it happened this particular pond had been shot very little, and the duck had come in earlier than their usual time. If, by chance, you have a duck pond of your own and you want to entice more duck to it—here is a useful tip: get some rabbits' guts, which should not be very hard to obtain, and strew round the edge of the pond, so that they lie just under the water. Personally I have found this method satisfactory in every way and well worth trying, as long as the entrails are not exposed. Another scheme that might be tried for the purpose of increasing your stock is to allow a few tame ducks on the pond, or, better still, a few pinioned wild birds, and then let any strange arrivals get well used to their new surroundings before attempting a shoot.

THE EFFECT OF CHANGES IN THE WEATHER ON WILDFOWL

Up to now I have only made mention of the normal habits of wildfowl under normal weather conditions. Let us see the effect of a hard frost on wildfowl. For the first two days or so of a frost, duck and geese are very wary and are harder to circumvent than at any other time, but as their food becomes more difficult to procure, so they lose their customary caution and fall an easy prey to the vigilant 'fowler. Further, the numbers of duck are considerably augmented by inland 'fowl who, by reason of frozen lakes and ponds, have no other alternative but to seek the marshes. If the frost extends over several weeks they become amazingly tame, and, being nothing but skin and bone, are not worth shot. During the frost there is a general migration south-wards, the movement of waders being especially noticeable; when, however, the thaw sets in, wildfowl return to their former haunts, and in a surprisingly short time attain their normal condition. The thaw period is the proper time for a chance of getting a good bag. As I have said, the birds have been very hungry, and now that their feeding-grounds are uncovered they are going to make up for lost time. They feed greedily and seem not to worry about sentinels; in fact I have known them shot at time and time again, and still they return to the same place. If by chance during hard weather you are fortunate enough to find a fresh-water stream that hasn't frozen, watch it carefully, because here duck will surely come. On the Severn I was lucky enough to find such a stream, and had one of the best day's shooting I have ever had.

Frost and snow so often go hand in hand that it needs but a few words to explain the effect of snow on wildfowl. Imagine it is day-time, the wind is westerly, and the normal routine is preserved, *i.e.* the ducks are on the sea and the geese feeding inland. Quite suddenly the wind veers to the north, dark clouds mass in the sky, and the air grows colder. Small parties of duck come in, the calling of waders becomes more incessant and flocks of them move quickly hither and thither over the marsh, while from somewhere the wind, which is rising now, carries the call of geese to your ears. Everywhere the sky is dark and sullen, and a few small flakes of snow brush against your face; from inland the call of the geese becomes louder and louder; from the sea come large bunches of duck flying at a height of 60 ft. or so. The snow drives into you—shapes of all kinds of wildfowl appear suddenly out of the white blanket, and disappear as quickly. During the storm 'fowl very rarely settle and, as long as you can keep yourself warm, your bag should be good and varied. The storm is over and a mantle of snow covers everything. The feeding-grounds are temporarily covered and sport for the moment is practically over, as the bewildered birds settle after, maybe, hours of flying unnatural for the time of day. The lull may not last long; this period, from the birds' point of view, is given to taking stock of the situation and to assembling their scattered senses. Soon, however, the pangs of hunger set them on wing again in search of food. The duck have, of course, gone out to sea and, but for a few exceptions, will not be seen till the evening, but not so the geese and waders who are daylight feeders; these move aimlessly over the saltings, the geese going inland only to return again shorewards. The advent of snow and frost is, I consider, the only time when geese become "silly," and all other wildfowl lose their customary wariness.

Shooting Under a Moon & its Effect on 'Fowl

I have not the space to deal in full with the moon and its effect on the tides; for practical purposes it will be sufficient to say that high tides coincide with the appearance of a new moon and occur again when the moon is full. In the spring and autumn the tides usually reach their highest.

Shooting duck under a moon is a sport that needs more patience than that advocated by Izaak Walton, primarily because the duck, obviously fearing the unnatural lightness of the night, choose any old time to come in to feed, and instead of flighting in a fixed period, their arrival is extended over several hours.

Now let us study the effect of a moon on geese. If the moon is up or is rising at sunset, they often prefer to stay in their feeding-grounds, and not till later in the night will they leave them. Again, supposing the moon rises during the night, the geese will leave their sand-bar or wherever they are roosting and fly inland to feed (for some reason best known to themselves they usually fly within easy gun-shot under a moonlit sky). During the night small flocks of adventurers will fly, apparently heedless of danger, all round the countryside; this activity is very prominent when a high tide washes them off their sleeping-ground.

Preferably it is best to choose a night when light clouds spread-eagle the sky, as such a background seems to magnify the forms of duck and geese.

As a general rule duck are irregular in their flighting habits, but geese on the other hand will often pursue their nocturnal excursions at very much the same time and in very much the same direction every night; it must, of course, be left to the observant 'fowler to find out when these things happen, as there is no specified time for all localities.

DOGS FOR WILDFOWLING

I know I shall be treading on many people's toes when I say there are only three kinds of dogs of real use for wild-fowling; they are the Irish water spaniel, the black curly-coated retriever, and the black or yellow Labrador. Whatever your choice, your dog must have three outstanding qualities, namely, courage, perseverance, and common sense. Steadi-ness is not always essential; I would much rather have an over-keen dog than one of those look-at-master-and-see-what-to-do dogs. Most of the species to-day have long narrow heads; it seems a pity that the old broad-headed Labradors are fast giving place to the modern creation. I myself am the fortunate owner of a strong-boned, broad-headed yellow Labrador, and though he would be black-balled at any field trial, I would back him anywhere in a battle of wits and common sense.

The great secret in training a dog for wildfowling is to teach him to mark and use his ears, though the latter is really instinct, and needs little encouragement. When my dog was about six months old I used every day to take him to a big field and make him sit. I then walked with a couple of stockings stuffed with hay or straw (something soft it must be) to a point about 150 yards away from the dog; in full view of him I threw one high in the air in one direction and the other one the opposite way. On walking back to him, I patted him and endeavoured to take his mind off the dummies; about two minutes after I made him sit in his place, and then told him to "hie lost." A month or so later I introduced a gun into the performance. "Yes, that is all very well," critics will say, "but he doesn't learn to use his nose." There, I think, they are mistaken, because a dog with "common sense" will go to the fall at once, and if he is unable to see his quarry he will automatically use his nose. I don't say that this method is always successful, because the bird might fall on the dog's blind side and then he will have to be taken to the fall, but nine times out of ten "marking" will save much time and energy, especially when a bird falls the other side of a river or big drain and it means a walk of a mile or so to get over it. I have personally never regretted the hours I spent training my dog to mark. At night-time you must train him to wait for a second or two after a shot, so that he can listen for the satisfying sound of a bird falling; this is most important, especially when the bird is winged, for if it is near water it will not be long in getting to it, and that is when a dog that marks by ear is most needed. I advocate a dog on the large side, primarily because he may be asked to retrieve a bird such as a goose, which will sometimes weigh as much as 10 or 11 lbs.; again, he may have to swim in icy water for some time in search of a winged duck, an effort which will test his strength and courage to the limit.

Last, but by no means least, must be considered the necessity of keeping him warm. Don't let him sit on wet ground or you will have a rheumatic dog on your hands; always remember to put down a piece of sacking or some similar material. When the flight is over, let him run about all the way home, or if you have a car give him a temporary rub down. At home dry him thoroughly all over and DON'T forget the ears, because water, and especially sea water, has a very damaging effect on them.

Colour Scheme of Clothes, Hats & Dogs

Many years ago the colour of clothes played a very important part in game shooting. Lord Spitzbang would write the usual invitation to his guns, adding the particular colour of clothes which they were expected to wear; he would even mention the tailor where they could obtain a suit made of this cloth. This latter incurred, of course, much extra expense, and merely suited the fad of the host, while at the same time it caused great inconvenience to the impecunious guest. Obviously this state of affairs was carrying things too far, but for all that the idea was good in principle. Birds that are designated to the intellectual species, in other words, the "larder" species, are quick to recognise a blot on the landscape, and if the blot is unnatural or does not conform with the general colour scheme, a change in direction of flight soon takes place. Going to the extreme, a suit made of black, white, or red would enable the wearer to put a clean gun to bed, but curiously enough a blend of these colours, would in many localities render him almost invisible. My advice, therefore, is to get a heather mixture coat and hat of strong cloth, and they will stand wear and tear for many years. I have purposely not mentioned trousers; first of all they are an extra expense, secondly nine times out of ten you are squatting or lying in cover. Whatever your nether garments are, let them be grey or brown. I remember wildfowling in Wales a short while ago; three of us were waiting in a marsh for the evening flight. A fourth member of the party soon joined us; he had dark hair and was hatless. As the shadows deepened, so all but one of my friends disappeared from view, but an outstanding feature was left, and that was the dark poll of the fourth member. The interesting point which we all noticed was that, like ourselves, his body had completely evaporated, leaving the impression of a dark blob suspended in mid-air. I am not going to say that our blank evening (we saw nothing at all) is to be credited entirely to the blob, but I think you will agree that it certainly didn't help matters.

By far the most important portion of one's anatomy to

be camouflaged is the face. How often have we all known those occasions when birds have passed over our heads from behind, and quite falsely have we remarked, "If only I had looked round and seen it in time . . . " I say "falsely" because if we had looked round the bird would have flown past out of range, and we cannot but admit that this is only too true. In order to circumvent these annoyances I am persuaded to offer two alternatives, either wear a mask of the same texture as your clothes or plaster your face with mud. The latter evil is a messy business and should only be used in cases of emergency. The former is worth trying and may turn the luck in your favour.

Another point which is worth mentioning is the glitter of the sun on gun barrels; standing above the gun, we may not notice it, but seen at a distance this glitter is most pronounced, and will assuredly catch the eye of any bird in the vicinity. I know of one or two "'fowlers" who have painted the barrels of their guns green. Personally I do not advise people to do this, for obvious reasons, but I have mentioned it in case anyone should be minded to experiment; but what I do lay stress on is the importance of keeping the gun out of sight till the last possible moment.

As regards camouflaged dogs, it does not matter a bit whether he has a bunch of marram grass tied to his tail or a teapot on his head, as long as he sits *still* on the approach of game; for nothing will do more to upset the course of a bird than sudden movement, whether it come from man or beast. For the tyro I give one or two suggestions which I hope will prove helpful.

(1) If a bird is coming head-on, follow the flight (without tilting the head upwards) till it has passed out of sight beyond the brim of your hat; wait a second or two, and when your judgment tells you that it is nearly overhead, then, and not till then, look upwards with gun at the ready.

(2) If birds are approaching, don't run madly to the nearest ditch for concealment, or hurriedly kneel down (such movements, as I have said, are disastrous), but stand perfectly still without so much as fingering the safety catch, till the bird or birds are within range, then raise the gun in a

leisured fashion (don't take that too literally); the movement must be regular, not hurried.

(3) Never go to the marshes without a pair of binoculars, because the approach of birds can be seen quickly and, more important still, their species identified, which will save the misery of a needless wetting, when with the naked eye you thought perhaps that gulls were curlew and teal were golden plover.

(4) A point which applies to all forms of shooting: have nothing to do with people who shout their directions and observations when in the vicinity of game or 'fowl. If you must talk, do it in whispers; birds have very keen hearing and won't wait.

(5) To my disgust, a friend of mine shot a goose out of a skein of twenty at evening flight while smoking a cigar! I must say that such an exhibition goes entirely against the grain, but the fact remains that the geese passed low over his head quite oblivious of the smoke screen beneath them. My own theory is that, from a bird's-eye view, the smoke mingled with the evening shadows and took the form of a light ground-mist, an occurrence to which the geese would be well accustomed.

A Gun for Wildfowling

I am one of those optimistic few who firmly believe that there are very few shots, whether on marsh or in covert, that cannot be made with the ordinary 12-bore and a $2\frac{1}{2}$-in. cartridge. After all, it is the man behind the gun, and not the length of a piece of gas-piping, that does the trick. Adversaries will say: "Ah, he hasn't used a gun that fires heavy charges." On the contrary, I possess a very useful single-barrelled 8-bore with which, on occasions, I have managed to bring off a lucky long shot, but I always liken large and small bore guns to salmon and trout-fishing: when you are fishing for salmon you see trout rising and wish for a trout rod, and vice versa. How often have most of us been waiting for geese with the heavy gun, and perhaps a single duck has passed overhead within easy range; we are not inclined to waste an expensive cartridge on it, but we do wish we had the lighter gun instead.

For people who have more confidence in heavy guns, I should definitely advise the Magnum 12-bore, which fires a cartridge up to 3 ins. in length, although the chamberless kind fire an even longer case. The Magnum has an advantage over heavier guns in that it will take the ordinary 2½-in. case.

SHOT SIZES

There has been more controversy over this subject than any other, and I can only in the matter give advice which has been my standby ever since I took up wildfowling. For snipe, golden plover, &c., use No. 6 shot. For curlew and duck No. 4 shot. Geese require No. 1 or B.B. shot.

This is not an enviable subject to write about, but I am merely quoting facts that have proved satisfactory to myself. I have entirely followed the theory that if two stones, one large and one small, were projected at the same velocity, the heavier object would be the most destructive. On the other hand, a good shot could, with regularity, kill duck and geese with No. 6 or 7 shot, because—and this, I think, the whole point of the question—he will in all probability hit the bird in the head or neck, either of which is the most vulnerable of spots. But supposing his shot was a little too far back, the pellets would then encounter armour-plating in the form of thickly compressed feathers, through which only heavy shot would penetrate. So for the average performer with the gun I advise the heavier shot.

No. 4 shot and larger would, of course, be quite unsuitable for birds of the size of snipe, as (and it often happens) the bird would fly through the pattern without being touched by a single pellet. The smaller the shot the closer the pattern.

MISCELLANEOUS

(1) Geese bunch together when disturbed.
(2) A wounded bird will avoid salt water; this is im-

portant to note, if one has been winged or received any other minor injury, for when he gets a chance he will come ashore and, provided you are concealed, may be easily gathered.

(3) All geese except brent and barnacle fly in skeins.

(4) Distances on shore and inland are very deceptive. Where a bird has been killed inland at a range of 30 yards, another bird, though giving the appearance of a similar shot on a marsh, may be found, if picked up, to be quite double the distance. The only way to accustom yourself to distances on a salt-marsh is to pick out various landmarks and pace them out.

(5) If you are 'fowling when snow is on the ground, a good plan is to slip a nightdress over your clothes, and adorn the whole with a nightcap: a white mask would not be out of the way.

(6) Duck coming in to frozen water usually fly low for the purpose of spotting an open stretch.

(7) Most wildfowl fly in the V or W formation, because the energy used up in flying is reduced at the expense of the leader. It might be imagined that the most advantageous position of birds in flight would be that of a straight line, on the corollary of the astute cyclist who takes up his position behind a 'bus; but as the accepted formation of the aeroplane squadron indicates, the majority of wildfowl naturally assume the position of the V shape, which enables them to utilise in flight the rush of wind from their leader's pinions. Under these conditions the leader of a skein can only remain at the head for a short while, at the conclusion of which he drops to the rear and his place is taken by another.

(8) A pair of light gum boots or waterproof boots are the best all-round footwear for marsh days.

(9) See that a cartridge extractor and a compass form part of your equipment.

(10) Except when flighting late at night, try to make a point of going to bed early.

For those who are already proficient in the art of wild-fowling, I can only hope that what I have said and suggested does not run contrary to what they have already experienced. For those by whom wildfowling is still to be enjoyed, I would hope that something I have written here may prove for them productive of many happy experiences.

AN ANTHOLOGY

COLONEL PETER HAWKER

HAWKER'S DIARIES—A DISCOVERY

COLONEL PETER HAWKER, author of *Instructions to Young Sportsmen in all that Relates to Guns and Shooting*, who died in 1853, from his sixteenth year kept a diary. In it he wrote full accounts of his daily doings, in work, sport, or travel.

After Colonel Hawker's death, these diaries remained in the possession of his family, unread and unknown to the general public. Then, after a lapse of nearly forty years, they were entrusted to the late Sir Ralph Payne-Gallwey, author of *Letters to Young Shooters* and other works on shooting, who, in 1893, published the diaries in two volumes, containing more than a quarter of a million words, prefaced by the statement that they were merely a fragment of the whole.

In the course of time the book went out of print. Shortly after the War of 1914–8, trying to buy a copy, I only obtained one with some difficulty from a second-hand bookseller. It seemed a pity that so valuable and fascinating a book should not be more readily accessible, and it occurred to me that it might be possible to extract from the published diaries the best of the sporting entries, and to put them together in a single volume that should provide a record of Hawker's autumns with partridges and pheasants, and his winters with wildfowl. But then, I reflected, the published diaries were merely extracts from a much larger whole. Would it be possible to make a new book working from the original manuscript?

So I set to work to try to find the owner of the diaries. And after some months, I was fortunate in finding the present representative of the family, great-grandson of Colonel Peter Hawker himself, in Mr. Peter Hawker, then living in France. Mr. Hawker, with the greatest generosity, offered to help me in any way he could. He had portraits, letters, books, prints and other matter of interest to the compiler of a new book dealing with his great-grandfather, and he offered to put all these at my disposal when he should next return to England. But he had in store for me, too, a great disappointment. Not only had the original manuscript of the diaries completely disappeared, but the typed copy from which Sir Ralph Payne-Gallwey had worked could not be found either.

And then the unexpected happened. When Mr. Hawker eventually returned to England, one of the first persons he met in London was a friend who told him that he had some papers belonging to him in a box—I do not remember how they had come into his possession. Anyhow, they turned out to be the typescript copy of the diaries from which Sir Ralph Payne-Gallwey had worked, in the exact condition in which it had been returned to him with proofs from the printers. So there, to my hand, came in a few days the original copy of the diaries for which I had been hoping.

Even so, the diaries were incomplete. There were obvious gaps, and there were references to events which were not in fact included in the entries. Mr. Hawker told me that he believed that his father, before handing the manuscript to Sir Ralph Payne-Gallwey to be typed, or possibly before sending it himself to the typist, had removed a number of pages and had destroyed them. They were pages relating to domestic affairs and of no public interest. But whether when the typed copy had been made the original manuscript was destroyed, no one knows.

At all events, here was the copy, and presently I found myself reading it with even greater interest than I had supposed possible. For here was the answer to a riddle that had puzzled me ever since I first read the diaries published in 1893. Why did Hawker so often, indeed nearly always, go out shooting alone? Why should he have preferred to walk his stubbles and turnips without a shooting companion? Why should he have deprived himself of the assistance of another gun? How was it that a man who was obviously genial and high-spirited preferred to be solitary in his sport? The answer to those questions is that he was not solitary, and often had a companion, but that the editor of his diaries—for some good reason, no doubt, but I cannot tell what it was—frequently removed the name of his companion and assigned the bag to Hawker. And not only did the editor erase the name of the second gun, but that of another companion, who was no less a person than the second Mrs. Hawker. On 1st September 1845, for example, Mrs. Hawker accompanied her husband and his servant, Charles Heath, walking after partridges. Charles Heath's share in the day's sport is deleted from the entry in the diary, and so is the statement that Mrs. Hawker was the only one who came home fresh and hungry after the ten hours' "expedition." On 3rd September, again, which Hawker describes as "another severely hard day," the entry in the typescript copy of the diaries ends with the remark, "All hands (except Mrs. H.) so dead-beat, again, that we could hardly get home from the hills." And this is printed in the published diaries with the words in brackets omitted. Is it not strange? For what could be more interesting than the notion of an early Victorian young woman, in days of crinolines, poke-bonnets, and white pantalettes, going out all day walking after partridges? What kind of skirt did she wear? What sort of boots?

But Mrs. Hawker is not only not allowed to go out shooting with her husband, she is not allowed anywhere with him. One day—9th May 1846—he sits on a camp-stool and shoots rooks, while the keeper loads his gun and Mrs. Hawker picks up the birds. On another day, 15th October of the same year, he records that he "started off with Mrs. Hawker in search of a rare bird which we had seen yesterday, when we ran home for a gun." He takes her with him to see Lancaster the gun-maker; he goes shooting with her alone; she is with him whatever he does. And yet in his diaries as published there is no mention of her; you would hardly know that she existed.

There are other curious alterations and omissions from the text of the diaries, which give oddly different accounts or impressions of what happened, sometimes as regards other people, sometimes as to Hawker himself. At one time, early in his career in the Army, for instance, Hawker was stationed at Ipswich, and organised a raid on the pheasant-coverts of a certain Parson Bond. The parson came out with notices warning the raiders off, and in the published diary you read that "The two first people he warned off were Pearson and myself." If you turn to the original typescript you will find that the two first people were "Colonel Hawker and myself." The organiser of the raid was then a captain.

Again, in the edited diaries, we do not get a really true impression of Hawker as a game shot. He was magnificent, indeed Sir Ralph Payne-Gallwey is perhaps justified in claiming that "in the style of game shooting he pursued he has probably no equal in these days." But he did sometimes miss, and when he did so he honestly chronicled the fact. On 6th September 1845, for instance, he writes that he "never shot better. Brought home 19 partridges and 4 hares, and lost 2 dead birds; and (except two second-barrel shots, much too far off) never fired a blank shot all day." And on 5th January 1846, we read in the typescript that it was "a wet morning, but fine in the afternoon; got two ducks (one from hut), a snipe and 2 jack snipes; fired at 5 more jacks, but it got so dark that I could scarcely see them, and consequently shot badly." In the published diaries the words in brackets in the first entry are deleted, and the second entry is omitted altogether. There are other similar omissions.

As a fisherman, too, Hawker in the printed diaries appears to do marvels. His river was the Test, and he seldom took out his rod without bringing back a good creel of fish. But reference to the typescript shows that occasionally, when he had a fishing companion, the trout which his companion caught are attributed to Hawker. Also, Hawker caught a very large number of his trout trolling with a minnow, and all references to trolling are carefully struck out of the diaries as printed. You would suppose that he never fished except with fly.

E. P.,
1931.

LONGPARISH REVISITED

"1st September 1827.—The greatest day on record—102 partridges and 1 hare (besides 3 brace more birds shot and lost!). I believe, under all circumstances, and at all events in our country, this nearly doubles any day on record in the annals of sporting history!"

And again:

"7th July.—(Longparish.) Took two hours' trolling this evening, and killed 25 large trout.

"9th July.—Made a droll trial of a new-stocked duck-gun which was well done by Carpenter Keil. I knocked down, in 7 shots, 6 bats and a moth!! A duck, at dusk-flight, may therefore know what to expect!

"10th July.—Trolled and killed 20 very large trout indeed, and I then left off, not wanting any more fish to-day."

I read those passages again on a day last summer, and was possessed again with a desire that had been for years in my mind—which was to be able to see for myself the fields through which Colonel Peter Hawker walked when he shot his fifty brace of partridges to his own gun, and the river in which he trolled his minnow for trout. And I shall always remember the pleasure of receiving, through the introduction of a friend, a letter from Major-General Guy Dawnay, the owner of Longparish House, giving me permission to visit the house on whatever day I pleased, and to walk where I liked by the river and about the fields. I do not know when I looked forward more eagerly to the prospects of a journey.

So, on a day of sunshine in October—St. Luke's Day, as it happened, and the air was of St. Luke's Summer—I drove down to Longparish by roads which Hawker must have

known, for our route lay through Basingstoke to Whitchurch, which would have been the road of the stage-coach
to London. Leaving Whitchurch we turned left-handed
down what must have been years ago a dusty little lane, and
within a few minutes we found ourselves among the
thatched roofs of the outskirts of a straggling village, little
changed in its essentials, I should guess, since the days when
Duchess and Sappho trotted at their master's heel, and
Carpenter Keil put a new stock to the duck-gun. Little
changed, too, except for age, must be the noble avenue of
lime trees that line the drive to the house itself, for I see
that in the engraving, by J. Childe, dated 1844, and entitled
"First of September," which illustrates the ninth edition of
Hawker's *Instructions to Young Sportsmen*, the limes already
show well above the distant roof of the house.

In the drive we were met by the keeper, Dobson, with a
Labrador puppy by his side, and I was reminded once more
of that passage in Hawker's diary, which I have not seen
quoted elsewhere when there has been discussion on the
origin of the Labrador. It is under the date 20th October
1814 that he writes of the death of his favourite Newfoundland dog Tiger:

"This dog was of the real St. John's breed, quite black,
with a long head, very fine action, and something of the
otter skin, and not the curly-haired heavy brute that so often
and so commonly disgraces the name of the Newfoundland
dog."

Did Hawker own a Labrador ancestor, "quite black with
something of the otter skin?" If so, here, perhaps, with
Dobson the keeper was a descendant of Tiger.

We walked through a gate in a wall, and found ourselves
on a lawn with the Test flowing beyond it as it flowed all
those years ago, clear between its cresses. Here was the
spot, might not one guess?—where the Colonel tried his
new-stocked duck-gun; and here ran the very water as
Hawker knew it, when he wrote his advice to those who
wished to become something better than a "*Fanatico*" or a
"frying-pan-fisherman," and told the beginner that with
four or five patterns of fly, with "a white moth for dark

nights," he should be able to do as he, Hawker, had done in the rivers he had fished, "vastly well."

But he would not do vastly well to-day. We walked down the river bank, and there in the runs between the cresses lay here a trout and there a trout. But thirty years ago, the keeper told us, in the stretch of water in front of the house it would have been easy to take twenty or thirty brace of fish in a day. You cannot do that to-day, but there are big trout in those sunlit reaches still.

Farther down the bank we stopped opposite an island. The keeper pointed across the river to a spot still known as "Rover's Larder." That is surely a dog's title to fame. Rover was one of Hawker's favourite retrievers. I believe he only mentions him in his diary once, as an old dog, on 5th September 1835, but he must have been a dog of character, for tradition still holds that it was to this spot that Rover took his bones, and Rover's Larder remains a place-name a hundred years after the old dog first retrieved partridges. And it was opposite Rover's Larder that we stood on the very spot chosen by the Colonel for his "First of September" sketch by Childe, with his "cavalry and infantry," and Siney, the rat-catcher, mounted on his donkey and waving a mug. Siney, by the way, was still a name in Longparish village up to a few years ago.

We crossed the river, to walk through a water meadow by a path which I do not doubt often took Hawker and his dogs to other fields and another reach of the river, a chalk path raised above the level of the drenched grass beside it, and we passed by the old mill to whose music he must so often have listened. And for the first time, farther down the road, I came in sight of that lovely half-mile of broad water, channelled and islanded between reeds and cresses, which lies above Longparish, and on the far side of which are the water meadows through which Hawker walked for his snipe and duck. We sat on the bank in the sun, high above the river, and listened to the crying of plover and the whimmering call of coots—sounds, I liked to think, that must have been in the ear of the sportsman with his muzzle loader or his hickory trout rod a hundred years before.

I was reminded, looking across the stream, of a character-istic passage in Hawker's *Instructions*, on the choice of a day for snipe shooting.

"Snipe shooting," he writes, "is like fly fishing: you should not fix a day for it, but when you have warm, windy weather, saddle your horse and gallop to the stream with all possible despatch. Should there have been much rain, allow the wind to dry the rushes a little before you begin to beat the ground, or the snipes may not lie well. Although these birds frequent wet places, yet the very spot on which they sit requires to be dry to their breasts, in order to make them sit close; or, in other words, lie well."

What is curious is that, although Hawker often writes of riding his mare or his pony in order to shoot partridges, I cannot remember any passage in which he writes of riding out after snipe. But the advice he gives has always attracted me; it is so impetuous, he is so eager to begin, and yet tells you that if there has been much rain, you must not do so. He gallops to the ground and then waits for the wind to dry the rushes.

One more passage came to my mind. It is from the first page of his diary, dated September 1802, when he was fifteen. He writes of uncertainty in killing jack snipes:

"The first 13 shots I had at these birds I killed without missing one; have since fired 8 shots at one and missed all."

We came back to the house, for the keeper had told us that in the hall stood the barrel of an old punt-gun with the lock blown away, and my mind went back to a passage in the diary—I had the book in my pocket—wondering whether I was to see the original weapon which so nearly cost Hawker his life. And I cannot doubt that it was the same gun, for we took it from the hall to photograph it, and it corresponds exactly to his description. Here is the passage:

"19th February 1818.—When firing at some geese, my stanchion-gun, of about 96 lbs. weight, was literally blown to atoms! from the breeching to nearly the end of the stock, and though the lock and other appendages were dealing death and destruction in every quarter, and I was for a considerable time on fire, with a pound of gunpowder in my pocket, thank God not the slightest injury was sustained further than the end of one of the oars being blown off. Nothing but the kind intervention of Providence, and my invention for fixing this gun, could possibly have saved my life! The barrel, a Birmingham one (and was to all appearance clean), proved to be scarcely better than unbeat ore or granite-stone! Let this be a caution to discard all barrels that are not twisted."

We stood there by the door looking at the remains of the old weapon. There came from a garden tree the song of a thrush, and I wondered whether Hawker, too, used to link in mind the first song of autumn with the sunlight of St. Luke's Summer.

Eric Parker:
October 1933.

The Three Best Days

1st September 1819.—I have now to record one of the most brilliant day's shooting I ever made in my life, when I consider the many disadvantages I had to encounter. I had but three dogs: poor old Nero who was lame when he started; Red Hector who was so fat and out of wind that he would scarcely hunt; and young Blucher, a puppy that never was in a field but three times before, and who till this day had never seen a shot fired. The country had been for some time clear of corn, and the stubbles in general afforded but thin cover. The scent was so infamously bad that at least two-thirds of the birds I killed were sprung without the dogs finding them. The wind blew quite fresh the whole day, and the coveys were wilder than ever I yet saw them in the first part of the season; and, what was unusual in windy weather, I could scarcely get a bird into the hedges. I had four shooting parties round me, and the best half of my ground was beaten before I took the field, which I never do till after eight o'clock, because I have found, by experience, that dew is death to the dogs, and that a covey, if disturbed on the feed, is much more difficult to disperse than when left till the dew is off the ground. My list of killed and wounded was fairly and precisely as follows:

Misses: 4 very long shots, two of which were struck and feathered.

Kills: 45 partridges and 1 hare, bagged.

The constant succession of long shots that my favourite old Joe Manton barrels continued bringing down, surpassed anything I had before done, or seen, in my whole career of shooting.

4th September 1826.—My first day. The weather mended considerably; but the country was so extremely barren as scarcely to afford a vestige of covert for the birds. The stubbles were all trod down by sheep and "leasers," and, owing to the previous dry weather, there were no turnips large enough to shelter the game. The birds were plentiful, but much wilder than ever I knew them in September; insomuch that scarcely one covey in ten would allow even the dogs to come within gunshot. I, however, by means of mustering a good army of markers, and harassing the birds by repeated charges of cavalry, so completely tired them down at last, that I performed this day the most that ever was done by me or anyone in the annals of Longparish sporting. I bagged 56 partridges and (for our country in one day, a miracle) 7 hares in nine hours: never lost a bird the whole day. Owing to the extreme wildness of the birds, I was, of course, obliged to fire many random shots; but notwithstanding I was so weak from having been so unwell, I may safely say I did not lose a bird through bad shooting the whole day, as the only two fair shots I missed were at single birds, both of which I secured with my second barrel. Taking everything into consideration, this is the greatest day I ever had in my life.

1st September 1827.—The greatest day here on record. One hundred and two partridges and 1 hare, besides 3 brace more birds shot and lost.

N.B.—A cold, dry, strong, easterly wind, with no scent; but I took care to have a fine army of cavalry and infantry, and made ample allowance for the wildness of the birds by the rapidity of our charges. I had no dogs but poor old

Duchess and Sappho, both, like myself, among the "has-beens." I started at nine, had the first "butcher's halloo," or three cheers, for twenty brace, at two. A second "butcher's halloo" twenty minutes before six, and then worked like a slave for the glory of making up fifty brace off my own gun, which I not only did, but, on turning out the game, it proved that I had miscounted, and had gone one brace over the desired number. I believe, under all circumstances, and at all events in our district, this nearly doubles any day on record in the annals of its sporting history.

COLONEL PETER HAWKER:
Diary.

RED LETTER DAYS

THE GREAT SWAN OF LOCH LEE

I had tried two or three days to get at the largest wild swan on Loch Lee, but without success. However, on the sixth, a fine sunny day, as I passed at some distance from the lake where the swans were feeding, they rose and alighted on the largest of the pieces of water; seeing this, and that they were not inclined to take to the sea immediately, I sent the boy who was with me round the lake where they were while I made my preparation for receiving them at their feeding lake, supposing that they would return to it if allowed to rest for an hour or so and then quietly moved; even if they did not alight, I knew that I was pretty sure of their line of flight to the sea, and they seldom flew very high. I waded across part of the loch to an island, where I determined to await them, and set to work to make up a hiding-place of long heather, &c. This done, I loaded my gun with large shot and cartridges, and established myself behind my barricade. With my glass I saw the boy and retriever go round towards them; the appearance of the swans floating quietly on the water was most picturesque, their white forms being clearly defined on the dark blue water, and their shadows almost as distinct as themselves. They all held their heads erect, watching the boy, who, as he had been instructed, walked to and fro opposite the birds and sufficiently near to put them up, but without appearing to be in pursuit of them. I hoped by this means to drive them over to the loch where I was concealed without frightening them so much as to make them take off to the sea; but they seemed so unwilling to rise, and so little afraid of the boy, whom they appeared to look at with curiosity rather than alarm, that I struck a light in order to smoke the pipe of patience and resignation, for, fine as the day was for March, my situation in a damp island and wet through above my knees began to be uncomfortable.

The latakia was not half puffed away when I heard the well-known warning cry of the swans, and immediately looking round saw them just flapping along the water preparatory to their flight. Cocking my gun, I waited anxiously to see in what direction they would fly. At first they made straight eastward, as if off for the bay of Findhorn, but after a short flight in that direction they turned, and I saw them coming three and three together, as usual, straight towards where I was concealed. In a few minutes they were exactly over my head, at a good height, but still within shot, flying with their long necks stretched straight out and their black feet tucked up, but plainly visible as they passed over me. I stood up and took a deliberate aim at the largest of them as he ascended higher into the air at my unexpected appearance. The first barrel seemed to have little effect on them, though I distinctly heard the shot rattle on his strong quills; the second, however, which was loaded with larger shot, was more effective: whilst his two companions continued crying to each other, he remained silent. However, he kept up with the rest, and they all went off towards the bay. In the meantime three smaller swans came within twenty yards of me or less, trumpeting and calling loudly.

With the glass I watched the bird I had fired at, as I knew he was hard hit. He still, however, held his way with the rest, and they were gradually getting indistinct when I suddenly saw him rise up into the air, his snowy plumage shining as it caught the rays of the sun. I saw him a second time rise perpendicularly to a great height; he then suddenly turned backwards in the air and tumbled headlong to the ground perfectly dead. He was above half a mile or more from me, in the direction of the bay, and the whole intervening ground was covered with sandhills and bent, so that I could not see the exact spot where he fell, whether on the dry ground or in the sea. However, I marked the direction as well as I could, and set off after him.

Large as he was, I had a long and for some time a fruitless search amongst the broken sandhills. At length I came to the swan, who was lying stretched out on the sand, and a noble bird he was. I shouldered him as well as his great length would enable me to do, and carried him back to where the boy was waiting for me. I found him, too, no slight burden; he weighed above 27 lbs.; the breadth between his wings 8 ft., and his length 5 ft. Of all the swans I ever killed he was by far the largest, the usual weight being from 15 to 18 lbs.

CHARLES ST. JOHN:
A Tour in Sutherland.

THE MUCKLE HART OF BENMORE

Sunday.—This evening Malcolm, the shepherd of the shealing at the foot of Benmore, returning from church, reported his having crossed in the hill a track of a hart of extraordinary size; and he guessed it must be "the muckle stag of Benmore." This was an animal seldom seen, but which had long been the talk and marvel of the shepherds for its wonderful size and cunning. They love the marvellous, and in their report "the muckle stag" bore a charmed life; he was unapproachable and invulnerable.

Monday.—This morning at sunrise, I with my rifle, Donald carrying my double-barrel, and Bran, took our way up the glen to the shealing at the foot of Benmore. Donald had no heart for this expedition. He is not addicted to superfluous conversation, but I heard him mutter something of a "feckless errand—as good deer nearer hame."

As night fell, we turned down to the shealing rather disheartened; but the shepherd cheered me by telling me that the hart was still in that district, and describing his track, which he said was like that of a good-sized heifer.

Tuesday.—We were off again by daybreak. Towards the afternoon, when we had tired ourselves with looking with our glasses at every corrie in that side of the hill, at length, in crossing a bare and boggy piece of ground, Donald suddenly stopped, with a Gaelic exclamation and pointed— and there, to be sure, was a full fresh footprint, the largest mark of a deer either of us had ever seen. There was no more grumbling. Both of us were instantly as much on the alert as when we started on our adventure. We traced the track as long as the ground would allow. Where we lost it, it seemed to point down the little burn, which soon lost itself to our view in a gorge of bare rocks. We proceeded now very cautiously and taking up our station on a concealed ledge of one of the rocks, began to search the valley below with our telescopes. It was a large flat, strewed with huge slabs of stone, and surrounded on all sides but one with dark rocks. At the farther end were two black lochs, connected by a sluggish stream; besides the larger loch a bit of coarse grass and rushes, where we could distinguish a brood of wild ducks swimming in and out. It was difficult ground to see a deer in, if lying; and I had almost given up seeking, when Donald's glass became motionless, and he gave a sort of grunt as he changed his posture, but without taking the glass from his eye. "Ugh! I'm thinking yon's him, sir: I'm seeing his horns." I was at first incredulous. What he showed me close to the long grass I have mentioned looked for all the world like some withered sticks; but the doubt was short. While we gazed the stag rose and commenced feeding; and at last I saw the great hart of Benmore!

He was a long way off, perhaps a mile and a half, but in excellent ground for getting at him. Our plan was so arranged. I was to stalk him with a rifle, while Donald with my gun and Bran, was to get round, out of sight, to the pass by which the deer was likely to leave the valley. My task was apparently very easy. After getting down behind the rock I had scarcely to stoop my head, but to walk up within shot, so favourable was the ground and the wind. I walked cautiously, however, and slowly, to give Donald time to reach the pass. I was now within three hundred yards of him, when, as I leant against a slab of stone, all hid below my eyes, I saw him give a sudden start, stop feeding, and look round suspiciously. What a noble beast! What a stretch of antlers! with a mane like a lion! He stood for a minute or two snuffing every breath. I could not guess the cause of his alarm; it was not myself, the light wind blew fair down from him upon me; and I knew Donald would give him no inkling of his whereabouts.

He presently began to move, and came at a slow trot directly towards me. My pulse beat high. Another hundred yards forward and he is mine! But it was not so to be. He took the top of a steep bank that commanded my position, saw me in an instant, and was off at the speed of twenty miles an hour to a pass wide from where Donald was hid. While clattering up the hill, scattering the loose stones behind him, two other stags joined him, who had evidently been put up by Donald, and had given the alarm to my quarry. It was then that his great size was conspicuous. I could see with my glass they were full-grown stags, and with good heads, but they looked like fallow deer as they followed him up the crag.

Wednesday.—We were up an hour before daylight. We struck at one place the track of the three deer, but of the animals themselves we saw nothing. We kept exploring corrie after corrie till night fell; and as it was in vain to think of returning to the shealing, which yet was the nearest roof, we were content to find a sort of niche in the rock, tolerably screened from all winds; and having almost filled it with long heather, flower upwards, we wrapped our plaids round us, and slept pretty comfortably.

Thursday.—A dip in the burn below our bivouac renovated me; and we started with renewed courage. About mid-day we came on a shealing beside a long narrow loch, fringed with beautiful weeping birches, and there we found means to cook some grouse which I had shot to supply our exhausted larder. The shepherd, who had "no Sassenach," cheered us by his report of "the deer" being lately seen, and describing his usual haunts. Donald was plainly getting disgusted and home-sick. For myself, I looked upon it as my fate, that I must have that hart; so on we trudged. Repeatedly, that afternoon we came upon the fresh tracks of our chase, but still he remained invisible. As it got dark the weather suddenly changed, and I was glad enough to let Donald seek for the bearings of a "whisky bothie" which he had heard of at our last stopping-place.

Friday.—From the state in which my trusty companion was, with his head in a heap of ashes, I saw it would serve no purpose to awake him, even if I were able to do so. It was quite clear he could be good for nothing all day. I therefore secured some breakfast and provisions for the day (part of them oatcake, which I baked for myself), tied up Bran to await Donald's restoration, and departed with my rifle alone.

It was getting late, and I made up my mind that my most prudent plan was to arrange a bivouac before it became quite dark. My wallet was empty except for a few crumbs, the remains of my morning's baking. It was necessary to provide food: and just as the necessity occurred to me, I heard, through the mist, the call of a cock grouse as he lighted close to me. I contrived to get his head between me and the sky as he was strutting and croaking on a hillock close at hand; and aiming at where his body ought to be, I fired my rifle. On going to the place I found I had not only killed him, but also his mate, whom I had not seen. It was a commencement of good luck. Sitting down I speedily skinned my birds, and took them down to the burn to wash them before cooking. In crossing a sandy spot beside the burn, I came upon—could I believe my eyes?—"the Track!" Like Robinson Crusoe in the same circumstances, I started back; but was speedily at work taking my information. There were prints enough to show that the hart had crossed at a walk leisurely. It must have been lately, for it was since the burn had returned to its natural size, after last night's flood. But nothing could be done till morning, so I set about my cooking.

Saturday.—Need I say my first object was to go down and examine the track anew? There was no mistake. It was impossible to doubt that "the muckle hart of Benmore" had actually walked through that burn a few hours before me, and in the same direction. I followed the track, and breasted the opposite hill. . . .

Looking through a tuft of rushes, I had a perfect view of the noble animal, lying on the open hillock, lazily stretched out at length, and only moving now and then to scratch his flank with his horn. I watched him for fully an hour, the water up to my knees all the time. At length he stirred, gathered himself together, and rose; and arching his back, he stretched himself just as a bullock does when rising from his night's lair. My heart throbbed, as turning all round he seemed to try the wind for his security, and then walked straight to the burn, at a point about one hundred and fifty yards from me. I was much tempted, but had resolution to reserve my fire, reflecting that I had but one barrel. He went into the burn at a deep pool, and standing in it up to his knees, took a long drink. I stooped to put on a new copper cap and prick the nipple of my rifle and—on looking up again he was gone! I was in despair; and was on the point of moving rashly, when I saw his horns again appear a little farther off, but not more than fifty yards from the burn. By and by they lowered, and I judged he was lying down. "You are mine at last," I said; and I crept cautiously up the bed of the burn till I was opposite where he had lain down.

I carefully and inch by inch placed my rifle over the bank, and then ventured to look along it. I could only see his horns but within easy shot. I was afraid to move higher up the bed of the burn, where I could have seen his body; the direction of the wind made that dangerous. I took breath for a moment, and screwed up my nerves; and then, with my cocked rifle at my shoulder and my finger on the trigger, I kicked a stone which splashed into the water. He started up instantly; but exposed only his front to me. Still he was very near, scarcely fifty yards, and I fired at his throat just where it joins the head. He dropped on his knees to my shot; but was up again in a moment, and went staggering up the hill. Oh, for one hour of Bran! Although he kept on at a mad pace I saw he was becoming too weak for the hill. He swerved and turned back to the burn; and came headlong down within ten yards of me, tumbling into it apparently dead.

Feeling confident, from the place where my ball had taken effect, that he was dead, I threw down my rifle and went up to him with my hunting knife. I found him stretched out, and, as I thought, dying; I laid hold of his horns to raise his head to bleed him. I had scarcely touched him, when he sprang up, flinging me back on the stones. It was an awkward position. I was stunned by the violent fall; behind me was a steep bank of seven or eight feet high; before me the bleeding stag with his horns levelled at me, and cutting me off from my rifle. In desperation I moved: when he instantly charged, but fortunately tumbled ere he quite reached me. He drew back again like a ram about to butt, and then stood still with his head lowered, and his eyes bloody and swelled, glaring upon me. His mane and all his coat were dripping with water and blood; and as he now and then tossed his head with an angry snort, he looked like some savage beast of prey. We stood mutually at bay for some time, till recovering myself I jumped out of the burn so suddenly that he had not time to run at me, and from the bank above I dashed my plaid over his eyes, and threw myself upon him.

I cannot account for my folly, and it nearly cost me dear. The poor beast struggled desperately, and his remaining strength foiled me in every attempt to stab him in front; and he at length made off, tumbling me down, but carrying with him a stab in the leg which lamed him. I ran and picked up my rifle, and then kept him in view, as he rushed down the burn on three legs towards the loch. He took the water and stood at bay up to his chest in it. As soon as he halted I commenced loading my rifle, when to my dismay I found that all the balls I had remaining were for my double-barrel, and were a size too large for my rifle. I sat down and commenced scraping one to the right size, an operation that seemed interminable. At last I succeeded; and, having loaded, the poor stag remaining perfectly still, I went up within twenty yards of him and shot him through the head. He turned over and floated, perfectly dead. I waded in and towed him ashore, and then had leisure to look at my wounds and bruises, which were not serious, except my shin-bone, which was scraped from ankle to knee by his horn.

CHARLES ST. JOHN:
Wild Sports & Natural History.

KEEPERS, POACHERS & FOXES

GROUSE IN THE STOOKS

Once, having received sure information that a certain farmer was poaching grouse, I, in the early morning, lay in wait in a ditch near an oat-field which was being reaped. Grouse were flying about, and presently I heard two shots from the neighbourhood of the reaper. The pack of grouse which had been shot at flew past me, and two birds dropped dead out of it, but from my position I could not see who had fired at the grouse.

The farmer continued to reap as I came up, and only stopped his team at my request. He was a good actor, for the manner he declared that he had heard no one shoot was almost convincing.

There was nothing to be learned from the farmer or his workpeople, but I walked along the first line of stooks, and, seeing a couple of grouse feathers at one, lifted a sheaf, when there lay two brace of warm grouse. An inspection of a neighbouring stook revealed the farmer's nice new hammerless gun, and with that under my arm, and the grouse in my other hand, I marched smartly away for home.

I had gone some distance when, hearing a call, I looked round to find a very humble farmer following me up. He seemed at a loss for a beginning, so I told him that I had found a nice gun and two brace of grouse in his stooks, and, as they seemed to belong to nobody, I was about to hand them into the Estate Office.

The farmer said:

"I'm no' goin' to deny the gun is mine, and I would be obliged if you give it to me back."

"Did you shoot those grouse?"

"I did that, but I'll never shoot grouse again, if you do not report me this time."

Of course I reported him, for otherwise it would be impossible for me ever to report a farmer again for game shooting.

DUGALD MACINTYRE:
Highland Gamekeeper.

THE LINCOLNSHIRE POACHER

When I was bound apprentice in famous Lincolnshire
Full well I served my master for more than seven year,
Till I took up to poaching, as you shall quickly hear:
 O! 'tis my delight on a shining night
  In the season of the year!

As me and my companions were setting of a snare,
'Twas then we spied the gamekeeper—for him we did not care,
For we can wrestle and fight, my boys, and jump o'er anywhere.

As me and my companions were setting four or five,
And taking 'em up again, we caught a hare alive,
We took the hare alive, my boys, and through the woods did steer.

I threw him on my shoulder, and then we trudgèd home,
We took him to a neighbour's house, and sold him for a crown,
We sold him for a crown, my boys, but I did not tell you where.

Success to every gentleman that lives in Lincolnshire,
Success to every poacher that wants to sell a hare,
Bad luck to every gamekeeper that will not sell his deer—
 O! 'tis my delight on a shining night
  In the season of the year!

OLD SONG.

POACHERS & PARTRIDGES

Partridges may very easily be preserved from poachers taking them at night with nets. It is a custom, generally speaking, when gentlemen take pains to preserve their game, to lay thorn bushes in the stubbles. I hold this custom to be of very little utility; for the two men who carry the net only halt a moment, when a third, who follows the net lifts it up over the thorn bush, and then they draw on; and they can always see the bush, unless the night be intensely dark; and even then, if careful, they can instantly feel that the net touches when they have but to halt and let the man behind free it.

There is a much better method; which is, to stick stakes about as big as your thumb, 3 ft. 6 ins. long, with one end well fastened, into the ground. These stakes they cannot see, unless of a moonlight night. But there is another method, preferable to all the rest, which I never as yet have heard to have been practised, and it is infallible:—Keep a boy mounted on a jack-ass; let him have two long-legged spring spaniels (not the small cocking spaniel) under his care, and feed them himself, that the dogs may know him well and follow kindly. Let him go out, not before it is quite dark, and hunt all the stubbles, and particularly the standing clover, for the breadth of half a mile all round your house. This will not take him much above three hours; he has only to lie in bed two hours longer in the morning. When a covey of birds is sprung at night, they separate and go various ways, and by far the greater part get to some hedge, if there be any, and the country be not quite open; for if it be ever so dark, they can distinguish the hedge by the darkness of its appearance: besides, as they fly very low, provided the hedge be of any moderate height, they are sure to see it. There they are perfectly safe; and also in the middle of a field, for no two birds will light together. Follow this method, and no netter, by night, can ever catch a covey; he may chance to catch a single bird.

COLONEL GEORGE HANGER:
To All Sportsmen.

Caught by the Wrist

One day I came on four poachers and three lurchers hunting a large root-field for hares, and I saw them get one hare. From the nature of the landscape it was impossible for me to get near the men, so I simply gave chase.

Off went three of the men at a great pace, but the fourth, a stout, square-built chap, was fifty yards behind the others, and I was gaining on him fast, when he threw away three rabbits, and began to run much better. It seemed that I must put on a spurt, and I did so, when my stout friend threw a hare away, and set off again at a great pace.

The men had had a good fright, so I was about to lift the hare and go back to pick up the spoils of war in the shape of the rabbits, when the stout man sent his lurcher for the hare. The well-trained lurcher lifted the hare almost out of my hand, and carried it off, bounding joyously along beside its master.

I put on a spurt, when the poacher again told his well-trained dog to drop the hare, and it obeyed. Once again I was about to lift the hare when the dog took it away, and, exasperated, I peppered the dog in the rump, and it dropped the hare for good. The animal had only been dusted with the small shot I had used, but it was out of action for a time, and I heard that its master was much enraged at me, and meant to give me the thrashing I deserved on the first opportunity.

The man was noted as a boxer, but I knew that if I once had him in a wrestling grip I had nothing to fear from him, as very few of the companions of my youth had managed to put me down.

The boxer lay for me on the public road one night, and we had it out. He hit me once on the left eye, and was in the act of repeating the blow when I caught his wrist, and it was then easy for me to work him into a good position for the final throw. He was gasping when I looked for a softer place than a stone wall to throw him down at, and I unclasped him, when he fell on his face. When in the act of rising he invited what he got, and I heard that the poacher had to keep to his bed for a fortnight after our encounter.

I heard that the man knew I was no boxer, and that, confident in his agility and power of dodging, he believed he could "mark me," that is, give me a couple of black eyes and get away with it. So he might, if I had been foolish enough to try to box with him, but, as it happened, I had it all planned what to do in the event of an attack by a boxer. My idea (of gripping the hand which attempts to strike) will always work out, if one is quick enough of eye, and strong enough of hand, to work the scheme properly.

DUGALD MACINTYRE:
Highland Gamekeeper.

How to Banish Foxes

It is well known that foxes destroy much game; not when the game is grown up and can fly, but by catching hen-pheasants and partridges when they sit on their eggs. If you doubt this, dig out a litter of young foxes and you will find, in the hole, the legs of many pheasants, partridges, and young hares. I would not, on any account, destroy a fox where hounds are kept; I think it a dishonourable and ungentleman-like act; but I would desire the master of the hounds to draw my cover frequently in the spring of the year, and I would dig in all the earths, and if a fox draws the holes open, which they will do, provided they are fond of and attached to the spot, then you should funk the earths with brimstone and assa-fœtida, or push a dead cat (stinking) as far as you can into the hole, or anything else which is filthy; for a fox is a clean animal, and will go somewhere else to breed.

COLONEL GEORGE HANGER:
To All Sportsmen.

Shooting Foxes

We perceived, as we coasted along, some men whom we had heard shooting; and hallooing to them, and approaching nearer the shore, found they were two fox hunters. They had just killed, as they informed us, a bitch fox and some cubs, and had earthed a wild cat, which, had there been any hopes of destroying, we should readily have joined in making the attempt; but, they assured us, they had sufficiently tried, and found it impracticable.

English sportsmen must not conceive that these men are mounted even on Highland *shelties*, or that they are furnished with caps, whips, horns, and thirty couple of hounds. They are merely on foot, dressed in Scotch bonnets, with *brogues*, by way of shoes, the rest as they can. They carry a very awkward gun, loaded with swan shot, have a brace of half-starved mongrel greyhounds, four or five couple of still worse fed hounds, called here *slow* hounds, in opposition to the *grey*-hound, and a couple or more of lame, but savage, bandy-legged terriers. One-half at least of these quadrupeds are eaten up with the mange, of which they must cure themselves, as little attention is paid to them.

We threw our brother sportsmen half-a-crown to drink the joys of a *tallyho*! but doubted much whether they clearly comprehended the cause of our bounty, though there could be little doubt but that they tasted the effects of it.

COLONEL THORNTON:
A Sporting Tour.

BROAD-TAILED KITES

There is no animal more easily caught than the large forked-tail kite; nor is there any animal more destructive to game, and especially to partridges. Suppose that they only destroy one partridge in a week, here is a direct loss of twenty-six pair of birds for the next breeding season.

Vermin destroy more game in the year than is ever shot on the manor. Recollect that there are numbers of their enemies at work by night as well as by day, and, provided the vermin be not destroyed, a manor cannot be well stocked with game. It is full as necessary to employ a vermin-catcher (but it is very difficult to find one who is skilful) as it is to keep gamekeepers, to preserve your game from poachers. The following methods, receipts, and lures, I assure you I have acquired the knowledge of, at a considerable expense, in a course of above thirty years, from the most experienced vermin-catchers; and, you may rely on it, you will find them succeed to your best wishes and satisfaction.

First, to the broad-tail kite: this bird is easily caught. I must first observe that a vermin-catcher should be provided with one dozen, or a dozen and half, of iron traps: the common warren-rabbit trap is the best; it should be about eight inches square (not round), a square trap will catch with much greater certainty than a round one. For the kite, set the trap against a bush which extends a little, so that you may place the end of it against the bush, and that the trap may be somewhat flanked on each side by the bush, that he must walk on to it. Bury the trap well, and fasten a piece of bullock's lights to the bridge of it; then strew about two handfuls of feathers round and over the trap; the feathers will lure him down from a great height, he supposing some bird lies killed there. All hawks are to be caught in the same way.

Magpies and jays destroy many partridges and pheasant nests by sucking the eggs. The best method of destroying them is to set a trap in the woods. You observe them frequently before the leaves are on the trees: lay a hen's egg on the bridge of the trap. These are both very cunning birds, therefore the trap must be well covered. A magpie is a most destructive animal, for he will kill young pheasants, partridges, and all sorts of young poultry; and, I have been informed, they will pick the eyes out of lambs not long dropped, and kill them.

Polecats, weasels, and stoats are thus to be destroyed: set a trap where you observe them run; let it be well covered with earth; take a small bird, sparrow, linnet, &c., &c. DIP THE TIPS OF THE BIRD'S WINGS IN TINCTURE OF MUSK; stick a pointed stick into the bird's throat, and suspend him directly over the bridge of the trap, about five or six inches high. The tincture of musk will lure all these vermin at a considerable distance.

There is an animal which, in Norfolk and Suffolk, is called a lobster; I know not why, for he certainly is of the same species as the weasel and stoat, but much larger: no vermin which run are so fatally destructive to all game as these animals; they will absolutely hunt a hare down which is above half grown. A gamekeeper assured me that, about three years ago, he saw one which was hunting a young hare, as regularly as a hound would do. The animal got away from him in a hedge. About two hours after, returning that way, in the next field, a turnip field, he observed a hare, above half grown, cross the path, and this devil of an animal following, and hunting it by the foot, a very few yards behind. He had a good dog for vermin with him, and killed it. This most destructive animal may be destroyed in the same manner as the polecat, stoat, and weasel.

COLONEL GEORGE HANGER:
To All Sportsmen.

DOGS & THEIR MASTERS

Comfort for Dogs

I ALWAYS make my dogs *my companions* in the shooting season; taking them into the room where I sit, after I am returned from the field; letting them bask themselves by the fire, which comforts them, and does them a great deal of good, especially when, after rain, the turnips are very wet. This method, I am certain, prevents many from having the rheumatism.

Would you like, when you return from shooting, to be put into a parlour, as they call it, at an ale-house, in which there has not been a fire lighted for a week?—I always request the favour that I may be permitted to have a small round table, near the fire, in the kitchen. There I sit and roast myself till I am nearly hot through; and I am certain that method has preserved me from disorders and maladies; particularly from the rheumatism, for I never experienced the smallest attack from it in my life, which is a very singular thing for an officer to assert, who has, for many years, slept under the canopy of heaven (generally speaking), and nothing above him but the skies.

Colonel George Hanger:
To All Sportsmen.

Language of Looks

Whenever speaking to a dog, whether encouragingly or

reprovingly, the sportsman should endeavour to *look* what he means, and the dog will understand him. The dog will understand the look, if he does not the words. The sportsman should never, with a smile on his countenance, punish a dog; nor commend him when he has done well, but with an apparent hearty goodwill: the dog will then take an interest in obeying him. Gamekeepers and dog-breakers are often odd fellows, and seldom natives of the place where they follow their avocation. Many of them are particularly loquacious to the dogs. Should one of these queer specimens jabber in a Cornish or Yorkshire dialect to a dog trained on the Grampians, the dog will understand from his look whether he is pleased or offended, but nothing more. The dog has not the gift of tongues, but he is a Lavater in physiognomy!

The Oakleigh Shooting Code.

FEED YOUR DOGS YOURSELF

I have ever, throughout life, fed my own dogs, after they came home from the day's sport. If I had twenty servants, one should prepare the food for them; but I would not so much as allow him to be present when they are fed. The advantages you acquire are very great by doing this yourself: first, you make the dog attached to you, and only to you; for which reason he will hunt the better for you, and infallibly be more obedient. If your servant feeds him, the dog is always looking after him, and cares not one curse for you. What a pretty situation you are in, with an ignorant groom, who knows not, in the smallest degree, how to hunt or treat a dog in the field. By heavens, you had as well stay at home, either for the pleasure or the sport you will have! It is different with gentlemen of fortune, who can afford to keep a regular gamekeeper and dog-breaker, who knows well his business. Then the master has nothing more to do than to go up and shoot, when his dogs stand: everything else is the keeper's business. This is going into the field in grand style, as it may be truly said; but a wandering, poor vagabond like myself, mounted on a mule, with a boy, hired for the time, riding behind me, cannot enjoy such luxuries.

COLONEL GEORGE HANGER:
To All Sportsmen.

COBBETT'S DOG

A *professed shot* is, almost always, a very disagreeable brother sportsman. He must, in the first place, have a head rather of the emptiest to *pride himself* upon so poor a talent. Then he is always out of temper, if the game fail, or if he miss it. He never participates in that great delight which all sensible men enjoy at beholding the beautiful action, the docility, the zeal, the wonderful sagacity of the pointer and the setter. He is always thinking about *himself*; always anxious to surpass his companions. I remember that, once, Ewing and I had lost our dog. We were in a wood, and the dog had gone out and found a covey in a wheat stubble joining the wood. We had been whistling and calling him for, perhaps, half an hour or more. When we came out of the wood we saw him pointing with one foot up; and soon after, he, keeping his foot and body unmoved, gently turned round his head towards the spot where he heard us, as if to bid us come on, and, when he saw that we saw him, turned his head back again. I was so delighted that I stopped to look with admiration. Ewing, astonished at my want of alacrity, pushed on, shot one of the partridges, and thought no more about the conduct of the dog than if the sagacious creature had had nothing at all to do with the matter.

WILLIAM COBBETT:
Rural Rides.

POINTER & PAINTER

Carrying the eye round to admire Loch Lomond again, and not sufficiently satiated with either view, we were about to sit down in order to examine both more minutely, when we discovered Pero, whom we had not attended to before, pointing. I remembered having shot two brace and a half of black-cocks, and several moor game, some years since on this very ridge; and I hoped this point would produce black-game rather than grouse, though my friends had never seen either, and were extremely anxious to gratify their curiosity. We soon came up to the dog, who still maintained his point; and so interesting was his attitude to Mr. Garrard, that he immediately set about preserving it by a sketch. He had just accomplished this when Pero moved forward, and, after footing a little, we sprang the brood, which consisted of twelve well-grown grouse.

COLONEL THORNTON:
A Sporting Tour.

POINTER, HORSES & PARTRIDGES

Mark, the pointer used by Captain Ross in his match with William Coke, was the best I ever had. When he stood he was a perfect model; he always raised his head as high as he could, with his tail perfectly extended, so that you could imagine he was looking at some object in the air. He was perhaps the staunchest pointer that ever stood; as an example, I will mention an instance which occurred when I was shooting with him alone: in a grass field with a good deal of bottom to it, Mark stood. Four or five horses were grazing there, and as soon as they saw the dog stand they surrounded him and kept striking at him with their forefeet. Mark took no notice; he never moved a muscle; he might have been a marble statue. I was so afraid the horses might kill him that, exasperated by the thought, I ran within fifty or sixty yards and gave them one of my barrels in their hindquarters. They all galloped away, and Mark remained in *statu quo* until I had reloaded and put the birds up.

SQUIRE OSBALDESTON:
His Autobiography.

The Falls of Foyers

These falls differ very much from each other; the lower one, I fancy, exceeds everything of the kind in Britain, and, I should think, is equal to the boasted Fall of Tivoli. The upper one is astonishingly rapid, and pent in between two sharp rocks which seem as if cut through to receive the water.

I had heard an absurd story that no Englishman ever dared venture this passage, and fully declared my determination to attempt it, regardless of the consequences. Mr. S. (a friend of mine), who was with me, not thinking it necessary to take a guide, we rode on, easily finding it by the noise it creates; tied our horses, and seeing a rough, unpolished fir-tree laid across, in spite of his admonitions I got over it by the assistance of some few broken hurdles that were partially laid across this dreadful chasm.

Having thus succeeded (I should have mentioned that a favourite pointer followed me), I recrossed it with some difficulty; but all the pains we could take would not induce Ponto to trust himself. Inconsiderately, I again crossed it, thinking thus to tempt him; but it was to no purpose, and I, still more rashly, determined to bring him, not a very large dog, in my arms. In this absurd way, deaf to Mr. S.'s entreaties, and dreading that my dog, a spirited one, on seeing us gone, would attempt it and be lost, I very cautiously began to recross, taking Ponto in my arms. Mr. S. was in the greatest distress at my situation, which I did not consider so hazardous as it proved; for, being about half-way over, the dog, through fear, sprang from me; I luckily fell flat on the fir, and throwing my arms and legs across, continued passively in this situation for some minutes, till, examining my position, I recovered my alarm, and crawled very slowly till I came so near that Mr. S. reached me a bough, without which I was so flurried that I might not have been able to have got over.

Never was joy painted more visibly on any countenance than on his upon seeing me safe. I began then to inquire after Ponto, who, I concluded, was dashed to atoms. It seems that, on my falling, he, at one bound from the fir, had made an immense leap and got safe; but was so terrified that he avoided us, and we found him waiting for us with the horses.

COLONEL THORNTON:
A Sporting Tour.

DOGS SHOULD RUN HARES

I am, as in most other things, a very irregular sportsman, of which you shall hear further in due time; and why I teach all my dogs to run hares. Even when put into my hands, so perfectly well broke that they will not look at a hare which gets up before them, I confess it mortifies me much; and their regularity, to me, is very unpleasant for a time; but I soon prevail on them to forgo those great regularities; then they become amiable, please me much, and are thoroughly useful to my method of sporting.

You shall now know my reason why I teach all my dogs to run hares. I will not defend the practice, for I well know it is very unsportsman-like, and contrary to all rule and order. I scarcely know the time when I have missed a hare, I mean when she gets up before me in a field, or out of a hedge; not when they are bobbing about in a cover; then it is very difficult to shoot them, and a man must shoot very quick indeed, a perfection which I never attained, I always take a long aim. In three days and three hours (for it began to rain on the fourth day, very heavy, by twelve o'clock) my partner and I shot eighty-six hares. I shot above fifty of them, and we neither of us missed one shot.

As I always shoot with uncommon large shot, Number 2, patent, from the first of September to the last day of January, I frequently mortally wound hares at a great distance. Knowing, when I hold them well, that I must have wounded them, I always follow them with my dogs, and many dozens have I recovered above a quarter of a mile distant, which otherwise would have crept into a ditch and died. I solemnly declare I have shot numbers of hares above seventy yards, when they ran across me, so as to shoot them in the forequarters; so that they never have run five yards: and once I saw a man with a gun of mine shoot a hare one or two yards above eighty, and she never ran above one hundred and fifty yards. These distances were measured, not computed.

COLONEL GEORGE HANGER:
To All Sportsmen.

SENDING DOGS NORTH IN THE 'SEVENTIES

I have frequently been asked for information on the following subject: What is the best means of conveying dogs to Scotland and other places as the trains terrify them?

I have constantly *sent* dogs very long distances—which is, of course, far more hazardous than *taking* them—and of the scores that I have transmitted by railroad only two have suffered from the journey when they were sent in baskets or boxes, and but one retriever was so injured (being sent with chain and collar only) as to die a few days after reaching its destination (Liverpool).

No dog ought to be without water in hot weather for more than six hours under any circumstances, although he can do without food for twenty-four hours without any inconvenience; and, unless he is to be exhibited, he should be fed at such intervals, and always at night.

I think a dog's comfort is studied best if he is carried either in a dog basket or a dog box. Let either of these cases be large enough, and you effectually prevent your dogs being stifled in one of those black holes which have stifled many a good brace of dogs on their way to Scotland. You secure your setters a place in the guard's van or a truck; at any rate, they are certain of air, and probably *in transitu* they will provoke the attention of some good-hearted railway official, who will give them a pan of water.

Whether your dogs travel in box or basket, there ought to be some easy plan for furnishing it. I have both baskets and boxes, which I will describe.

I have wicker cases of various sizes, and, provided they are strongly made and the dog has no inclination to gnaw his way out, they answer very well. They are cheaper than travelling boxes, and cooler also. They should be, to use the terms of the trade, "randed" up and not "slewed" up; that is, the withes should be put in singly (the lateral withes), and not three or four together, as in wine hampers. For one dog this basket ought to be three feet six inches long, twenty inches high, and two feet wide. The opening is best made at the end, and there should be a hole at one corner with a tin or wooden trough, by means of which contrivance water is easily furnished. I have baskets with a partition for two dogs, and then the doors are at opposite ends. The single baskets, made stout enough, cost from twelve shillings to a guinea each, but boxes cost a little more. They are to be had of deal or elm, the latter wood the best, and the door is an iron grating. I have no double boxes—they are too cumbrous; and except that they are, when properly made and banded with small hoop iron, more enduring than wicker-work, they are for the transport of dogs in every way inferior to the basket.

Unless dogs are sent to the north by rail, they must go up by sea, and they are exposed in steam vessels to greater risks, and for a longer time, whilst the master or the servant in charge remains in such a prostrate condition that they receive no care or attention from their natural protectors.

The Idstone Papers.

NERO

26th February 1820.—This evening poor old Nero died, having never recovered the French illness with which we were all such sufferers. He was the best dog I ever had, ever saw, or ever heard of.

I killed during this extraordinary dog's service, and almost entirely to him, game, &c., as follows:—

Up to 1812, 356; 1813, 244; 1814, 402; 1815, 320; 1816, 378; 1817, 503; 1818, 463; 1819, 253; 1820, 344; to the day of his illness. Total, 3,263 head.

I almost always used him single-handed for every purpose as he would of his own accord "down charge" and bring the game when told. At a hedge he would stand till I came, and then, if ordered, go all the way round and drive the game to my side; for a river, for a boat, for everything, he was a perfect wildfowl dog, although a high-bred pointer with a cross of foxhound. The game that I calculate has been killed to this dog, including that shot by my friend as well as myself, I estimate at about 5,000 head, but to be widely under the mark, I will say 4,000; supposing then we take each head of game one with another at two shillings apiece, which would be low price among those who deal in such things, I may say the poor old dog has earned me £400 besides trifling wagers.

COLONEL PETER HAWKER:
Instructions to Young Sportsmen.

THE SINNER

For the sake of a very noble memory you will forgive me if I omit the name of the beloved sinner and content myself and you with the mere statement that he was a retriever and a very good one.

I was fishing one morning in the late May and the big black dog, my Achates, sat, among the buttercups, like a graven image. And when I hooked a trout, then would he stroll forward and, with a quizzical patronage, approve my treatment of it. And so we lazed along the banks in all peace and amity. And presently I saw my companion stand stiffly still. Then (I can hardly write the words) he pounced and picked a sitting partridge off her eggs. Then he, who was so big and gentle, killed her, realising perhaps his abominable sin and desiring that no witness of it might survive. But I had seen and I put my rod down and came and spoke to him. I laid no hand on him. He crawled into a hedge and he lay there. It was late afternoon when I came home, and I came alone. "Where is so-and-so?" said his mistress. I said, untruthfully, that I neither knew nor cared and I talked to her of what had been. "We will take the car and go back," said she, "for though he knows the way home he may be too unhappy to take it."

And so we went back. And still the penitent lay under

the white may bush, and as his two friends came to him he crawled upon his belly, and he cried.

PATRICK CHALMERS:
At the Sign of the Dog & Gun.

TO A GOLDEN RETRIEVER

Wendy: April–December 1927

You came to your first home only in June,
  And changed the current of our summer days,
    When in your puppyhood your mistress found
New joy of life, and in your brown eyes' gaze
    Read all your heart, so that the world went round
      And filled with a new tune—
Wendy, a woolly baby dog that rolled
  And ruffled a soft coat, waved a broad paw,
  And heard from one loved voice all puppy law;
Golden retriever Wendy, nine weeks old.

And so through August days to strength you grew,
  Gay with your mistress, learning at her side;
    Questioning, dancing, slender and light as she,
Following her by field and road and ride:
    And watching I would wonder which could be
      The happier, she or you—
The happier?—Ah, such happiness to keep!
  Day takes away the gift that day bestows:
  Death called predestined through December snows,
And laid you, young, obedient, to sleep.

So short, the life has passed. The dream remains.
  Still may I watch you with an inward eye,
    Still may I love you with unwounded heart,
Forgetful for an hour that dogs must die,
    Choosing of memory just this small part,
      So that by Surrey lanes
Wherever once you ran in rain and sun,
  There still by rew or ride your light foot falls,
  Still from the summer lawn your mistress calls,
Still through the August garden blithe you run.

E. P.

TIME WAS

Hats in the 'Seventies

I CAN only say from experience that in August and September there is nothing better than straw. A straw hat, if it is a good one, is better than any other. I confess that it is not without its defects, or rather its *one* defect. It is not a protection against rain. In all other points can you tell me anything that will equal it? If you get a good one (which you can do by going to a good maker), it will last you two or possibly three years, after being annually cleaned, lined afresh, and stiffened, at the cost of eighteen-pence; and if I get one I like I am very chary of getting rid of it. The black-and-white answer best. They don't get brown like the unstained one, and don't attract the sun like a self-colour. They should have nothing thicker than gauze for lining, and a ring of flannel or serge where it touches the head.

In a broiling day you may get a young cabbage leaf tacked inside the crown; and if you forget this comfortable arrangement you can put a handful of grass instead. The brim should not be more than 2¼ ins. wide, and I seldom have mine over 2 ins. If the straw is moderately coarse the wind will not affect this margin, and the eyes will be thoroughly protected.

The crown should be $3\frac{1}{4}$ ins. exactly. This allows enough circulation above the head, and is not acted upon by the wind. I have been out in very heavy rains with such a hat, and have experienced very little inconvenience from the percolating of the water; and as soon as the storm passed away I gave my hat a shake, and felt no inconvenience.

If you don't like a straw, you have to choose between two evils—the soft wide-awake and the hard one.

The soft one is by far the most comfortable for the open, provided there is no wind; but when there is even a breeze, if the brim is a couple of inches too wide, you are always put out by its flapping in your face. As these soft brims are made to turn up, you can't very well shear them down without making yourself "an objec'," otherwise a sewing-machine and a pair of scissors would put all right. These soft hats do not attract the sun so much as the stiff ones, even if they are black; and we have our choice from white to brown or grey. White are too great a contrast to the heather; and for fishing, which goes hand in hand with the gun in Scotland, a white hat is most objectionable. Well, certainly, it is advisable to have as few traps as possible on our expeditions, and it would be well that a hat should answer all purposes if possible: suppose we say neutral grey or lavender is the best colour of all.

For covert, the stiff, hard hat will do, as the brims slip through the underwood; and, though objectionable in the sun, they are cool enough beneath the leaf in October, or when the heat of summer is past. Yet I prefer much the soft skull and stiff brims; and I have worn them with great comfort even in September.

The Idstone Papers.

A GAMEKEEPER OF THE 'EIGHTIES

I deem myself fortunate in obtaining for publication in the pages of this magazine the following correspondence as to the duties and responsibilities of a gamekeeper.

Very little alteration has been made in the letters. With a few necessary corrections, they make their appearance just as they were written, the real names of the parties being, of course, changed. There are those who may think Sir Robert Campsie's demand too absolute in asking, from a person who had applied for the situation of keeper on his estate, a detailed account of his career; but I am able to assure the readers of *Baily* that many gentlemen are now in the habit of doing so. A friend of mine, who owns a Scottish estate of some magnitude, tells me that he never engages a servant without knowing the story of his life, including, of course, a chronological account of his previous services.

"Why should he not tell it to me?" said my friend. "I make him, so to put the case, one of my own family whilst he remains in my service; he may have to teach my boys to shoot and my daughters to use their fishing-rods—at any rate, they must all, as a matter of course, be frequently thrown into his company, as he will have to advise my wife about her poultry, and also be consulted a good deal by her with regard to supplies for the table and so forth. Besides, a respectable, well-trained man, and I want no other, can have nothing to conceal, and should, therefore, be willing to give me his pedigree and recite his experiences. A keeper's place, as you know, Ellangowan, is one of great trust, which should only be filled by respectable men who will be satisfied to remain for years in the service of a good master. My present coachman, for instance, has been with me since he entered the stables as a boy of thirteen, that is to say, nineteen years since; my chief gardener has remained in my service for over seventeen years; and my forester was born on this estate in 1846—his aunt is my wife's housekeeper. I dislike very much to see new faces, and am only too glad to be good to old servants who perform their work faithfully and well."

So spoke my friend and there will be many, I dare say, who will echo his opinion—at all events, I can certify that he is well served by really good men.

ELLANGOWAN.

Application from JOHN KILPAITRICK *to* SIR ROBERT CAMPSIE, Bart., *of Torrance, for the situation of gamekeeper.*

SIR ROBERT,—Having heard through my brother-in-law, William Grieve, who is coachman to the Dowager Lady Torrance, that you want a trustworthy keeper—a middle-aged man—to enter your service at Martinmas next, I beg leave respectfully to apply for the place. I was head keeper for four years to the late Mr. Jeffrey, of Calixter, and am still kept on by Mrs. Jeffrey; but, as she has announced the estate for sale, I am anxious to get a new situation, in case I may not be wanted by the gentleman who may buy Calixter.

I am, SIR ROBERT, your obedient servant,

JOHN KILPAITRICK.

From SIR ROBERT CAMPSIE, Bart., *desiring additional information.*

JOHN KILPAITRICK,—Your letter of application for the situation of keeper on my estate has been received by me, and I am pleased so far with it that I wish you to send me additional particulars. When I engage a confidential servant it is desirable that I should know something about his history, and, as I observe from the letter you have addressed to me that you write very well and spell your words correctly, I wish you to inform me in writing who your parents were, and to give me a note of the date at which you first entered service, and some account, it may be short, of every situation you have filled since then. I have learned from William Grieve that you are married and have three children. I wish you then to say how long you have been married, and in whose service your wife was employed when you married her.

ROBERT CAMPSIE, Bart.

From JOHN KILPAITRICK *in answer.*

SIR ROBERT,—I have duly received the letter which you have written to me, and beg respectfully to say, that as I have nothing to be ashamed of, or to conceal, there can be no objection on my part to give you all the information which you ask me for. My father's name is Peter Kilpaitrick, and he is still living, being now sixty-eight years of age and very strong and healthy; he has a pension of ten shillings a week from the son of a master in whose service he was as coachman for forty years. I was educated at the parish school, where I took prizes for writing, arithmetic, and geography. When I was twelve I used to carry the bag every September for General Blaikie, my father's master.

After I had been in the service of Major Matheson for two years, his keeper was unfortunately shot by one of a gang of pheasant poachers, and the Major then asked me to take his place for a month or two till he could find a successor to the man who had been murdered, and I very willingly did so, having a fancy for that kind of work.

As keeper, however, I remained for five years, and the Major was so pleased with my work that he recommended me to the Marquis of Uddingstone as forester, a situation which I liked very much, having considerable knowledge of trees and plants. At the end of ten years, the Marquis, as you are likely aware, Sir Robert, was accidentally shot on a moor in the Highlands by one of his greatest friends.

I am married, and have three children, two girls and a boy, one thirteen, the other eleven, and the boy will be nine on his next birthday. My wife was head dairymaid at Uddingstone Castle, where her father was for a long time the house carpenter.

I hope, Sir Robert, these particulars of my various places will be satisfactory to you, and I now remain your obedient servant,

JOHN KILPAITRICK.

Slockenham, Calixter.

From SIR ROBERT CAMPSIE, Bart., *in reply*.

JOHN KILPAITRICK,—Your letter, I am pleased to state, is very satisfactory, and your dates, I am glad to find, all fit in correctly so as to make up the period of your age. As writing seems quite easy to you, perhaps you will not find it difficult to give me some notion of how you will arrange your duties here, in the event of your being engaged as my keeper.

ROBERT CAMPSIE, Bart.

Torrance.

JOHN KILPAITRICK *complies with* SIR ROBERT'S *request.*

SIR ROBERT,—It will take a long reply to go over all the points mentioned in the letter which I have had the honour to receive from you, but I will do my best to answer all your questions, first of all saying that I am very pleased my little history has satisfied you.

SIR ROBERT CAMPSIE *engages* JOHN KILPAITRICK *as his keeper.*

JOHN KILPAITRICK,—Having read and considered your three statements, and being told by Lady Campsie of your respectful manners, and clean, orderly appearance, I have resolved to engage you as keeper on my estates of Torrance and Campsie (it is a very responsible situation) on the following terms, which I think are liberal and just:—

(1) Your wages will be at the rate of £60 a year, and will be paid monthly.

(2) Your wife will receive 10s. every month, for her assistance in breeding the pheasants and partridges, and for helping with the incubators and preparing the food of the dogs, ferrets, &c.

(3) You will have an excellent house of four apartments (one of which I have furnished for my own occasional use), with washing-place, &c., as also a daily supply of milk for your family, or, if you prefer it, grass or other fodder for a cow of your own. There is a demand for milk by the villagers.

(4) Coals and firewood will also be allowed—one ton of coals every month for all purposes.

(5) You will keep a note of the food purchased for dogs and poultry, and pay the persons who supply it, handing me

the vouchers for the payments every month. No objection will be made to your breaking a dog for any of my friends.

(6) You will have the aid of one permanent assistant and two men during the shooting season.

(7) I shall allow you one pair of breeches and long leather-gaiters every season.

(8) Powder and shot will be supplied to you in moderation, and you will be at liberty to shoot one pair of rabbits every week for the use of your family.

These are my conditions, and I think them fair and reasonable; I say nothing whatever on the question of gifts made by my guests; the giving of such perquisites is a practice I dislike, but I fear it cannot be prevented.

ROBERT CAMPSIE, Bart.

Extracts from original letters, with the names altered, quoted in an article in Baily's Magazine, *October 1888, entitled "The Gamekeeper of the Period, his Duties and Responsibilities."*

BATTUE SHOOTING

Battue shooting is the sport of wealthy men, and it would be better named "something to do" than sport. We must agree to an enormous outlay for a few hours' sport. *I state deliberately that I have frequently formed one of a party where I believe the sport to have cost little less than one hundred pounds an hour.* I put the outside value upon the pheasants when I say they were worth £40, the hares £12, the woodcocks £6, and rabbits there were none worth mentioning—all of which game was given away. I have commenced shooting this large covert at half-past one or later in the day with some such results as those I name, and the staff of keepers, the barley, and various expenses were never met by the sum of £600 per annum. Occasionally the covert has been shot a second time, but not with equal results. This, however, would reduce the cost of the sport per hour by one-half, and I am, I admit, putting an extreme case. I am alluding to a pheasant preserve on which no expense was spared, to give some notion of what these large bags cost.

You must have men well disciplined and well protected, and you must expel all babblers and skirters from the pack. If they are not well protected from thorns by long leggings, they not only will not go through them, but they cannot. Every man should have a white "slop." This protects his clothes and shows him to the guns; besides which, the ground game see and move from him more readily than if he were in dark clothes.

He ought also to have gloves and a stick. He must use his stick and not his tongue; and on the silence of the beaters, the constant rattle of their sticks, and their keeping in line and not shirking "the stick," the success of the beating depends. The under keeper should be at one end of the line of beaters, and an intelligent man— a night-watcher, for example, who knows the wood, or someone who comprehends the arrangements—should be at the other. Frequently the under keeper is required to superintend the running of the nets, and then the beaters are left with a very inferior head or leader, unless the owner of the covert or some friend who knows the ground walks with the beaters at the end and keeps them in order.

The head keeper has to "place the guns," and (according to John Leech, himself a good sportsman and unrivalled satirist) to order "two lords on the right, two more lords on the left, a couple more forward, and the commoners to walk with the beaters."

Three or four men are required to carry the game; they walk a few paces behind the beaters, bring the game out at the end of each strip, and consign it to the head keeper, who places it in a row, counts it, and consigns it to his cart in waiting just beyond—sometimes not beyond—the guns.

Some head keepers (I am supposing the head keepers to be the general manager of the sport) place stops at the end of every important strip; and if the strip faces the open, or is contiguous to an enemy's country, they should be so placed. This function is generally performed by an old ex-keeper, an invalid, or a cripple, who keeps tapping the trees with his stick as he walks to and fro; and any small boy is equal to this situation, provided that a man is left to take care that he performs it!

In this battue shooting it is desired to drive the pheasants to a particular spot where they may be easily shot, and where an *abattoir* has been prepared from which they will rise a few at a time. This is managed in various ways. Sometimes the underwood is cut and "splashed" down into a mass or mat about two feet high. Sometimes long fir poles are fixed horizontally at intervals, and fir branches are leant against them so as to form a sort of large tent, beneath which the birds will run.

If you "go in" for this "sport," a great deal depends upon the way the birds are flushed; and there is need of great experience to get them to the place and to put them up for slaughter when they have reached the shambles.

Some men are indifferent as to the day's sport provided they get a good finish, which, by the way, often is put off until it is too dark to distinguish cocks from hens.

When this good finish is desired, no nets are placed at the ends of the squares of covert into which the preserve is marked out, and numbers of birds and hares run on, never presenting a mark for the guns, which are posted in front of the beaters, and are shooting towards the advancing line. I need hardly say that when the beaters come near the guns, and rabbits are thick and pheasants fly low, or are shot by "snap shots" directly they appear above the scrub or brushwood, I have frequently envied these men their position, especially when I have observed a little group around one or more of their body who owes his life to the thickness of his head, and is made fit to be shot at again by a half-crown and a pull at one of the gentlemen's flasks. It may be want of taste, but I confess that I consider no cock-fighting could have been equal to this—especially when the gun that "potted" him is very severe with him for being "in the way when he pulled."

The Idstone Papers.

The Twelfth, 1838

Morning dawns—the morning of the Twelfth—and "heavily with mists comes on the day." The occupiers of benches and chairs are first on the alert—the landlady is called—breakfast is prepared—the dogs are looked at—all is tumult, noise, and confusion—reckless must he be that can rest longer in bed—"the cootie moorcocks crously crow," little fearing that many a bold mountaineer amongst them must ere night, be

" Whistled down with a slug in his wing ! "

The dram-flasks are filled—the sandwiches cut—some provision is made for the dogs—the shot-belts are buckled around the waist, being less irksome carried thus than when slung over the shoulder—a multitude of other matters are arranged and orders given. Next is heard the howling and yelping of dogs—the cracking of whips—the snapping of locks—the charging, and flashing, and firing of guns—and every other note of preparation!

The march is sounded, and away they wend, true *peep-o'-day boys*, far, far from the busy money-getting world, to breathe empyreal air, and to luxuriate in a sport which wealth is but too prone to monopolise. The sportsman's shooting dress this day is a shibboleth, which introduces him alike to his superiors, to his fellows, and his inferiors: there is no outpeering of arrogance or coldness; but a generous rivalry exists to eclipse each other in the number and size of birds killed! To the shooter in training, full of health and strength, and well appointed, it is of little consequence whether game be abundant or not. The inspiriting character of the pursuit, and the wild beauty of the scenery, so different from what he is elsewhere in the habit of contemplating, hold out a charm that dispels fatigue! He feels not the drudgery!

To him the hills are lovely in every aspect; whether beneath a hot autumnal sun, with not a cloud to intercept the torrid beam, or beneath the dark canopy of thunder-clouds—whether in the frosty morn or in the dewy eve—

whether when through the clear atmosphere he surveys, as it were in a map, the counties that lie stretched around and beneath him, or when he wanders darkly on, amidst the volumy vapour that rolls continually past him—still a charm pervades the hills! The sun shines brighter, and the storms rage more furiously than in the valleys! The very sterility pleases: and to him who has been brought thither by the rapid means of travelling now adopted, from some bustling mart of trade, or vortex of fashion, the novelty of lonesomeness is agreeably exciting! The stillness that reigns around is as wonderful to him as the solidity of land to the stranded sailor! Scarcely is there a change of scene; silence and solitude—hill and ravine—sky and heather universally prevail!—the outline is everywhere bold—and where the view terminates amidst rocks and crags, frequently sublime!

His noon-day bivouac may be in some quiet dell shut out from the world; or near some rocky summit, perchance on the boundary of the muir-lands, whence on the one hand he beholds an unbounded expanse of heathery hills, by no means monotonous if he looks at it with the eye of a painter, for there is every shade of yellow, green, brown, and purple; the last is the prevailing colour at this season, the heather being in bloom; nor are the hills monotonous if he looks at them with the eye of a sportsman, for by this time he will have performed many feats, or at any rate will have met with several adventures, and the ground before him is the field of his fame; he now views with interest many a rock, and cliff, and hill, which lately appeared but one of so many "crags, knolls, and mounds confusedly hurled"; he contemplates the site of his achievements, as a general surveys a field of battle during an interval of strife; the experience of the morning has taught him a lesson, and he plans a fresh campaign for the afternoon, or the morrow, or probably for the next season, should the same hills be again destined to be the scene of his exploits: and on the other hand he looks down, and, in bright relief, sees the far-off meadows, and hamlets, the woods, the river, and the lake!

He rises and renews his task. The invigorating influence

of the bracing wind on the heights lends him additional strength — he puts forth every effort — every nerve is strained—he feels an artificial glow after nature is exhausted —and returns to the cot where he had previously spent a sleepless night, to enjoy his glass of grog, and such a *snooze* as the citizen never knew!

The Oakleigh Shooting Code.

An Old Game Book

Gamonia was printed in 1837, and we may guess that it owes its name to the fact that some ten years earlier Sir Humphrey Davy, the great chemist, had published his book, *Salmonia, or Days of Fly-fishing*. Colonel Rawstorne spends his days with game, and like Sir Humphrey, he writes from personal experience. He is not content, as so many of the earlier sporting writers have been, to copy out the observations of others; he has observed and found things out for himself.

How wide and varied was his experience may be judged from the record of his shooting as kept by him in his *Game Book*. I have been privileged, through the kindness of his son, Lawrence Rawstorne, Esq., J.P., D.L., of Lyncote, Parkstone, Dorset, to examine this volume, and have done so with the interest which any shooting man must naturally find in handling the actual document penned by a sportsman of a hundred years ago. The book is bound in half morocco, and contains some 170 leaves of good cartridge paper, with the right-hand pages of the first half of the book ruled for entries of game. A page goes to a month, so that the figures of each season's shooting occupy five or six pages—six when, as sometimes happened, there was shooting in March. The left-hand pages are used for notes jotted down for names and details of this or that day's bag.

There are seven columns marked for varieties of game, and Colonel Rawstorne sets them in the order: partridges, pheasants, woodcocks, snipes, wildfowl, hares, rabbits.

Partridges are placed first, doubtless, because they come first in the seasons of the year, but if we analyse the bags of the twenty years of which this book is the record, it looks as if the chief interest of the estate in the later years centred in pheasants. The numbers of pheasants rise gradually from a total of 38 in 1820 until we come to 250 in 1825, 344 in 1826 and 653 in 1828; after that the bags are mostly between five and six hundred. Partridges vary as we should expect; indeed, the bags are as instructive as are those recorded by Colonel Hawker in his Diaries, and show that a hundred years ago partridges were just the incalculable birds which they remain to-day, that once in ten years, perhaps, comes a bumper season when all goes well, but that the average season is one in which the gamekeeper in September looks back upon the losses caused him by the weather of June and July.

Rawstorne's best partridge year is 1827, and that, we may remember, is the year in which Hawker made his record for Longparish, when shooting single-handed on 1st September, he wrote afterwards in his Diary of "the greatest day on record—102 partridges and 1 hare, besides 3 brace more birds shot and lost." This is the only year in which Hawker bagged 100 partridges in a day and it is the only year in which Rawstorne can record the same number—156 on 18th September. It was altogether a remarkable season. From 1st September to 5th October, the *Game Book* shows sixteen days' shooting, with the three smallest totals, 12 on 1st September, 11 on 15th September, and 3 on 30th September; the best day 156, and the other twelve totalling 457, or an average of nearly 20 brace a day.

The column headed "Wildfowl" makes some interesting reading, particularly in the early years, when each species is carefully recorded. Later, we get merely an entry of numbers, but we can sometimes reconstruct a day by referring to the notes jotted on the left-hand pages. "Wildfowl" include not only duck, but "various." In September 1819, for instance, there are entries of 6 landrail, 2 teal, and 1 wigeon, and on 4th October we find the column filled by " 5 curlew hilts." These are not curlew, for curlew have their separate entry; are they, perhaps, "half curlew," or "curlew jack," that is, whimbrel? But if so, they were sometimes given their other name, for in 1822 we read: "16th Sept., Booth (the gamekeeper), 3 wimbril; 17th, do., 6 wimbril; 19th, Booth, 2 hares, 3 wimbril, 3 teal; 21st, Booth, 1 wimbril, Taylor, 2 golden plover; 28th, Taylor, 2 teal, 3 wimb; 3 golden pl." The Colonel's spelling varies, for on 4th October we find a pleasant old form in the entry, "Booth, 3 wimbril, 1 curlieu, 1 snipe, 2 hares."

A more unusual "various" occurs in a left-hand page note for 20th October 1834. The entry runs on the right-hand page: "Wildfowl 3." On the left we get: "20th, L. R., 5 snipes, 1 spoonbill: Blackburn (keeper), 6 snipes, 2 spoonbill."

The keepers seem to have shot regularly, either in company with their employer, as above, or by themselves; and also to have brought in game, shot or otherwise brought to bag, out of the shooting season. Thus, for instance, on a left-hand page opposite the entries for September 1837, we read: "Keepers in September, 3 snipes, 3 wildfowl, 1 hare, 26 rabbits," and "Keepers from 1 Feb. '37 to 1 Sept. '37, 5 pheasants, 2 woodcocks, 21 snipe, 1 wildfowl, 33 hares, 681 rabbits." This entry of game killed between February and September occurs every year.

There was a fixed scale for head of vermin, whether limited to keepers or extended to others. This was the scale in 1819:—

"Foumets, 6d. each; cat, 4d.; polecat or weasel, 6d.; carrion crow, 4d.; hawk, 6d.; magpie, 3d."

It was changed in 1823, in which year we find a note that there was to be "no allowance for cats, but that for foumets and polecats to be 1s."

It looks as if cats had become too frequent an item in the list. Vermin money must have been a somewhat large charge on a shooting estate, at all events if the numbers entered in the books were comparable with those which were accounted for by the keepers at Knowsley, where Colonel Rawstorne often shot with Lord Stanley, afterwards 13th Earl of Derby. Lord Stanley also was a frequent guest at Penwortham, and the two estate owners must often have talked over questions such as vermin money. Here is a note made by Colonel Rawstorne of the vermin accounted for at Knowsley in the four years 1829–32.

Date.	Foxes.	Polecats.	Weasels.	Cats.	Hawks.	Crows.	Magpies.	Jays.	Herons.	Total.
1829	1	50	498	349	54	160	148	99	9	1,369
1830	–	31	526	309	67	90	136	122	–	1,281
1831	3	49	548	330	49	190	114	109	13	1,405
1832 (to end of August)	8	17	302	129	34	51	82	81	3	707

We have riddles of nomenclature in these lists. "Foumet" is "foumart," or "foulmart," another name for the polecat, as opposed to "sweet-mart," the pine marten. Then what was the distinction at Penwortham between "foumet" and "polecat," and why are polecats bracketed with weasels? And does the term "weasels" embrace stoats, which otherwise are not mentioned? At all events, we can see that even allowing nothing for cats, and only 6*d.* each for polecats or weasels, the vermin bill at Knowsley in 1829, for instance, may have amounted to some £20. With cats at 4*d.* it would have been a good deal more.

Another page in the game book, with notes on the employment of gamekeepers, throws some light on the changes and chances of a keeper's life of the period. Under the heading, "Gamekeepers with the time when they first came," we find the entry, "Novr. 13, 1818. John Booth from near Farington," and five years later "Booth died April 4, 1823 from the overturn of a coach on the Penwortham Bridge." On 1st July 1818: "Taylor for Longton (part of the estate) 3 months from Aug. 1, and the remainder of the year as he may be wanted." On 1st Nov. 1820: "Godbert to go out at nights when wanted, and to look after the Grange." And on 12th Aug. 1825: "Robt. Cross came for Longton and to go out at nights. Taylor only occasionally at 51 yrs." Taylor at the age of 44 presumably was out after poachers every night.

The keepers were provided with a considerable armoury. Here is the list for 1820:—

> Guns, pistols, traps, spring guns.
> Double gun, Manton's—Booth.
>   Do.   late Bannister's—Taylor.
> Single gun, Parker—keeper's son.
>   Do. bought from Troughton—Bacon.
>   Do. 2 of his own—Blackburne.
>   Do. musket—Ireland.
>
> Pistols:—
>   1 with bayonet—Booth.
>   1 with bayonet—Bacon.
>   1 without bayonet—Ireland.
>   3 humane steel traps.
>   1 large steel trap
>   3 spring guns.
>   11 vermin traps.

There was a difference evidently between "humane" and "large" steel traps. The former, perhaps, had no teeth. Both were for men.

A most carefully detailed account was kept in the *Game Book* of all game sent away. The name of every recipient was written down, sometimes with the address, under the heading "Partridges sent, 1827," or whatever the description of the game might be. In 1827 one page is filled with names of persons to whom partridges were sent, nearly two pages are occupied with names for "pheasants sent," and half a page goes to hares. But how any reference could be made to the list, even by its compiler, I cannot imagine, for a page measures only $7\frac{1}{2}$ ins. by $4\frac{1}{2}$ ins., there are no lines or rules, the names are in rough columns, and there are some 250 of them on the page.

Here, finally, is the analysis made by Colonel Rawstorne of the bags of the game seasons at Penwortham from 1820 to 1839.

GAME KILLED IN EACH SEASON ENDING 1ST FEBRUARY
AT PENWORTHAM, &C.

Season.	Partridges.	Pheasants.	Wood-cocks.	Snipe.	Wild-fowl, &c.	Hares.	Rabbits.	Total.
1820	260	38	9	41	29	163	72	612
1821	271	80	6	31	22	229	267	906
1822	347	141	12	25	11	301	345	1,182
1823	190	162	28	66	44	366	477	1,333
1824	168	231	6	66	17	240	160	888
1825	182	250	24	45	11	281	318	1,111
1826	316	344	11	58	42	249	510	1,530
1827	451	653	1	55	13	345	978	2,496
1828	711	683	7	87	37	230	695	2,450
1829	269	435	10	126	69	212	275	1,396
1830	205	387	12	54	10	335	395	1,398
1831	53	85	10	120	37	224	175	704
1832	197	664	20	36	19	273	133	1,342
1833	209	663	8	63	23	270	266	1,502
1834	73	515	10	152	39	364	571	1,724
1835	143	528	12	278	56	263	438	1,718
1836	127	551	9	157	48	241	632	1,765
1837	76	356	22	201	32	236	1,225	2,148
1838	188	636	16	73	20	242	1,999	3,174
1839	104	230	18	45	23	145	1,647	2,412

There are other entries of ferreted rabbits, which seem
sometimes to be included in the totals, sometimes not. In
1828, for instance, there is a separate entry of 3,153 ferreted
rabbits, so that it must have been a great year. But the
tables show that partridges and pheasants were the chief
interest, the former naturally varying largely, the latter as
constant an entry as good keeping could make them.

E. P.:
Note to Gamonia.

THE TRUE SPORTSMAN

The shooter who ranges for grouse in November, and
beats for cocks in March, deserves the appellation of

sportsman. He who is only to be seen in the turnip fields and stubbles in September does not.

THE SHOOTER'S CALENDAR, 1838

January.—All kinds of game, except grouse and black-game, are in season in January. When the weather permits, the cover-shooting in this month is very good; the brambles being dead or trodden down, the thickest woods are passable. Partridges begin to pair this month when the weather is mild: they should not then be fired at. This is the prime month for wildfowl shooting.

February.—The 1st of February is the last day of the season for shooting partridges and pheasants. The fowling-piece may be cleaned and put aside, for it is too late to shoot hares and snipes. Cocks will very rarely be found in the inland covers this month. In severe frosts wild ducks will leave the lakes and pools frozen over, and will be found on rivers and in gutters in the vicinity of fresh-water springs.

March.—The shooter may in March beat the covers for cocks.

April.—The sporting year may be said to expire, with the game certificate, on the 5th of April. The shooter should now renew his certificate. This month he will not use, but may occasionally oil, his fowling-piece. He should now select young dogs for the ensuing season. March, April, and August are the best months for running dogs, previous to shooting over them. In May partridges and pheasants lay their eggs, on which they sit in June, and the young ones are too small to avoid dogs in July, therefore they should not be disturbed in those months by the incursions of the dog-breaker.

May.—The shooter should now purchase a fowling-piece, if not already suited. He should likewise furnish himself with strong boots or shoes, in order that they may be seasoned by being often greased, and that they may fit easily by being worn at intervals before the shooting months.

June.—The shooter can do little this month, except in the way of preparation. If he has taken Time by the forelock, as he ought to have done, there will remain nothing for him to do.

July.—Little can be done this month, except what was omitted to be done in April, May, or June. The gun-locks, &c., should be examined, and if the gunsmith's services are required, no delay should take place.

August.—Grouse shooting commences on the 12th of August; blackgame shooting on the 20th. The finishing lesson should be given by the breakers to dogs, from eight to twelve months old, intended for partridge shooting; that is, the finishing lesson before shooting over them. Snipes and leverets are killed this month.

September.—Partridge shooting is now what those who like to take things easily wish it to be. It is followed chiefly in stubble, potato, and turnip fields. Hares may be killed in September. A young dog may be taught more in a fortnight in September than in any two of the winter months. So may the young shooter learn more this month than in any other.

October.—All kinds of game that can be met with are now in season. The woods are generally too full of underwood, and the foliage is too dense to allow the shooter to beat comfortably or to obtain many shots until towards the end of the month. Many pheasants are found on the outskirts and under bushy hedges near fields of potatoes or high stubbles. Cocks arrive on the moors in the beginning of October and in the woods near the end. Snipes also arrive in abundance.

November.—With the exception of August this is the best shooting month. All kinds of game are in season. Cover shooting is in perfection. The trees are leafless and the woods somewhat trodden. Cocks are abundant. Pheasants and blackgame are well grown, well fed, and in full plumage; the pheasant is scaled with gold to the throat, and the black cock is feathered to the foot! Partridges are wild; but the shooter will find more hares this month in the open fields than earlier in the season, and snipes are more plentiful. Hares are often found in stubble fields this month.

December.—Shooting this month is similar to that of last

month. Large shot or wire-cartridges are now indispensable: game is not only wild but strong, and well protected by feathers or fur. Grouse and blackgame shooting end on the 10th.

With this retrospect of the shooter's monthly duties, and an injunction that it may never be forgotten that Field Sports are contributory to health, long life, and sociality; and are an antidote to care, ennui, melancholy, misanthropy, and a thousand other ills that flesh is heir to, we conclude these our HINTS ON SHOOTING!

VIVAT REGINA!
The Oakleigh Shooting Code.

TO THE MEMORY OF
LIEUT.-COL. PETER HAWKER

Beside the stream new-fangled spring
Has cast the April clothes she wore,
Whetstones in water-meadows ring,
Through falling grass the carriers pour,
Twittering swallows swoop and soar,
Drakes over sedges, greens and greys,
Dance their cotillion as of yore—
O memories of Hampshire days!

Along the lane the robins sing
Summer is gone. The snipe no more
Bleats from the blue down-curveting,
There are the coveys on the floor
Of wheat and oats—you can't ignore
That call to new September ways;
Look how your spaniel's eyes implore—
O memories of Hampshire days!

November, when the pheasants swing
  Over the larch-wood corridor,
December, when north-easters fling
  Bernicle, greylag, blown before
  Gales from the Needles to the Nore,
And underneath a white moon's rays
  The gunner drags his punt ashore—
O memories of Hampshire days!

  Prince, for what skill we have, or lore
Of guns or game, be yours the praise,
  And ours the happiness, who store
Your memories of Hampshire days!

E. P.

TO-DAY

PHEASANTS YESTERDAY & TO-DAY

HOW MANY men who shoot in October have heard of Colonel George Hanger? He is unread, he lacks his *vates sacer*; you will not find him among the new editions.

Yet he published his book, *To All Sportsmen, and Particularly to Farmers and Gamekeepers*, in the same year, 1814, in which Peter Hawker, just gazetted out of the Army on account of wounds received at Talavera, gave the world his *Instructions to Young Sportsmen in the Art of Shooting*: and it was he who first wrote detailed advice as to the preservation of pheasants. It is true that some of his suggested methods have a rather full military flavour; for instance, he recommends that, in order to be sure of keeping poachers out of your wood, you should mount a six-pounder cannon on the top of your house, and fire a few rounds of glass marbles and perforated clay balls into the wood by night, two or three times a week.

The perforated ball, he says, would "make a most terrible whizzing noise, and, together with the marbles buzzing about a fellow's ears, would make him think that the very devil was in the wood." This is a little old-fashioned, but otherwise the Colonel has plenty of advice which would suit gamekeepers to-day. It is he who first prescribes the proper proportions, five hens to a cock, for the laying-pens; and as to diet for the young birds, some of us a few years ago were given, as a new and valuable "tip," that young pheasants should be given green onion tops. Hanger printed the "tip" in the year before Waterloo.

But who, before Hanger, wrote anything practical about breeding pheasants? The *Sportsman's Dictionary*, which went into a fourth edition in 1792, has nothing to say; and yet, in 1790, Pye, the Laureate, wrote a poem, "Amusement," in which he pours scorn on the effeminacy of the day, and writes of "the winged tribe" which

> "*by care domestic bred,*
> *Watch'd with attention, with attention fed,*
> *Where'er the sportsman treads in clouds arise,*
> *Prevent his wish, and sate his dazzled eyes.*"

That can only mean pheasants; and yet Hawker, greatest of authorities on shooting, writes of pheasants twenty years later as if he had never heard of any but wild birds. It is a curious lacuna in the history of shooting, and it would be interesting if it could be filled, for with the introduction of the system of rearing pheasants by hand we come to the beginnings of pheasant shooting as it is understood to-day; and to the difference, too, between the pheasant shooting of October and the modern, carefully planned covert shoots of November and later in the season.

Our great-grandfathers, with Hawker and Hanger, shot their pheasants—sometimes other people's—anywhere and anyhow; and, except that we are more careful as to our neighbours' boundaries, that is the way in which pheasants are shot in October to-day. The pheasant season opens, of course, on the first, but not in the same way in which the grouse season opens on the Twelfth of August, or partridge shooting begins on the First of September.

The date is a convenience rather than an occasion; we may shoot if we please, though probably we shall not; and if we do, it will be hardly so much for the sake of sport as frankly for the pot. True, the gamekeeper welcomes the legal date, for he can then have an honest shot at the hardy old cock of last season, who likes to get some of the young fellows putting on their new feathers to follow him away from the coverts to the blackberries and other delicacies of distant hedges.

But, generally speaking, we are all agreed that the young cock pheasant of early October is an immature, callow creature, more likely to run away from the gun, or, indeed, towards it, than to fly as cock pheasants should. At the end of September he is still moulting, and he will not get the splendid blues and scarlets and bronzes of his full plumage, much less the strength that goes with firm wing-muscles and a long tail, until November, when, moreover, frost and wind will clear the leaves from the trees so that it is easier to see to shoot him.

And there is another reason for waiting. Pheasants can be expensive birds. Wild pheasants, it is true, cost little to keep; a stack of barley-rakings is enough to attract them, morning after morning, to the same clearing in the wood. But pheasants that have been reared under domestic hens cost money, both to buy as eggs and to feed as chicks; and that being so, it is waste to bring them to an end before they have filled their purpose, which is to give the gun a sporting chance of hitting them and themselves a sporting chance of escape.

Later in the year, hurled down a thrashing November gale, it may be, or rising high over January snow-fields, the bird which to-day bustles ignobly from the hazel hedgerow will swing over a line of guns to test the quickest hand and the straightest eye. If he is to justify his keep, he must fly far and fast; otherwise, you might with almost as much satisfaction add him to the bag from the poulterer's window.

When we go pheasant shooting in October, then, we are after wild birds: we shall leave the main stock of the covert till a later day. And beating round the "outsides"—the coppices, the hedgerows, and the rough fields that lie away from the central coverts—can be as pleasant a day's shooting as any man need look for with a gun and a dog. It is the sunshine that makes the day. Summer is surely not over when we can still watch the small copper and the red admiral butterflies balancing themselves on the wild scabious; or when the harebells still hang fresh side by side with the toadflax and the campion.

But autumn is here, with the acorns slipping from their cups, and the great splashes of yellow in the crowns of the elms, like light poured through a church window; with the birches fluttering half-bare, and the bryony red and orange, and traveller's joy turned to old man's beard in the roof of the hedge. Or we glance at the blackberry bushes, and have to look closely to pick fruit that is not over-ripe; or, as we stoop, we get the scent of crushed crab-apple from the path trodden under the fence. These belong to October, and so, too, does that clatter of wings which comes from the gorse-clump where a moment or two before we heard a whimper from the spaniel.

Out he flusters, in his early bravery of bronzes and greens, one of the young cocks of a brood hatched by his wild mother in that boundary hedgerow, it may be; and as he gets to a fair distance from the gun, down he crashes into the brambles. He is the first of the day, and he will be followed by others, young and ancient, to make a bag which adds an entry to the game book none the less happy in that it belongs to the old fashions.

E. P.

Caper in the Sunset

I remember one day, to be marked for ever with a red underline in the game book of memory. There was snow on the Norsk hills, not deep, but it was freezing, and a cold wind was blowing in the isolated edges of the forest. One outlying gulley—so my hunter told me—generally held an elk. As the travelling was very noisy owing to the frost, I instructed him to go round and drive the place, as it was probable that any animal which might be disturbed would seek the lower levels rather than face the gale on the heights. Meantime I found a fallen tree, a fir, behind which I en-sconced myself. The time was late afternoon and the sun was giving its last lights to the desolate upland world before sinking behind the forest. It was very, very cold. Looking ahead I saw a raven rise from the woods that were being driven by the single beater, and go swinging down the wind. A long wait followed, and then one by one three cock caper rose, at first small as bats against the white backgrounds, but developing as they came into enormous black fowl, which whizzed by me so close that I could see the red in their eyes, and even the startled optics themselves. Later, another hustled out of a pine and followed them. I had nothing but my rifle, and no wish to shoot at any game save elk, but I rarely think of capercaillie without seeing again that chill Norwegian sunset and the great sudden birds looking so large that they might be such fowls as Thor hunted on his journey through Jotunheim.

HESKETH PRICHARD:
Sport in Wildest Britain.

NOVEMBER PARTRIDGES

"It's closing itself; it generally does," an old Tweed fisherman remarked one late November evening, gazing at the darkening river, and hoping in vain for the "back end" salmon which should fitly finish the season. And the same is true of the season of partridge shooting. When the roots are pitted there is no more cover into which the keeper with his line of beaters can drive the coveys before sending them over the fence to the waiting guns. The days of the fields and the hedgerows are over, and the thoughts of the country house shooting parties turn to the woods.

But how pleasant the day may be before the season closes! These morning hours of late autumn, with the elms and the larches yellow under a cloudless sky—are there any others with a more buoyant pulse of wind and sun? Hope begins with the light. An air blows in at a bedroom window from dew on the lawn; the garden smells of frost, of oak leaves, of wet soil under a southern wall. And we are to be out after breakfast on stubbles and grass and plough, waiting for the keeper's distant whistle that means coveys speeding forward to the hedge of hawthorn or the belt of spruce. What could a shooting morning promise more?

Memory goes back to other such mornings, each with its different outlook. Which would you choose, if you could be back again? An hour of Hampshire, would it be—with the chalk stream under the stony hill, and the junipers studding the turf, and the reek of turnips down wind from the fence? Or Salisbury Plain and its long white roads, and hares cantering over the skyline—an acre of hares, perhaps, such as Cobbett saw at Netheravon and wrote of in *Rural Rides*? Better than Salisbury Plain the Sussex Weald, with the downs twenty miles away to the sea; or one of those big flinty fields of Surrey, where you can drive partridges over strips of pine; or that strange and fascinating breckland of the Eastern Counties, where partridges are the best crop the ground grows, and where you may shut your eyes and people the desert horizon with bustards dead and vanished from England a century since. It is the breckland we are nearest to to-day; in Norfolk, and on a morning that seems to belong typically to the county, with a rain-washed sky blue above spruces and elms, and blue wet ruts along the cart-tracks, and tinkling water in hidden ditches, and broad fields shining with flints and mangold-wurzels. And with fields, too, that wear an aspect new to some of us, untidy spaces of broken soil and littered green and yellow leaves, and outside the field gate piled at the roadside a heap of whitey-brown roots crusted with mud, which—oddly enough—have been topped but not tailed. It is the new crop, beet; and the sugar, it seems, goes to the very tips of the roots—a new accompaniment, these unsightly saccharines, of partridge-driving.

We take our places for the first drive. The beaters have walked in three or four fields of stubble and fallow, pushing before them any coveys they have found into the roots which we can see through the fence in front of us. They are now lining the far hedge, and silence lies over the field. It is much to the waiting shooter to hear the coveys get up before they come to the fence, for if he is a judge of distance he knows what time he has got; and we listen intently in a quiet, broken by the bark of a jay jinking from an oak, and the meditative carols of answering robins. A wren, beak and tail sharply cocked, interpolates his fiery little jet of song; and from a mile or more away raps out another sound of Norfolk mornings. "Pat—pot"—the guns on the next manor are earlier to work than we.

Suddenly we pick out another sound. A familiar creaking in mid-field is followed by the keeper's whistle—a second whistle. Two coveys have risen and are on their way—our way? No. A scattered group of grey specks is mounting to clear the trees on the right of the line; we hear the quick reports of the guns, but we dare not do more than glance aside; there may be a whistle sounding for us too. The second covey, we realise, has come over the middle of the line, and as they flee behind it two grey balls curve down to the stubble floor, bounce and are still. Someone has scored a pretty right and left. Our neighbour to the right is less lucky, but a minute later drops a crossing single bird neatly into the hedge. Another covey breaks over the right, and the beaters are out of the field.

Now comes a different task. Five of the guns go forward to line a distant fence; two remain on the right and left of the beaters, who are to walk some big fields with the right flank forward swinging round at right angles to the fence lined by the guns. It is an interesting if not very exacting job, for we are really driving pheasants rather than partridges, and the two guns with the beaters are to take any birds that break back. But the attraction is to watch the birds we flush. We cover a wide front, with the beaters dragging lengths of rope between them over the heads of the roots and seeds, and as we flush pheasant after pheasant we see them fly steadily forward, high or low, but always, as they catch sight of the guns, mounting suddenly higher—a disconcerting flight which enables more than one of them to reach their chosen covert behind the line.

That, too, is a typical drive, but it is not the best. We get that later in the day, from a large field of roots into which partridges have been put to join the pheasants already there. Does that not make for an exhilarating contrast of pace and angle and the purpose of the bird? For the pheasant is faster than the partridge, as you can tell if you see the two on the wing together; but he is the easier, driven like this. He may swing and curl, but it is on a wide arc. The partridge is a bird incalculable. He is surprised to find you there, he surprises you when you try to find him. To the left, to the right, swerving up, across, back where he came from, and screaking and chattering at you as he alters his mind and perhaps succeeds in altering yours—it is he on whom memory lingers, he, as the second of a right and left, who leaves his image on the inward eye. The last two barrels of the day—if those have closed the Norfolk afternoon as they should, we can be almost content to have seen the last of the November partridges.

E. P.

Taking a Shoot

Never you take a shoot without going and seeing it first, and, if possible, the fellow who has had it before you.

Let me illustrate by anecdote. Once upon a time there was a Sassenach who took a shoot in the Highlands without a previous inspection of it even by proxy. When he would go into residence there, he drove upon a public coach for there was no railway. He was fortunate in getting a seat next the driver, and, without disclosing himself, he sought local information about his bargain. He asked the coachman then, "Do you know Auchenflichity?" "Aye," was the uncompromising answer. "And what sort of a place is Auchenflichity?" "Gin the Deil was tethered on it ye'd just say 'puir brute!'" said Donald Beg.

Patrick Chalmers:
At the Sign of the Dog and Gun.

Grey Geese Alert

Few sights are finer than that of a great flock alighting. In the air the glory of their flight lies in its strength and in the wonderful formation of the feathered phalanx; but once a single cautious bird has alighted, watch the rest swinging and swooping in aerial gymnastics which one would fancy all too light and undignified for such grave and reverend birds. They swoop and swing like plover, and then, as they begin to feed, mark the short alert step, and, above all, mark that sentinel in whose care lies the safety of the feathered republic. Often have I lain watching geese for hours at a time. Once I saw a sentinel remain unrelieved for fifty-five minutes. They may remain longer, certainly sometimes the period is shorter, for I have known the watcher to be relieved three times within the hour.

There he stood on his point of vantage; presently some other birds came feeding towards him. One of them stood up, and the sentinel resigned his duties and vanished into the private life of the flock. I have never seen the sentinel goose ask for relief by plucking at a comrade with his bill, as some observers record; yet of one thing I am certain, the geese understand each other, and, I verily believe, converse together.

HESKETH PRICHARD:
Sport in Wildest Britain.

TO-MORROW IN WALES

I will set out, not next year, or the year after, but to-morrow for Wales. I will choose the same train which I chose last—how many years ago!—and I know when and where it will land me. I shall find myself in the cold dark of a December morning—the day after to-morrow morning, just as near as that—at a little grey railway station with the wind blowing through it, and in the wind the smell of the sea. I shall get up into a farm gig, and I shall be driven off into the dark; we shall go splashing for miles down narrow roads, and come to a ford with the stars in it, black and surely too deep to drive through; we shall drive through that and come to the inn, with the ducks quacking in the stone-lined runnel in front of it, and there we shall find the mistress of the inn as smiling and the bread and butter as white and as yellow as they used to be, and the blankets and the curtains as clean and warm, and the hills as far and desolate; and we shall go out for all the day on the hills and the marshes and the little green fields between them.

We shall walk through grey heather and brown heather, through miles of rushes and tussocks and hags and mosses; we shall stride up lanes down which rivers are flowing, and wade about meadows which are half lakes; snipe will start into the wind from the rim of the flood-water, and teal clatter up from the reeds of hidden pools, and cormorants go sailing out over the river to the sea. We shall go for our lunch to a farmhouse, and be given home-made bread and home-made cheese by the farmer's daughter, in the pleasantest way in the world; and for tea we shall knock at the door of a little cottage tucked in a dip in the hills, and we shall sit in the parlour by the big chimney with the tea stewing on the hob, and a lump of clay red-hot in the fire, and two old ladies nodding at us with grey curls. It will be the same cottage where we first had tea many years ago, and the two same old ladies will fetch their two tall Welsh hats and white frills, and we shall look again from the nodding hats to the big pumpkin drying in the chimney corner, and think again of fairy godmothers and Cinderella with her pretty feet among the ashes. We shall shoot all through the winter morning and afternoon, and empty our boots and wring out our stockings before we walk home in the dark; and in the warm inn bedroom, with the single sheet spread under the white blankets, we shall fall asleep thinking of the long day, and all its shooting; the right and left killed in the corner of the first grass field as we left the road; the wisp driven by one of us to the other over a fence of sallows; jack snipe flitting up like moths from the rushes; sunset fading from the bog-water of the marsh.

ERIC PARKER:
Shooting Days.

CURLEW OVER THE CITY

Although he is more essentially, perhaps, than any other bird a denizen of the wild, yet sometimes he may be seen near the centres of civilisation. In the evening, flocks often fly by Ravelston Dykes over Edinburgh, and we may believe that Alan Breck heard them as he waited for David

Balfour at Rest-and-be-Thankful, that spot which is nowa-days the Mecca of the Writer to the Signet's Sunday constitutional. The curlew is not out of place there, nor out of the picture which includes the high Corstorphine Woods, as well as from another vantage point, that view which drew out the word-picture: "I saw all the countryfall away before me down to the sea, and in the midst of this descent, on a long ridge, the City of Edinburgh smoking like a kiln . . . and ships moving or lying anchored in the Firth."

But the curlew occasionally appears in other places; at the heart of populous cities where one would scarcely expect to see him or on wharf-surrounded expanses of black mud in the shadow of giant houses of merchandise. Once, near Glasgow, a single bird rose from a pool of slime in the vicinity of a huge gasometer—he rose and headed away for the Clyde; let him reach it and pass over the tossing water, flying above giant liners until, far away, his sharp eyes discern the Kyles of Bute.

HESKETH PRICHARD:
Sport in Wildest Britain.

RABBITING WITH BEAGLES

In February only the rabbits are left. To-day we are to shoot them over beagles—or in front of beagles, rather, the idea being to station the guns at one end of the covert and to put the beagles in at the other. It is a form of shooting which does not belong to every part of the country, but has long flourished in Kent, Sussex, and others of the southern counties. Moreover, to those who love the sound of a huntsman's horn and the cry of hounds, the opening of the pack unseen and far away in the covert is the most inspiriting music.

The meet is at the farm, which lies on the skirt of the park, and, while the guns collect, the keeper has news to give of the work he has had in the past day or two in laying out the rabbits. There are various ways of ensuring that the little beasts, or a good proportion of them, shall be above ground instead of in their buries when the day comes for shooting. Running ferrets through the buries is one way, for the rabbits will not go back if they can help it till the scent has cleared; but it is a slow and tiresome job, for the ferret may kill below ground, and then you have the weary business of finding the kill with a line-ferret and possibly digging out the two into the bargain. A much better plan, though it entails some hard work and needs an energetic man, is to go the round of every bury and to place in every hole, as far down as possible, a small quantity of some evil-smelling mixture—there are nauseous compounds sold for the purpose. During the following night, if it is fine and dry, the rabbits will come out to feed, and the next morning the keeper, with the stroke of a spade and the stamp of a heavy boot, fills in the entrance to each hole. The rabbits, preferring clean bramble and fern to tar and paraffin, will be found above ground later in the day.

And here are the hounds! A closed cart, drawn by a rough-coated skewbald farm pony, lumbers up the hill. There descends from it begaitered, grey-smocked, grey-locked, of the cheerfullest habit—Falstaff. You will find nothing ruddier, nothing more nobly round, among hunts-men of beagles. *Ore rotundo* he addresses his hounds, and his figure suits his mellow voice. Will he stay the day with his pack? You will see. Down comes the tailboard of the cart, and out tumbles a cataract of black and white and tan, all sizes, all shapes, from the "little singing beagle," standing perhaps twelve inches, to what may be a mixture of otter-hound and foxhound with a touch of Toby—seven and a half couples guaranteed to nose out any rabbit on four legs in the nearest hundred acres of Sussex wood.

The guns, eight of them, move off across the park to take up their stands in a ride traversing the slope of a hill. The pack, apparently given a moment's law before being taken up the road, is suddenly seen streaming in full cry towards a little dip in the park grass. A rabbit has been put up which goes to ground there, and as the guns turn to look and laugh, a cock pheasant gets up with a prodigious crowing from the very middle of the pack and flies low and fast to the wood on the hill. The huntsman's horn calls back the hounds, and the guns cross a fence to the ride beyond.

How pleasant to wait at the corner of a covert, with green rides running two ways, a blue sky over hazel catkins, a west wind blowing, sunlight in clay puddles in the ride, and the scent of wet earth rising rich and warm from moss and root and hazel-stub! And how melodious the outcry far up the hill, as the first rabbit (you guess) is on foot before the pack—a sound broken by the report of a gun, and followed by silence till the pack opens again! Hounds are lower down the hill now, and—is that a rabbit? A blur of grey and white, a joyous tongue behind it, the black nose is too close and you cannot fire; the rabbit doubles among the stubs, doubles again, dashes across the ride, and rolls over and over among rain-rotten leaves.

We move off to other rides and other coverts, taking oblong after oblong of wood and leaving each in turn, as we hope, rabbitless behind us. Now and then you may catch sight of a beagle actually finding his quarry, checking, stiffening, nosing forward and dashing in as he scents and sees. And behind and with his hounds, stalking through the morning among chestnut and hazel and oak and gorse, the grey-smocked huntsman will be seen in glimpses and his horn and his high and sonorous hallooing will be heard. "Aie! Aie! Forrard, forrard, forrard! Push 'em out there, push 'em out! Truelove, Truelove! Rummager boy! Rummager boy!" All through the morning, all through the afternoon, that cheery, mellow voice and the music of the horn sound about these Sussex rews and ghylls; through hour after hour small grey forms dart over the floor of the woods to the crackle of guns. Once or twice a hare is afoot. "Ware hare!" you hear. "Don't shoot 'em here, I think," the huntsman mutters to his smock, his brow glistening ruddy in the sun. "Call 'em off, anyhow." But a moment afterwards, once more the melodious horn, and that prolonged and haunting echo of "Rummager bo-oy! Rummager bo-oy!"

E. P.

GOLDEN PLOVER

And how he captivates one's thoughts, this most soft-eyed of all birds, for the golden plover has a gentler eye than any of his kind, and nothing of the hard, darting glance common to almost all his cousins. Upon what strange scenes does he look in the short span of his life? He flies high over northern towns into cold mists bred about the Pole. There during the brief summer he struts in the splendour of his black-breasted breeding plumage beside meres in wastes unvisited by man. When the time comes for his southward move, he again proves himself a great traveller. His advance guards break their journey in Scandinavia and in our Isles, but his main battalions sweep on over the Giralda Tower and Seville to the marshes and vegas of Andalusian rivers. From there he makes his traverse of the narrow seas to Africa; thus the plover that was hatched in the Arctic waste in June may in November fly over the minarets of the sacred cities of the desert.

HESKETH PRICHARD:
Sport in Wildest Britain.

HILL-MEN

Apropos of experts, I'll tell you a tale. To this same forest where I have to-day been bidden there came as I did, for the first time, a guest. He was as distinguished a hill-man and as knowledgeable a sportsman as ever held a rifle straightly. He was sent out to stalk with a first-class professional forester who as yet knew not what angel his employer entertained.

The pair sat down to spy. The professional was noted, among many other things, for the falcon keenness of his vision. "I see staags," he said. The "gentleman" put his glass upon the spot indicated—a far distant corrie. "I see *deer*," he said at last, "but how you can tell that they are stags I do not know." Said the tolerant Gael didactically and in the sad and gentle sing-song of his kind, "Staags hass horrns."

PATRICK CHALMERS:
At the Sign of the Dog and Gun.

SEVENTY DRIVEN GROUSE

My butt was No. 4. The four top butts were sited fifty

yards from the skyline, the remainder falling away over the shoulder of the hill into a deep corrie.

Immediately in front of No. 4, and breaking the horizon at about fifty yards, was a small knoll. "Yon knowl's the making of the butt," observed my loader. "The early birds all come to it, as do most of those on the flat above when the drivers get nearer—'tis a long drive; and then, too, you will find them coming up from the left and down from the right."

Settled at last, I prop my shooting stick at a comfortable angle and gloat in satisfaction over good work well performed during the past drive, when a whistle from No. 3 butt galvanises me into sudden life. I glance quickly up the hill, and as I do so, with the tail of my eye glimpse a black circle with two projections, motionless apparently and suspended in the air and some few feet above the knoll. In a flash I realise that it is the first grouse of the drive roaring down upon me on stiffened pinions. Nearly caught napping, but not quite! Crack! and the black circle loses its firm outline, becoming a lifeless, irregular lump of ruddy brown flecked with white, which with undiminished speed hurtles between me and my loader to fetch up with a bump against the back of the butt. Another whistle and here comes the covey that the old cock was leading. I get the first, I miss another, change guns and, oh folly! turn round for a despairing tail shot as he swoops down the hill. Two barrels I fire, the second when the bird must have been two hundred yards away; meanwhile three or four more come over and disappear unscathed, for by this time, what with changing guns, turning round and falling over my own feet, I am all hot and bothered.

At this critical juncture I recall the advice of a friend, viz.:—

"Never turn round when grouse are coming thick and fast." Pulling myself together I regain confidence by downing a couple of sitters coming up from the left, besides crumpling up a very fast bird swinging down from my right. All the guns are busy now, and I can no longer count upon a warning whistle. My usual practice, when time permits, is to mark the general fall of birds killed by placing one empty cartridge in the appropriate position on the butt wall; to-day, however, this is impossible—they are coming, and, I rejoice to think, falling too fast, so I count as I shoot. Three in front, one behind, four in front, two behind, &c., but even this will not keep tally of the fallen, so thickly do they come and so well am I shooting. I therefore content myself with numbering each bird out loud as I see it hit the heather. Fifteen are down when a confiding covey swings up from my left in "column of lumps." I get the leader, and in my haste brown the rest and two more fall. Changing guns, I get two more as they flap up the hill. Obviously they had intended alighting, and it took them some time to get under way. Twenty the score is, and birds coming on all the time.

This is the real thing, this is grouse driving at its best. I must confess that most of the early birds came very nicely, and bar the first covey the majority of them seemed to contemplate finding a "lee" from the beaters behind the knoll. There were exceptions, however, just to remind me that a driven grouse can use himself when flying downhill and with a slight wind.

And so the tale goes on, and the count creeps up by ones and twos to 27—a pause, and I miss a real screamer flying straight and high over the butt, but am compensated immediately by crumpling one in front out of a covey that comes equally high from the right, and turning quickly I get the last bird almost out of shot. I see him bounce right back off the ground, and then go rolling over and over down the slope. A succession of single birds follow, most of which collapse in front, and then comes a rush of coveys in quick succession; the skyline is pitted with black dots, rising and falling, hovering apparently at times, or turning sideways with a deceptive twist to slant away down the hill, seeking shelter in the corrie behind me. These birds are really flying for the beaters, and are much nearer. Crack, crack, a right and left, the leading bird dies between me and the knoll; his fellow-sufferers some forty yards away to his left. A single bird comes straight at my head, so close that he should have been blown to pieces. He dies, too. I add a wounded straggler, who flies jerkily down from one of the upper butts, and then snap an old cock behind, who apparently had come from nowhere; and the tally reaches 45.

And now the tragedy. "Man, have ye any cartridges? If not, we have but four left, two in each of the guns!" "What, none? I'll away to the next butt." Laying the spare gun on the butt wall he darts down the hill. A single bird, a somewhat weakly cheeper, brings the score to 46; the leading grouse of the next covey makes it 47, and I have but two cartridges left. I put down the empty gun and prepare to defy the oncoming hordes—"*Jusqu'à la derniere cartouche.*" A big covey appears round the upper side of the knoll, sweeping downward and crossing my front. This time no shame is mine for the fluke when the leader and the next grouse fall at the same shot, and then to my joy I get a third with my last cartridge. Fifty all told and an empty gun.

Oh, awful tantalising moments! Grouse streaming overhead, not as single spies, but in battalions (a watcher from afar said that they flew over the butts like flocks of rooks, so great were their numbers) down from the right, up from the left, in front or passing behind, I with an empty gun and my neighbours blazing away as though repelling a counter attack. I gaze frantically down the hill, and see my loader come out. Thank heaven! Oh, d——! They must be short, too; he is going farther down. I could almost cry with rage, and the moments pass like hours. There are more grouse than ever. At last he reappears, crouches a moment to allow my neighbour to shoot, and then, purple, sweating, and panting, struggles up the hill. So blown is he that I take the bag and load for myself while he recovers his wind, and very good shooting I make. My right-hand neighbour misses clean a covey that, starting well above him, are proper birds when they reach me. I get my two. Good shooting though I says it as shouldn't!

The beaters are near now and the birds not so plentiful, but coming quicker and higher, with no intention of stopping this side of the corrie. I can recall also killing a snipe although this latter phase is a little blurred, while the score creeps up into the 60's. One spectacular left and right I do recollect, and always shall, by which I pulled a couple of grouse out of the stratosphere, or so it appeared to my excited imagination.

Sixty-five we have. Shall we reach 70? And by single birds we creep up to 68, 69, and—hurrah!—70. Incidentally, there are four dead birds in the butt, and my none-too-steady dog is alternately nuzzling them or raving at the flutterers which he can see outside. I can hear the beaters' shouts, the very snapping of their flags, so I let off a blue hare within easy range as he sits up and looks back, even though I know that my hostess wants some for soup. At this moment the last bird, as did the first, comes over the knoll, and I kill him behind me, and the drive is over. I have counted 71, so I stick to that figure, but I know there were more, and anyway, I am more than satisfied; yet, with the perverseness of human nature I shall never cease to speculate upon what my bag might have been had I not run out of cartridges.

LORD DORCHESTER:
One Crowded Hour.

TO-MORROW

To be back again to the glen, my Dear!
to the hill and the lodge in the glen!
To winds blowing cold from quartz and ling
And grouse in the morning challenging,
To the lodge and the glen wild roses—
When shall we come there again?
Harebells, horizon seas,
Blossom-powdered bees,
And grass of Parnassus opening white
And the low burn singing through the night,
Far tides and redshank flying,
Curlew from wet moors crying—
To the hills and the curlew crying—
Shall we ever come there again?

And to ride side by side down the long rough road,
where the little white cabins are,
And red geraniums, and the sweet
Unforgettable reek of peat,
To swing down the long grey road with you,
in Pat's old jaunting car!
Don't you remember the tune
In the August afternoon
Of the piper calling to the bridge
And girls from the hazy, lazy ridge
Barefoot coming and gay?
(O the light on Galway Bay!)
O my Dear! in Connemara, Connemara—but how far!

But best in our own South Country,
where the carts go large and slow,
Where hayloads catch in hazel boughs
And dusty nettles smell of cows,
To walk in our own South Country,
by the ways we used to know!
To find it all again
In April sun and rain,
When primroses are under the stiles
And the Downs are blue for twenty miles,
And Chanctonbury there
With his crown in Channel air
Lifts our hearts into the springtime of all those years ago!

E. P.

EXPERIENCE TEACHES

THE BETTER SHOT

IT IS generally the mistaken idea of those who are no judges of shooting, that if a man kills a certain number of times without missing, he is to be put down as a first-rate shot; and that another person, because he has been seen to miss, is to be considered as his inferior.

For example, the one man goes out and springs birds enough to fire fifty times, within forty yards, and perhaps, being a *reputation* shooter, only twenty of these shots happen to suit his fancy. He never fires a second barrel unless the birds rise one at a time, or a covey happens to spring from under his feet; and, in short, he kills his twenty birds with twenty shots. The other man takes the whole of the fifty shots, many of which may be very difficult ones, and under extreme disadvantages; he kills thirty-five, and misses fifteen. A fair sportsman and really good judge, I conceive, would not hesitate to say that the latter has claim to be considered the better shot of the two.

We will then bring a first-rate shot into the field, and he shall kill forty-five out of the fifty (never failing, of course, to work both his barrels on every fair occasion): he will then have missed five times; and would any old sportsman judge so unfairly as to place *before him* the *never miss gentleman* with his twenty trap shots running?

COLONEL PETER HAWKER:
Instructions to Young Sportsmen.

HUNTERS & SHOOTERS

There is an important distinction to be made between *hunters* (including coursers) and *shooters*. The latter are, as far as relates to their exploits, a disagreeable class, compared with the former; and the reason of this is, their doings are almost wholly their own; while, in the case of the others, the achievements are the property of the dogs. Nobody likes to hear another talk *much* in praise of own acts, unless the acts have a manifest tendency to produce some good to the hearer; and shooters do talk *much* of their own exploits, and those exploits rather tend to *humiliate* the hearer. Then, a *great shooter* will, nine times out of ten, go so far as almost to lie a *little*; and, though people do not tell him of it, they do not like him the better for it; and he but too frequently discovers that they do not believe him: whereas hunters are mere followers of the dogs, as mere spectators; their praises, if any are called for, are bestowed on the greyhounds, the hounds, the fox, the hare, or the horses. There is a little rivalship in the riding or in the behaviour of the horses; but this has so little to do with the personal merit of the sportsmen that it never produces a want of good fellowship in the evening of the day. A shooter who has been *missing* all day must have an uncommon share of good sense not to feel mortified while the slaughterers are relating the adventures of that day; and this is what cannot exist in the case of hunters. Bring me into a room, with a dozen men in it, who have been sporting all day; or rather, let me be in an adjoining room, where I can hear the sound of their voices, without being able to distinguish the words, and I will bet, ten to one, that I can tell whether they be hunters or shooters.

WILLIAM COBBETT:
Rural Rides.

PENALTIES

Where game is not slaughtered indiscriminately, it is customary to consider persons committing certain unsportsmanlike actions, whether done purposely or accidentally, liable to certain penalties, which, however, are seldom exacted on account of their being fixed too high. The delinquent thus escapes scot-free with a bagful of hen pheasants, as criminals are acquitted when the punishment is out of proportion to the offence. It is the amount of the penalty, and that alone, which renders such bye-laws a dead letter. The penalties should be on a reduced scale; no excuse whatever should avail the person becoming liable; but they should be claimed, and paid *instanter*.

Table of Fines payable on Oakleigh Manor

	s.	d.
Killing a grey-hen, or hen pheasant	5	0
For a second, the same day	7	6
For a third, fourth, fifth, &c., each . . .	10	6
Dropping two or more birds from one barrel . .	2	6
Shooting at blackgame, red grouse, pheasants or partridges on the ground	5	0
And for every bird killed on the ground . . .	5	0
Killing a bird not in season	5	0
Shooting at a bird not in season	2	6
Shooting at a hare (leverets allowed) between 10th of February and 1st of September	5	0
Shooting at a snipe between 10th of February and 1st of August	2	6

The Oakleigh Shooting Code.

OLD POKERS

Such is my opinion of a slow poking shot, that I would rather see a man miss in good, than kill in bad style. For instance, if I saw one man spring a covey of birds close to his feet, and keep aiming at one till the covey had flown thirty or forty yards, and even bring down his bird dead, and another man miss both barrels within the same distance, I should say perhaps the latter, if in good nerve, may be a good shot; but I was quite sure that the former never could be one, because he was a hundred years behindhand in the art of using a gun. I know many old pokers who would feel sore at this assertion, but this I cannot help: it is my humble opinion and therefore I have a right to give it.

Colonel Peter Hawker:
Instructions to Young Sportsmen.

Family Shots

However orderly the array of a covey, however favourable the opportunity may be, the partridge-shooter must not be tempted to "rake" them; a rule, we suspect, "more honoured in the breach than the observance." The grouse-shooter need not be so punctilious. The following practicable method of obtaining such a shot as shall, in all probability, secure a plurality of birds at each discharge, will be found in one of the papers of "Quartogenarian." As regards grouse shooting we think the justification of the practice is fully made out in the passage we are about to quote, when it is remembered that the writer is speaking of a wet and windy day in November—of that season when grouse leave the high hill-tops altogether, and resort to the braes, and broken bases of the hills, whence on the approach of the shooter, they take flight long before he is within range, and wing round the turns of the knolls or rocks. He says, "In such cases the best way will be to station yourself previously down wind, where your dear-earned experience has led you to expect them, and send a person, or persons, to take a good circuit, and walk carefully through the lea sides and sheltered bields of the hills. The best *family* shots are often to be thus obtained, and under such circumstances are perfectly justifiable, though in common shooting there is nothing I more detest doing, or seeing done, than to drop more than one bird to a barrel; to avoid which the outer birds should always be fired at. But here the case is quite different: always take the middle birds—'Father, mother, and Suke,' down with them, the more the merrier—and this is what I term a family shot!"

The Sporting Magazine, vol. vi.

CHOOSING THE DAY

Snipe shooting is like fly fishing: you should not fix a day for it, but when you have warm windy weather, saddle your horse and gallop to the stream with all possible despatch. Should there have been much rain, allow the wind to dry the rushes a little before you begin to beat the ground, or the snipes may not lie well. Although these birds frequent wet places, yet the *very spot* on which they sit requires to be *dry* to *their breasts*, in order to make them *sit close*; or, in other words, lie well.

If they spring from nearly under your feet, remain *perfectly unconcerned* till they have *done twisting*, and then *bring up your gun and fire*; but, if you present it in haste, they so tease and flurry that you become nervous, and from a *sort of panic cannot bring the gun up* to a proper aim. If, on the other hand, they rise at a *moderate* distance, *down with them before they begin their evolutions*. When they cross, be sure to fire *well forward*, and (if you possibly can) *select*, as I have before said, a windy day for this amusement; as snipes then usually *lie better*, and, on being sprung, *hang against* the wind, and become a good mark.

COLONEL PETER HAWKER:
Instructions to Young Sportsmen.

A SHOOTER'S NOTEBOOK

THE COMPANYES OF BESTYS & FOULES

An Herde of swannys.
An Herde of cranys.
An Herde of corlewys.
An Herde of wrennys.
A Nye of fesauntys
A Bevy of quayles.
A Sege of herons.
A Sege of bytourys.
A Sorde or a Sute of malards.
A Mustre of pecockys.
A Walke of snytes.
An Exaltynge of larkys.
A Cherme of goldfynches.
A Flyghte of dovves.
An Unkyndnes of ravens.
A Claterynge of choughes.
A Dyssymulacion of byrdes.
A Bevy of conyes.
A Cowple of spanellys.
A Tryppe of haarys.
A Gagle of geys.

A Brode of hennys.
A Badelynge of dokys.
A Covy of pertryches.
A Sprynge of telys.
A Desserte of lapwynges.
A Falle of wodcockes.
A Congregacion of plovers.
A Coverte of cootes.
A Duell of turtylles.
A Tygendis of pyes.
A Flyght of swalowes.
A Buyldynge of rokys.
A Murmuracion of stares.
A Nest of rabettys.

DAME JULIANA BERNERS:
The Boke of St. Albans.

THREE HUNDRED YEARS LATER

The modern terms as applied to waterfowl are as follows:—

A herd of swans.
A gaggle of geese (when on the water).
A skein of geese (when on wing).
A paddling of ducks (when on the water).
A team of wild ducks (when flying in the air).
A sord or suit of mallards.
A company of wigeon.
A flight or rush of dunbirds.
A spring of teal.
A dropping of sheldrakes.
A covert of coots.
A herd of curlews.
A sedge of herons.
A wing or congregation of plovers.
A desert of lapwings.
A walk of snipes.
A fling of oxbirds.
A hill of ruffs.

A small number of wildfowl, as ducks and geese (about thirty or forty), is termed a "trip." The same of wigeon, dunbirds, or teal, is termed a "bunch"; and a smaller number (from ten to twenty) is called a "little knob."

Of swans it would be said, a "small herd"; and sometimes of geese a "little gaggle," or a "small skein"; and so of ducks, a "short" or "long team."

Let us hope the character of the English sportsman is not so far degenerated, or the respect he owes to ancient diversions so far forgotten, as to permit him any longer to persist in such cramped and improper slang as to use the inapplicable term "flock" to every, or any, description of wildfowl.

H. C. FOLKARD:
The Wildfowler.

THE BEST

If the partridge had but the woodcock's thigh
'Twould be the best bird that e'er did fly.

OLD PROVERB.

THE CRIME

On the First of September, one Sunday morn,
I shot a hen pheasant in standing corn
Without a licence. Contrive who can
Such a cluster of crimes against God and man!

RICHARD MONCKTON, 1ST LORD HOUGHTON.

AN ACRE OF HARES

Not far above Amesbury is a little village called Netherhaven, where I once saw an *acre of hares*. We were coursing at Everly, a few miles off; and one of the party happening to say that he had seen "an acre of hares" at Mr. Hicks Beach's at Netherhaven, we who wanted to see the same or to detect our informant, sent a messenger to beg a day's coursing, which, being granted, we went over the next day. Mr. Beach received us very politely. He took us into a wheat stubble close by his paddock; his son took a gallop round, cracking his whip at the same time; the hares (which were very thickly in sight before) started all over the field, ran into a *flock* like sheep; and we all agreed that the flock did cover *an acre of ground*.

WILLIAM COBBETT:
Rural Rides.

AT THE END OF THE GUN

A guest of mine once gave me a fright while shooting in Yorkshire. He was a very good and, generally, a careful shot; but on this occasion he lapsed from his usual discretion. I was exceedingly lame at the time, and having no shooting pony, I shot off a donkey who stood fire like an artilleryman. My friend was walking a short distance before me when some partridges flew up; he turned round and levelled at a bird which was flying in a direct line for my face. A donkey is not a nimble animal, at least you cannot make him move aside very quickly, and I thought my last moment had come. I was not much reassured when, in answer to my shout to take care what he was doing, my friend answered: "Oh, I saw you at the end of my gun. There is no danger." It did not occur to him, apparently, that when a man has his finger on the trigger and is intent on a partridge, he may fire before he realises that there is another victim a little farther away than the bird. I was not more than fifteen or sixteen yards from him.

SQUIRE OSBALDESTON:
His Autobiography.

THE POINT OF VIEW

The curlew, be he lean or fat,
Carries a shilling on his back.

OLD PROVERB.

To Robert Louis Stevenson, of Scotland and Samoa . . . I dedicate these tales of that grey Galloway land, where about the graves of the martyrs the whaups are crying—his heart remembers how.

S. R. CROCKETT:
Dedication of the Stickit Minister.

24TH DECEMBER & CHRISTMAS DAY, 1843

Weathercock with head where tail ought to be; dark, damp, rotten, cut-throat-looking weather; flowers blowing; bluebottles buzzing; doctors galloping in every direction; a Philharmonic of blackbirds and thrushes; an armistice from guns and shooting; the poor punters driven to oyster dredging, eel picking, day labour, or beggary; not even the pop-off of a Milford snob to be heard in that unrivalled garrison of tit shooters.

COLONEL PETER HAWKER:
Diary.

DREAMS

From the lone shieling of the misty island
Mountains divide us, and the waste of seas,
Yet still the blood is strong, the heart is Highland,
And we in dreams behold the Hebrides.

Canadian Boat Song:
Blackwood's Magazine,
September 1829.

RED PARTRIDGES FROM FRANCE

21st March 1666.—To the Duke of York, and did our usual business with him; but, Lord! how everything is yielded to presently, even by Sir W. Coventry, that is propounded by the Duke. Sir Robert Long told us of the plenty of partridges in France, where he says the King of France and his company killed with their guns, in the plain de Versailles, three hundred and odd partridges at one bout.

SAMUEL PEPYS:
Diary.

GLOSSARY OF TECHNICAL TERMS

Allowance: in firing at a crossing bird "allowance" is the distance ahead of it at which the gun calculates he should aim. The faster the bird is travelling the greater "allowance" is needed.

Anvil: a small piece of brass shaped like an arrowhead which is placed inside the cap of the cartridge so that when the striker hits the cap the composition contained in the cap is forced against the point of the anvil and explodes, igniting the powder in the cartridge.

Backing: when pointers or setters are "down," *i.e.* searching for game, together, one is said to "back" the other when, seeing his companion check and point, he immediately checks and points also.

Ballistics: the science of projectiles: literally, of things thrown. From the Greek *ballein*, to throw. Used of shots, powder, &c.

Barrel: the metal tube of a gun, through which the shot is discharged.

Beater: a man employed to "beat," *i.e.* walk through, usually with a stick, the covert, with the object of driving out game. Beaters or drivers on a grouse moor are provided with flags, which they wave when coveys rise in order to send them forward.

Blank: to drive in "blank." To beat a covert in a chosen direction, with the object of pushing game out of it, but without immediately offering shots to the guns.

Blink: to shut the eye to, pass by, ignore; used of pointers, &c.

Bore: the bore of a gun is measured by the number of spherical balls of lead, each exactly fitting it, which go to the pound.

Brace: two taken together; a pair; a couple, *e.g.* a brace of pheasants, partridges, grouse; a brace of pistols.

Brown, To: to fire indiscriminately at a covey, without selecting one particular bird at which to aim.

Butt: (1) the thicker end of anything, especially of a fishing rod, a gun, or a rifle; (2) originally an erection on which a target for archery practice is set up; and so, later, a mound in front of which targets are placed for rifle practice; (3) a screen, usually built of sods of heather, to hide the shooter when grouse are driven towards a line of guns.

Cheeper: an immature grouse or partridge belonging to a late brood, too young to be worth shooting. "Cheeper," because of the weak cheeping call of the young chick to its parent. In the same way partridge chicks are known as "Squeakers."

Choke: full and half choke. Constriction of the bore of a gun barrel near the muzzle which thus keeps the charge of shot together.

Covert, Cover: woods, undergrowth, &c., which shelter game. *Coverts:* feathers that cover the bases of the wing and tail feathers of a bird.

Decoy: a pond or pool with arms covered with network into which ducks are lured so as to be caught. Decoy ducks are used for this purpose.

Detonation: a more than usually rapid explosion.

Doll's head: an extension of the top rib of a gun let into a corresponding hole in the top of the breech.

Driving: partridges, grouse, &c., are "driven" by a line of beaters towards guns stationed in a line behind a hedge or in butts on a moor.

Drumming: (1) the noise made by snipe in the nesting season, whether vocally or by the air passing through the outer tail feathers during flight is a disputed point; (2) the noise made by a cock pheasant beating his wings in the nesting season. A pheasant crows and then drums: a barndoor cock drums and then crows.

Energy: the work contained in a moving body, measured in weight and velocity.

Erosion: the wearing away of the surface of a barrel. See under *Pit*.

Euston System: a system, named after the well-known estates of the Duke of Grafton, by which gamekeepers collect the eggs of partridges day by day as they are laid, substituting dummy eggs, and then returning the eggs which have been brooded by hens or in an incubator when on the point of hatching.

Field Certificate: a certificate awarded to game farmers by the *Field* newspaper guaranteeing that the pheasants stocked by the farmer are kept and lay their eggs under healthy conditions.

Field Trial: a meeting held on a shooting estate at which pointers or setters or retrievers are tested under practical conditions by qualified judges.

Flanker: the two outside men of an advancing line of beaters or drivers are the flankers. They are usually provided with flags of a different colour from those of the drivers and are chosen for their knowledge and skill in waving their flag at the right moment to send the birds forward and prevent them from breaking out at the side.

Flapper: young wild duck.

Flighting: the flight of duck at morning and evening towards their feeding grounds or quarters for day or night.

Flip: a secondary, lateral movement of recoil.

Frenchman: the red-legged partridge (*Caccabis rufa*), introduced into England from France in the reign of Charles II.

Grit: fragments of quartz or other hard substance swallowed and used by birds for grinding food in the gizzard.

Ground Game: hares or rabbits.

Hanging Game: pheasants, grouse, partridges, &c., need hanging in the larder before being fit to cook. The period of time required for hanging varies with the weather.

Heather Burning: in order to provide a succession of young heather for grouse food, heather needs to be burnt from time to time.

Improved Cylinder: a barrel which is slightly choked.

Jump: a secondary, vertical movement of recoil.

Leash: (1) the thong in which hounds or dogs are held; (2) a set of three, *e.g.* a leash of hares.

Load: the component parts of the charge of a gun, *e.g.* a light load of powder, a heavy load of shot.

Loader: the attendant carrying the second of a pair of guns, who loads both guns in turn.

Lock: the mechanism of a gun by means of which the charge is exploded.

Magazine: a case or box for carrying a quantity of cartridges.

Netting: of coarse string, used for stopping pheasants running, &c., or of wire, for fencing out rabbits.

Nitro-proof: See under *Guns and Rifles,* by Major Gerald Burrard.

Over and Under Guns: in these the two barrels are placed one over the other instead of side by side.

Pattern: the grouping of discharged shot, usually measured on a target; patterns may be close or scattered, even or uneven.

Pick Up: birds which, not gathered immediately after the conclusion of a drive, are picked up next day.

Pit: a barrel is said to be pitted when, owing to not being cleaned, holes are worn in its inner surface by rust.

Point: a dog "points" game when, getting the scent of it on the wind, he suddenly checks, stiffens, and looks in the direction of the game; at the same time he usually lifts a front paw and stiffens his tail.

Point-blank Range: the distance at which a gun may be fired at a mark before the shot drops below the horizontal.

Poking: a shooter is said to "poke" when he points his gun awkwardly and indecisively before firing.

Ranging: setters and pointers "range" when they traverse the ground in different directions in front of them when searching for game.

Recoil: longitudinal movement of the gun in the reverse direction from the movement taken by the projectile.

Ride: a path through woodland.

Saloon "Rifle": a small, smooth-bore gun for firing at short range.

Sear, Scear: the catch in a gun-lock which keeps the hammer at full cock or half-cock.

Setter: a dog which "sets" or "points" game. Setters are of three varieties—English, Irish, and Gordon Setters.

Sewelling: lengths of thin cord or stout string in which are tied at short intervals brightly coloured strips of cloth; stretched across strips of covert to scare back approaching pheasants.

Single-trigger Guns: in these, instead of a trigger for each lock, only one trigger is fitted, so that the two barrels can be fired one after the other by consecutive pulls.

Sizes of Shot: ordinary sizes vary from the smallest, No. 10, to No. 1, or, larger still, A, B, SG, and so on. See separate tables. Sizes commonly used are for snipe, No. 8; partridges, No. 6; grouse, No. 6; pheasants, Nos. 6 and 5½.

Snap Shot: a shot fired in the quickest possible space of time, when the shooter can only get a sudden glimpse of his mark.

Stance: a standing-place; to shoot well a firm, level stance is needed.

Stand: the place marked out for each gun when awaiting driven birds.

Stock: (1) the wooden portion of a gun; (2) the amount of game on any area of ground.

Stop: a person posted in a particular place to prevent pheasants, &c., breaking away past him.

Swing: a shooter swings his gun so that the muzzle follows the line of flight of the bird aimed at.

Towering: a bird towers when shot in the lungs; the air passages become choked, the bird throws its head further and further back, mounting perpendicularly as it does so. A towered bird is usually found fallen on its back, but sometimes on its breast, with wings outspread. *A False Tower:* sometimes a bird whose head has been grazed by a shot seems to tower and falls; but may recover from being stunned and fly away.

Trajectory: the curve described by a projectile in its flight through the air.

True Cylinder: a barrel of exactly the same diameter from end to end, without any choke.

Try Gun: a gun of which the stock can be so adjusted as to measure the amount of "cast off" or "cast on" required by the individual shooter.

Tunnel Trap: a long box, either end of which can be propped open, in which traps can be set for stoats, weasels, &c.

Vermin: animals or birds which prey upon preserved game.

Walking Up: as opposed to "driving"; walking in line through crops, heather, &c., and putting the game up as the line advances.

Wave-pressure: an unequal pressure of confined gases.

SHOOTING BOOKS & WRITERS

ALINGTON, CHARLES.—*Partridge Driving* (1904); *Field Trials and Judging* (1929).

BACON, CAPTAIN ALBAN F. L.—*Enchanted Days with Rod and Gun* (1926).

BADMINTON LIBRARY.—*Shooting: Field and Covert; Moor and Marsh.* PAYNE GALLWEY, SIR R. F.; and WALSINGHAM, LORD (1886).

BANKS, A. G.—*Book of the Rifle* (1940).

BARTON, F. T.—*Pheasants in Covert and Aviary* (1912).

BLANCH, H. J.—*A Century of Guns* (1909).

BONNETT, FRANK.—*Mixed and Rough Shooting* (1914).

BRYDEN, H. A., and TOZER, BASIL.—*How to Buy a Gun* (1903).

BUND, J. WILLIS.—*Oke's Game Laws* (1861–97).

BURRARD, MAJOR GERALD.—*Notes on Sporting Rifles* (1920); *In the Gunroom* (1930); *The Modern Shotgun*, 3 vols. (1931–2); *The Identification of Fire-arms and Forensic Ballistics* (1934).

BUXTON, EARL.—*Fishing and Shooting* (1902).

CARLTON, H. W.—*Spaniels, their Breaking for Sport and Field Trials* (1915).

CHALMERS, PATRICK.—*Green Days and Blue Days* (1913); *A Peck of Maut* (1914); *The Frequent Gun* (1928); *At the Sign of the Dog and Gun* (1930); *Mine Eyes to the Hills* (1932); *Gun-Dogs*; *Deer-Stalking* (1935); *Field Sports of the Highlands*; *The Shooting Man's England* (1936).

CHAPMAN, ABEL.—*Bird Life of the Borders* (1889); *The Art of Wildfowling*.

CHARLESWORTH, W. M.—*The Book of the Golden Retriever* (1933).

CLAPHAM, RICHARD.—*The A.B.C. of Shooting* (1930).

CLARK, ATWOOD.—*Gun-dogs and their Training* (1935).

COCHRANE, ALFRED.—*Collected Verses* (1903); *Later Verses* (1918).

COLQUHOUN, JOHN.—*The Moor and the Loch* (1840).
CORNISH, C. J.—*Wild England of To-day* (1895); *Nights with an Old Gunner* (1897).
DAWSON, MAJOR KENNETH.—*Son of a Gun* (1929); *Just an Ordinary Shoot* (1935).
DEWAR, DOUGLAS.—*Game Birds* (1928).
DEWAR, GEORGE A. B.—*The Faery Year* (1906).
DORCHESTER, LORD.—*Sport, Foxhunting and Shooting* (1937).
DROUGHT, CAPTAIN J. B.—*Partridge Shooting* (1936).
DUNCAN, STANLEY, and THORNE, GUY. — *The Complete Wild-fowler* (1911).
ELEY, MAJOR W. G.—*Retrievers and Retrieving* (1905).
EVERITT, NICHOLAS.—*Shots from a Lawyer's Gun* (1901).
FALLON, W. J.—*Practical Wildfowling* (1907).
FOLKARD, HENRY COLEMAN.—*The Wildfowler* (1859).
FORTESCUE, JOHN WILLIAM.—*The Story of a Red Deer* (1897); *My Native Devon* (1924).
GATHORNE HARDY, A. E.—*Autumns in Argyllshire with Rod and Gun* (1900).
GLADSTONE, HUGH S.—*Record Bags and Shooting Records* (1922); *Shooting with Surtees* (1927).
GOODWIN, LIEUT.-GEN. SIR JOHN G.—*Making a Shoot* (1935).
GORDON, SETON.—*Hill Birds of Scotland* (1915); *The Land of the Hills and Glens* (1920).
GREENER, W. W.—*The Gun and Its Development* (1881).
HAIG BROWN, ALAN.—*My Game Book* (1913).
HANGER, COLONEL GEORGE.—*To All Sportsmen* (1814).
HARDY, CAPTAIN H. F. H.—*Good Gun-dogs* (1930).
HARTING, JAMES EDWARD.—*Essays on Sport and Natural History* (1883); *The Rabbit* (Fur, Feather, and Fin Series) (1898).
HARTLEY, GILFRID W.—*Wild Sport and Some Stories* (1912).
HAWKER, LIEUT.-COLONEL PETER.—*Instructions to Young Sportsmen* (1814); Ninth Edition (1844); *Diary*, 2 vols. (1893).
HIPGRAVE, WALTER.—*The Management of a Partridge Beat* (1922).
HUTCHINSON, HORACE.—*Shooting* (Country Life Library), 2 vols. (1903).
HUTCHINSON, GENERAL W. N.—*Dog Breaking* (1848–1928).
"IDSTONE."—*The Idstone Papers* (1872).
JEFFERIES, RICHARD.—*The Gamekeeper at Home*; *Wild Life in a Southern County.*
JONES, OWEN.—*The Sport of Shooting* (1910).
JONES, OWEN, and WOODWARD, MARCUS.—*A Gamekeeper's Note-book* (1911); *Woodcraft* (1910).

KIRKMAN, F. B., & HUTCHINSON, H.—*British Sporting Birds* (1924).
"KLAXON."—*Heather Mixture* (1922).
LACY, RICHARD.—*The Modern Shooter* (1842).
LANCASTER, CHARLES.—*The Art of Shooting* (1924).
LEGGATT, ASHLEY.—*Stalking Reminiscences* (1921).
LESLIE, A. S.; SHIPLEY, A. E.; and others.—*The Grouse in Health and in Disease* (1912).
LONSDALE LIBRARY.—*Shooting by Moor, Field & Shore* (1930); *Lonsdale Keeper's Book* (1938); *Game Birds, Beasts & Fishes* (1935).
McCONNOCHIE, A. INKSON.—*Deer-Stalking in the Highlands* (1924).
MacINTYRE, DUGALD.—*Round the Seasons on a Grouse Moor*; *Scottish Gamekeeper* (1941).
MACKENZIE, E. G.—*Guns and Game* (1906).
MACKENZIE, OSGOOD.—*A Hundred Years in the Highlands* (1922).
MACKIE, SIR PETER.—*The Keeper's Book* (1907–24).
MACRAE, ALEXANDER.—*A Handbook of Deer-Stalking* (1880).
MALMESBURY, LORD.—*Shooting Journals* (1905), F. G. Aflalo (editor).
MAXWELL, CAPTAIN AYMER.—*Grouse and Grouse Moors* (1910); *Partridges and Partridge Manors* (1911); *Pheasants and Covert Shooting* (1913).
MEYSEY THOMPSON, COLONEL R. F.—*A Shooter's Catechism* (1907).
MILLAIS, J. G.—*Game Birds and Shooting Sketches* (1892); *British Deer and their Horns* (1897); *The Wildfowler in Scotland* (1901); *The Natural History of British Surface-feeding Ducks* (1902); *The Natural History of British Game Birds* (1909); *British Diving Ducks* (1913); *Deer and Deer-Stalking* (1913).
MILLARD, F. W.—*Game and Foxes.*
NICHOLS, J. C. M.—*Birds of Marsh and Mere* (1926).
"OAKLEIGH."—*On Shooting* (1838).
"OLD STALKER, AN."—*Days on the Hill* (1926).
PAGE, RICHARD.—*New Ways with Partridges* (1924).
PARKER, ERIC.—*Shooting Days* (1918); *Elements of Shooting* (1924); *Partridges Yesterday & To-day* (1927); *Field, River & Hill* (1927); *Shooting* (Lonsdale Library, 1930); *An Alphabet of Shooting* (1932); *Game Birds, Beasts & Fishes* (1935); *The Shooting Week-end Book* (1942); *Predatory Birds of Gt. Britain* (1939).
PAYNE GALLWEY, SIR RALPH.—*The Fowler in Ireland* (1882); *Letters to Young Shooters*, 3 vols. (1891–6); *High Pheasants in Theory and Practice* (1913).
PORTAL, MAJOR MAURICE, and COLLINGE, DR. W. E.—*Partridge Disease and its Causes* (1932).

PORTER, ALEXANDER.—*The Gamekeeper's Manual* (1907).

PRICHARD, MAJOR HESKETH.—*Sport in Wildest Britain* (1921).

ROUTLEDGE, VINCENT.—*The Ideal Retriever* (1929).

RUSSELL, R. L.—*The Whole Art of Setter Training.*

"SCOLOPAX."—*A Book of the Snipe* (1904).

SCOTT, LIEUT.-COLONEL LORD GEORGE.—*Grouse Land and the Fringe of the Moor* (1937).

SCROPE, WILLIAM.—*The Art of Deer-Stalking* (1838).

SEDGWICK, N. M.—*The Young Shot* (1940).

SEIGNE, J. W.—*Irish Bogs* (1928).

SEIGNE, J. W., and KEITH, E. C.—*Woodcock and Snipe* (1936).

SHARP, HENRY.—*The Gun Afield and Afloat* (1904).

"SIXTY-ONE."—*Twenty Years' Reminiscences of the Lews* (1871).

SMITH, SYDNEY H.—*Snowden Slights, Wildfowler* (1912).

SOBIESKI, JOHN, and STUART, CHARLES EDWARD.—*Lays of the Deer Forest* (1848).

SOMERS, PERCIVAL.—*Pages from a Country Diary* (1904).

SPEEDY, TOM.—*Sport in Scotland with Rod and Gun* (1920).

SPRAKE, LESLIE.—*A Shooting Man's Calendar* (1927); *The Art of Shooting and Rough Shoot Management* (1930).

ST. JOHN, CHARLES.—*Wild Sports and Natural History of the Highlands* (1846); *A Tour in Sutherland* (1849).

STUART WORTLEY, ARCHIBALD J.—*The Partridge* (1893).

TAYLOR, L. B.—*A Brief History of the Westley-Richards Firm* (1913).

TEASDALE-BUCKELL, G. T.—*The Complete Shot* (1907).

TEGETMEIER, W. B.—*Pheasants: their Natural History and Practical Management*, Fifth Edition (1920).

TENNYSON, JULIAN.—*Rough Shooting* (1938).

THORNTON, COLONEL THOMAS.—*A Sporting Tour through Northern England* (1804).

TIPPINS, L. R.—*Modern Rifle Shooting* (1900).

WALSINGHAM, LORD.—See Badminton Library.

WATSON, A. E. T.—*The Young Sportsman* (1900).

WINANS, WALTER.—*Practical Rifle Shooting* (1906).

WORMALD, J.—*How to Increase a Stock of Partridges* (1912).

YEATES, G. K., and WINNALL, R. N.—*Rough Shooting* (1935).

LOAD	PATTERNS					Striking Velocity in F.S.	Striking Energy per pellet in ft. lb.	Forward Allowance in ft. on bird crossing at 40 m.p.h.
	Improved Cylinder	Quarter Choke	Half Choke	Three-quarter Choke	Full Choke			
Standard—								
1 1/16 oz.—No. 6	145	160	175	187	200	623	1·40	8·5
High Velocity—								
1 oz.—No. 6	*	*	145	165	187	664	1·59	7·9
High Velocity—								
15/16 oz.—No. 6	*	*	*	*	175	664	1·59	7·9
Low Velocity—								
1 1/4 oz.—No. 4	106	117	128	139	149	612	2·14	9·1
Low Velocity—								
1 1/4 oz.—No. 4 1/2	125	138	150	163	175	597	1·73	9·1

Load not recommended for this boring.

MINIMUM NECESSARY PATTERNS

The following table gives the minimum density of pattern required to ensure reasonable certainty of killing different species of game birds.

Bird	Minimum Pattern
Blackcock . . Cock Pheasant	60
Mallard . . Hen Pheasant	70 / 80
Grouse . . Partridge . . Wood Pigeon . Woodcock . , Teal . , . ,	130 / 145
Snipe . . . ,	290

For birds not given in this table, the following formulæ may be adopted .—

For birds under 1 lb. weight:—

Minimum Pattern $= \frac{1,760}{W}$ where W is the weight of the bird in ounces

For birds over 1 lb. and under 2 lb. :—

Minimum Pattern $= \frac{3,000}{W}$ where W is the weight of the bird in ounces

For birds over 2 lb. and under 4 lb:—

Minimum Pattern $= \frac{165}{W}$ where W is the weight of the bird in pounds.

For birds over 4 lb. :—

Minimum Pattern $= \frac{220}{W}$ wnere W is the weight of the bird in pounds.

N.B.—The table and formulæ given above are quoted with special permission from Volume III of *The Modern Shotgun.*

EXTREME RANGE OF SHOT

The extreme range of a charge of shot is obtained when the gun is pointing at an angle of between 30 and 33 degrees with the horizontal and not at an angle of 45 degrees, as is very commonly supposed. The

SIZE OF SHOT.

The question of shot size for ordinary shooting is probably as much psychological as anything else. Some shooters like to have a pattern sufficiently dense to ensure hitting the head and neck of a bird and so use No. 7 ; while others are inspired with confidence by the extra smashing power of pellets of No. 5. The truth is that for the great majority of shots, at driven game at all events, the range is sufficiently close for No. 7 to give ample penetration, and No. 5 ample density of pattern.

The following table gives the minimum effective striking velocities necessary to ensure penetration on an ordinary game bird, and the ranges at which they occur when using standard, high and low velocity loads.

Size of Shot	Minimum Effective Striking Velocity in F.S.	Range at which in yards Minimum Effective Velocity occurs with :		
		Standard Load	H.V. Load	L.V. Load
BB	240	over 100	not used	over 100
1	287	over 100	not used	90
2	314	100	not used	80
3	340	80	not used	70
4	374	over 60	not used	over 60
4 1/2	406	over 60	not used	over 60
5	426	over 60	over 60	88
5 1/2	445	59	over 60	54
6	472	55	57	52
6 1/2	496	50	53	not used
7	529	46	49	not used

extreme range would be given by an elevation of 4 degrees in a vacuum.

It can be assumed, without material error, that for ordinary shot sizes the extreme range is just under 250 yards.

When fired vertically upwards No. 6 shot attain a range of about 120 yards.

THE NUMBERS OF PELLETS IN DIFFERENT CHARGES OF SHOT.

Size of Shot	Ounces					
	1½	1¼	1⅛	1 1/16	1	¾
LG	9	7	7	6	6	4
MG	11	9	8	7	7	5
SG	12	10	9	9	8	6
Special SG	16	14	12	12	11	8
SSG. ..	23	19	17	16	15	11
SSSG ..	30	25	22	21	20	15
SSSSG ..	38	31	28	27	25	19
SSSSSG or AAAA..	45	38	34	32	30	22
AAA ..	53	44	39	37	35	26
AA	60	50	45	43	40	30
A	75	63	56	53	50	38
BBB ..	90	75	67	64	60	45
BB	105	88	79	74	70	53
B	120	100	90	85	80	60
1	150	125	113	106	100	75
2	180	150	135	127	120	90
3	210	175	158	149	140	105
4	255	213	191	181	170	128
4½	300	250	225	212	200	150
5	330	275	248	234	220	165
5½	360	300	270	255	240	180
6	405	338	304	287	270	202
6½	450	375	338	319	300	225
7	510	425	383	361	340	255
8	675	563	506	478	450	338
9	870	725	653	616	580	435
10	1,275	1,062	957	903	850	637

COMPARISON OF DIFFERENT BORES.

The only true comparison of the powers of different gauges of guns is that given by comparing the weights of their standard shot charges. The velocities developed by the different bores are the same, and consequently the penetration will be the same for any given shot size at any given distance. If the degree of choke is the same the patterns must vary with the weights of the shot charges, and other things being equal, the pattern density is the correct indication of power.

USUAL GAME GUNS. LOADS.

Bore and Length of Case	33-Grain Powder	42-Grain Powder	Black Powder
	Pdr. Shot	Pdr. Shot	Pdr. Shot
Bore—In	Grains Oz.	Grains Oz.	Drs. Oz.
4—4	90—3	112—3¼	9—3¼
8—4	73—2⅜	85—2½	7½—2½
10—2⅝	38—1 5/16	49—1 5/16	3½—1⅜
12—3	40—1 5/16	50—1½	3¾—1½
12—2¾	36—1¼	46—1¼	3¼—1¼
12—2½	33—1 1/16	42—1 1/16	3—1⅛
14—2½	31—1	38—1	2¾—1
16—2½	28—⅞	36—⅞	2¾—⅞
20—2½	24—¾	31—¾	2¼—¾
28—2½	20—9/16	25—9/16	1¾—9/16
410—2½	10½—⅜	12½—⅜	1—⅜
410—2	9—5/16	11—5/16	¾—5/16

For a condensed powder such as Sporting Ballistite a special case has to be used. The recommended loads are as follows:—12 in.—2½ in., 25 grains, 1 1/16 oz. shot; 16 in.—2½ in., 21 grains, ⅞ oz. shot; 20 in.—2½ in., 18 grains, ¾ oz. shot.

SIZES AND WEIGHTS OF GUNS.

The size of the bore, or gauge, of a shotgun is measured by the number of spherical balls of pure lead, each exactly fitting the bore, which go to the pound, e.g., a 12-bore gun is one on which the barrels are such a size that twelve spherical balls of pure lead which fit the bore will together weigh 1 lb.

For gauges smaller than No. 32, the size is usually given by quoting the diameter of the bore in decimals of an inch, e.g., .410.

The following table gives the gauges, diameters of bores and weights of double-barrelled guns for weapons chambered for different lengths of cartridge cases.

Gauge	Diam. of bore in inches	Length of Cartridge in. inches	Weight of Double-Barrelled Gun
4	1·052	4 & 4½	19 to 22 lb.
8	·835	All lengths	13 ,, 15 lb.
10	·775	,, ,,	8½ ,, 9½ lb.
12	·729	.3	7¾ ,, 8 lb.
12	·729	2¾	7 lb. 2 oz. to 7½ lb.
12	·729	2½	6 to 6½ lb.
16	·662	3	6¼ ,, 6½ lb.
16	·662	2¾	6 ,, 6¼ lb.
16	·662	2½	5¾ ,, 6⅛ lb.
20	·615	3	6 lb. 2 oz. to 6 lb. 6 oz.
20	·615	2¾	5¾ to 6 lb.
20	·615	2½	5½ lb. to 5 lb. 10 oz.
28	·550	2½	5 lb. 2 oz. to 5½ lb.
410	·410	2½	4 lb. 6 oz. to 4¾ lb.

N.B—In Great Britain the size of the bore is determined by the diameter at a point nine inches from the breech end.

OUNCES IN GRAINS, POUNDS, AND GRAMMES.

Shot Charge in Oz.	Grains	Lbs. Av.	Grammes
1½	656·3	·0937	42·52
1 7/16	629·1	·0899	40·75
1⅜	601·8	·0860	39·00
1 5/16	574·2	·0821	37·22
1¼	546·9	·0782	35·44
1 3/16	519·5	·0743	33·67
1⅛	492·2	·0703	31·89
1 1/16	464·8	·0664	30·12
ONE	437·5	·0625	28·35
15/16	410·2	·0586	26·58
⅞	382·8	·0547	24·81
13/16	355·5	·0508	23·03
¾	328·1	·0469	21·26
11/16	301·8	·0430	19·50
⅝	273·3	·0391	17·72
9/16	246·1	·0352	15·94
½	218·8	·0313	14·17
7/16	191·3	·0274	12·40
⅜	164·0	·0234	10·63
5/16	136·7	·0195	8·86
¼	109·4	·0156	7·09
3/16	82·0	·0117	5·32
⅛	54·7	·0078	3·54
1/16	27·3	·0030	1·77

AVERAGE WEIGHT OF GAME.

Blackcock	4 lbs.
Capercailzie	14 lbs.
Common Snipe	4 ozs.
Golden Plover	7½ ozs.
Grouse	1 lb. 12 ozs.
Hare	7 lbs. 8 ozs.
Jack Snipe	2 ozs.
Lapwing	8 ozs.
Partridge	14 ozs.
Pheasant	3 lbs.
Ptarmigan	1 lb. 3 ozs.
Quail	3½ ozs.
Rabbit	3 lbs. 12 ozs.
Widgeon	1 lb. 8 ozs.
Wild Duck	2 lbs. 4 ozs.
Woodcock	12 ozs.
Wood Pigeon	1 lb. 6 ozs.

PHRASEOLOGY.

The following terms were in the past and are sometimes still used.

A *nye* of pheasants (a brood); a *badling* of ducks (a gathering); a *fall* of woodcock (a flock); a *skulk* of foxes (a troop); a *cete* of badgers (a company); a *sounder* of swine (a herd); a *singular* of boars (a pack); a *pride* of lions (a group); a *sege* of herons (a flock); a *herd* of swans (a large number of swans feeding or travelling together); a *spring* of teal (a flock); a *covert* of coots (a flock); a *gaggle* of geese (a flock of wild geese); a *sord* or *sute* of mallard (a flock); a *bevy* of quails (a flock); a *covey* of partridges or grouse (a flock); a *pack* of grouse (a gathering of coveys); a *congregation* of plovers (a flock); a *walk* of snipe (a flock); a *wisp* of snipe (a flight); a *building* of rooks (a company or rookery); a *murmuration* of starlings (a flock).

OTHER POPULAR LOADS

Gauge	Length of Case	"Smokeless Diamond" "E.C." or "Empire" 33-gr. Pdr.		"Schultze" or "Amberite" 42 gr. Powder		"Sporting Ballistite" condensed Powder	
		Pdr.	Shot	Pdr.	Shot	Pdr.	Shot
	Ins.	Grs.	Ozs.	Grs.	Ozs.	Grs.	Ozs.
12	2½	38	1¼	47	1¼	29	1¼
12	2½	33	1½	42	1½	26	1½
12	2½	36	1	46	1	—	—
12	2½	35	1	45	1	—	—
12	2⅝	34	1	44	1	—	—
12	2½	33	1	43	1	—	—
12	2½	34	1⅝	42	1	—	—

Where 1-oz. shot charges are required for 12-gauge cartridges, the use of 33-grain powders is recommended in preference to 42-grain powders.

POPULAR PUNT GUN LOADS

Bore	Black Powder	Shot	Weight of Gun (approx.)
Inch	Drs. Ozs.	Ozs. lbs.	lbs.
1⅛	25=1½	8=½	64
1½	48=3	16=1	128
1¾	64=4	20=1¼	163
2	96=6	32=2	234

The ordinary ratio of punt powder to shot is 1 in 5.

All the above loads are for the usual sporting shot sizes. The charge of powder may be slightly increased when large sizes of shot, e.g. letter shot, are loaded.

GRAINS TO GRAMMES
1 Grain = ·0648 of a Gramme.

Grs.	Grms.	Grs.	Grms.	Grs.	Grms
20 * 1·30		34 * 2·20		48 * 3·11	
*(½ Dram)		*(1½ Drams)		*(1¾ Drams)	
21 — 1·36		35 — 2·27		49 — 3·18	
22 — 1·43		36 — 2·33		50 — 3·24	
23 — 1·49		37 — 2·40		51 — 3·30	
24 — 1·56		38 — 2·46		52 — 3·37	
25 — 1·62		39 — 2·53		53 — 3·43	
26 — 1·68		40 — 2·59		54 — 3·50	
27 * 1·75		41 * 2·66		55 * 3·56	
*(1 Dram)		*(1½ Drams)		* (2 Drams)	
28 — 1·81		42 — 2·72		56 — 3·63	
29 — 1·88		43 — 2·79		57 — 3·69	
30 — 1·94		44 — 2·85		58 — 3·76	
31 — 2·01		45 — 2·92		59 — 3·82	
32 — 2·07		46 — 2·98		60 — 3·89	
33 — 2·14		47 — 3·05		61 * 3·95	
				*(2¼ Drams)	

INDEX

313

THE LONDSDALE LIBRARY
of Sports, Games & Pastimes

Edited by LORD LONSDALE & MR. ERIC PARKER.

NEW VOLUME.

FLAT RACING. EDITOR, RT. HON. EARL HAREWOOD. Qr. Lthr. 42s.
Buckram. 21s.

Earlier Volumes—

HORSEMANSHIP. GEOFFREY BROOKE. Qr. Lthr., 42s. Buckram, 21s.*
TROUT FISHING. ERIC TAVERNER. Qr. Lthr., 42s. Buckram, 21s.*
SHOOTING. ERIC PARKER. Qr. Lthr., 42s. Buckram, 21s.*
COARSE FISHING. ERIC PARKER, &c. Qr. Lthr., 35s. Buckram, 12s. 6d.
LAWN TENNIS. WALLIS MYERS. Qr. Lthr., 35s. Buckram, 12s. 6d.
CRICKET. D. R. JARDINE, &c. Qr. Lthr., 35s. Buckram, 15s.
FOXHUNTING. SIR C. FREDERICK, BT., M.F.H. Qr. Lthr., 45s. Buckram, 25s.
WINTER SPORTS. LORD KNEBWORTH, &c. Qr. Lthr., 35s. Buckram, 15s.
GOLF. ROGER & JOYCE WETHERED, &c. Qr. Lthr., 35s. Buckram, 15s.
SALMON FISHING. ERIC TAVERNER. Qr. Lthr., 45s. Buckram, 25s.*
BOXING. VISCOUNT KNEBWORTH. Qr. Lthr., 35s. Buckram, 12s. 6d.
ANTHOLOGY OF SPORT. ERIC PARKER. Qr. Lthr., 30s. Buckram,
10s. 6d. Pocket Edition. Cloth, 7/6.
HOUNDS & DOGS. A. CROXTON SMITH, &c. Qr. Lthr., 35s. Buckram, 15s.
BIG GAME—AFRICA. MAJ. H. C. MAYDON, &c. Qr. Lthr., 45s. Buckram, 25s.
CRUISING. E. G. MARTIN & JOHN IRVING, &c. Qr. Lthr., 42s. Buckram, 21s.
RACKETS, SQUASH RACKETS, TENNIS, FIVES & BADMINTON.
LORD ABERDARE, & others. Qr. Lthr., 35s. Buckram, 15s.
SEA FISHING. A. E. COOPER & Others. Qr. Lthr., 35s. Buckram, 15s.
MOUNTAINEERING. SYDNEY SPENCER, &c. Qr. Lthr. 42s. Buckram, 21s.
MOTOR CRUISING. K. M. MILLER & J. IRVING. Qr. Lthr., 42s. Buckram, 21s.
GAME BIRDS, BEASTS & FISHES. E. PARKER. Qr. Lthr., 42s. Buckram 21s.
POLO. LORD KIMBERLEY, " MARCO," &c. Qr. Lthr., 45s. Buckram, 25s.
DEER, HARE & OTTER HUNTING. BY MAJ. GEN. GEOFFREY BROOKE,
THE EARL OF COVENTRY. Qr. Lthr., 35s. Buckram, 15s.
HISTORY OF HUNTING. PATRICK CHALMERS. Qr. Lthr., 42s. Buckram, 21s.
RIVER MANAGEMENT. H. E. TOWNER COSTON. Qr. Lthr., 25s.
Buckram, 15s.
THE LONSDALE BOOK OF SPORTING RECORDS. THE EARL OF
KIMBERLEY, LORD ABERDARE, SIR GEORGE THOMAS, BART., &c. Buckram, 15s.
THE LONSDALE KEEPERS' BOOK. BY ERIC PARKER & MANY
FAMOUS GAMEKEEPERS. Qr. Lthr. 35s. Buckram, 15s.
MOTOR RACING. EDITORS, LORD HOWE & S. C. H. DAVIS, & BY REID
RAILTON, G. E. T. EYSTON, JOHN COBB &c. Qr. Lthr., 35s. Buckram, 15s.

* *Also Large Paper Edition de Luxe, £5 5s.: and the ordinary edition of all the volumes are bound in the same de luxe style, price £3 3s.*